W. B. YEATS AND IRISH FOLKLORE

Mary Helen Thuente

W. B. YEATS
AND
IRISH FOLKLORE

GILL AND MACMILLAN
BARNES & NOBLE BOOKS
Totowa, New Jersey

First published 1980 by
Gill and Macmillan Ltd
15/17 Eden Quay
Dublin 1
with associated companies in
London, New York, Delhi, Hong Kong,
Johannesburg, Lagos, Melbourne,
Singapore, Tokyo

7171 1020 6

First published in the USA 1981 by
Barnes & Noble Books
81 Adams Drive
Totowa, New Jersey, 07512

ISBN 0-389-20161-8

Printed in Great Britain by
Bristol Typesetting Co. Ltd, Barton Manor, St. Philips, Bristol

To
Frances Ernst
Frank A. Ernst
Helen Mulcahy Ernst

Contents

Acknowledgments

Grateful acknowledgment is made to the holders of copyright for all matter quoted in this book. If I have committed any involuntary infringement of copyright, I apologise for my apparent negligence. Special acknowledgement is made to Miss Anne Yeats and Senator Michael B. Yeats, and to A. P. Watt and Son, for permission to quote from the works of William Butler Yeats.

Quotations from Edward Garnett's reader's report about W. B. Yeats's *Irish Adventurers* appear with permission from the Henry W. and Albert A. Berg Collection; The New York Public Library; and the Astor, Lenox and Tilden Foundations. Quotations from *Fairy and Folk Tales of Ireland* appear with the permission of Mr Colin Smythe. Quotations from *The Collected Poems of W. B. Yeats, The Autobiography of W. B. Yeats, Essays and Introductions, Explorations, Mythologies, Variorum Edition of the Plays of W. B. Yeats,* and *Variorum Edition of the Poems of W. B. Yeats* appear with the permission of Macmillan Publishing Co. Inc., New York.

Some material in this book has already appeared in print and I gratefully acknowledge permission from the following: the editors of *Anglo-Irish Studies* to use some materials from my article, 'W. B. Yeats and Celtic Ireland: 1885–1900', *Anglo-Irish Studies* IV (1978); the editors of *The Journal of Irish Literature* to use materials from my article, 'W. B. Yeats and Nineteenth-Century Folklore', *JIL* VI (September 1977); the University of Manitoba Press and the editors of *Mosaic* to use some materials from my article, 'Traditional Innovations: Yeats and Joyce and Irish Oral Tradition', *Mosaic* XII /3 (April 1979); Mr Colin Smythe to use materials from my Introduction to his new edition of W. B. Yeats's *Representative Irish Tales* (1979).

A*

Special thanks are due to Mrs Ruth Harrod of the Indiana University-Purdue University at Fort Wayne Library for the excellent Inter-Library Loan service she has provided me. Thanks are also due to Miss Alexandra Mason and her staff at the Kenneth Spencer Research Library, the University of Kansas; to the staff at the National Library of Ireland; to the staff at The Berg Collection of the New York Public Library; and to the staff at the Lilly Library of Indiana University.

Much of the research for this book was supported by a Dissertation Fellowship at the University of Kansas, and by Indiana University-Purdue University Faculty Research Grants for the summers of 1977 and 1979. I am also grateful to Mrs Marci Irey for typing the manuscript and to Professor Steven Hollander and Professor Frederick Kirchhoff for their editorial assistance.

Special thanks are also due to Sister Mary Adorita Hart of Clarke College, who first inspired me to study literature, and to Professor Harold Orel of the University of Kansas, who supervised my doctoral thesis and the early stages of my research for this book. Finally, my family, especially my husband David and son Danny, deserve special appreciation for their interest, encouragement and patience while I was writing this book.

M. H. Thuente
Indiana University-Purdue University at Fort Wayne

Preface

'All the words that I gather,
And all the words that I write'
W. B. Yeats

W. B. Yeats began his dedicatory poem to his second anthology of Irish folklore, *Irish Fairy Tales* (1892), with the above lines.[1] The precedence he gave in these lines to the words which he had 'gathered' as a reader, collector and anthologist of Irish folklore is indeed appropriate because much of what Yeats 'wrote' or created as a poet and playwright was inspired by his omnivorous and eclectic reading and study of traditional Irish literature. A. N. Jeffares' declaration that Anglo-Irish literature needs 'to be seen in the context of its own growth, its own literary relationships, its own social and political history, its own cultural patterns' is especially true with regard to Yeats.[2] Yeats never ceased in his efforts to define a specifically 'Irish' literary tradition and place himself within it. His 'General Introduction for My Work', which he wrote less than two years before his death, emphasised the Irish literary backgrounds of his subject matter and declared that stylistically 'even what I alter must seem traditional'.[3] His early reading and interests, of course, extended well beyond Irish literary tradition; nevertheless that tradition, especially Irish folklore, remains one of the most neglected areas of scholarship on Yeats.

Irish folklore was the central impulse behind one of the most distinctive literary movements of the century, the Irish Literary Renaissance. Yeats and his associates repeatedly claimed that it was a revival of interest in Irish folklore that had made their work possible. As early as 1893 Yeats declared: 'Folk-lore is at once the Bible, the Thirty-nine Articles, and the Book of Common Prayer, and well-nigh all the great poets have lived by its light. Homer, Aeschylus, Sophocles, Shakespeare, and even Dante, Goethe, and Keats, were little more than folk-lorists with musical tongues.'[4] Yet in 1975 Birgit Bramsbäck pointed out in her essay 'W. B. Yeats and Folklore Material' that there is no full-scale comprehensive investigation of Yeats's relationship to Irish folklore as a tradition or of the significance of his numerous borrowings from folklore.[5] Approximately six thousand items are listed in the most recent bibliography of scholarship about Yeats, yet Richard Finneran is able to discuss all the scholarship on Yeats and Irish folklore in three short paragraphs he categorised as 'Irish Mythology' in the course of his one-hundred page critical survey of Yeats scholarship.[6] The articles which Finneran does cite are scattered source studies.

Several studies of Yeats have recognised that the rediscovery of traditional Irish literature inspired the literary revival at the end of the nineteenth century, but ancient Irish literature, especially what critics loosely refer to as 'mythology', has attracted much more attention than Irish folklore has. 'Folklore' and 'mythology' have been commonplaces in literary criticism about Yeats but seldom have the two terms been used precisely or examined in depth. Folklore as a subject matter and nineteenth-century Irish folklore as a literary tradition of oral and of written dimensions have remained relatively unknown to literary critics. Yeats himself had a far keener and more comprehensive understanding of the distinctions between 'folklore' and 'mythology' than scholars who have frequently confused the two elements in their discussions of his work. 'Folklore' and 'mythology' should be viewed as two related but ultimately distinct elements in Yeats's literary development.

'Folklore', in this book, will refer to the broad range of oral traditions which belonged to the nineteenth-century Irish peasantry—narratives, songs, beliefs, customs—which Yeats studied so thoroughly in both oral and written form during the 1880s and 1890s. The terms 'peasant' and 'peasantry' will be used because, although they can evoke unpleasant and false images in the Irish sense of identity, no synonym—such as 'countryman' or 'folk'—will do as well. 'Mythology' will refer to the narratives about ancient Irish gods and heroes available primarily in written form in old manuscripts and in nineteenth-century translations. The subject matter of ancient Irish myth still survived in nineteenth-century Irish oral tradition but generally in a very fragmented and debased form. Myth is a kind of traditional literature and represents one genre of traditional folk narrative—the other two being legend and folktale.

The following chapters will demonstrate that Yeats was much more involved with Irish folklore than with Irish mythology during the 1880s and 1890s. Previous studies which have considered Yeats's involvement with Irish literary tradition, such as Phillip L. Marcus's *Yeats and the Beginning of the Irish Renaissance*, have generally been source studies or have focused on ancient Irish myth and ignored his intense early involvement with Irish folklore. Daniel Hoffman's discussion of Yeats in *Barbarous Knowledge: Myth in the Poetry of Yeats, Graves and Muir* is an exception : Hoffman distinguished between folklore and mythology and argued Yeats was more indebted to folklore than to mythology, but Hoffman is only able to begin to explore the topic of Yeats and ballad poetry. Folksong and folk poetry represent the one area of folklore that has begun to receive some attention in literary criticism about Yeats. Michael Yeats's article 'W. B. Yeats and Irish Folk Song', Colin Meir's book *The Ballads and Songs of W. B. Yeats: The Anglo-Irish Heritage in Subject and Style*, and Sean Lucy's article 'Metre and Movement in Anglo-Irish Verse' have demonstrated how the metrical and rhythmical patterns of Irish folk poetry and song influenced Yeats.

This book will focus on how the narrative traditions of Irish folklore, in particular legends, influenced Yeats in subject, theory and style. In addition to exploring Yeats's involvement with Irish folklore, it will also consider other relatively unknown aspects of Yeats's early career: his early activities as an editor and anthologist, as a folklore collector, and as a writer of prose fiction. The reading Yeats did when he prepared his anthologies exercised a significant influence on his later work, although his early reading in Irish folklore and its influence has never been adequately explored. Indeed, John V. Kelleher has argued that the Irish books which Yeats read during the late 1880s and 1890s were so important that they had a disproportionate influence on him.[7] T. R. Henn declared of Yeats that, 'All that he saw and read and thought must one day be examined.'[8] Yeats's anthologies reflect his early reading and thought. The chronological examination of Yeats's study of Irish folklore reveals several concurrent developments: that an intense interest in Irish folklore preceded any significant involvement on Yeats's part in ancient Irish myth; that his developing interest in Irish folklore and mythology was determined largely by the folklore and mythology available to him as well as by his personal and professional interests; and that his activities as an editor and collector of Irish folklore evolved through four successive Irish subjects—fairies, contemporary peasants, eighteenth-century rogues and rapparees, and ancient heroes—and through several genres —folk belief legends, Anglo-Irish fiction, folk hero legends, and ancient myth. The study of Yeats's involvement with Irish folklore suggests new perspectives on his developing conception of the hero, on his early poetry, plays and prose, and on his literary theory and style.

I

Yeats and Nineteenth-Century Irish Literary Tradition: From Poetry to Folklore

Yeats's earliest poems, dramatised lyrics set in India and verse dramas in imitation of Shelley and Spenser, demonstrate his early interest in pastoral characters and themes based on fairy lore but they were not Irish in subject or setting. While the Indian setting of some of these poems probably reflected his interest in Eastern religions, neither Arcadia, the vague pastoral setting of 'The Island of Statues' (1885), nor Inquisition Spain, the setting of 'Mosada' (1886), came to life for Yeats or his readers. Yeats often wrote of his childhood repulsion for the nineteenth-century materialistic world of progress, realism, intellect and science, for all of which he considered England to be the prototype. The far-away settings of his early work illustrate his need for another world removed from the actual world he despised. The same situation appeared again and again in Yeats's early verse dramas and poems : earthly beings encountered supernatural beings, the world of time confronted the timeless world of the imagination. However, the vague settings and static characters of these early dramas and poems were not adequate vehicles for Yeats's themes.

'The Island of Statues', subtitled 'An Arcadian Faery Tale', is the characteristic result of the young Yeats working derivatively and self-consciously within the traditions of the classical pastoral and of English romanticism. The fairies are disembodied voices, the fairy enchantress is a 'goblin queen', the shepherds play lutes, the chivalric quest is to an enchanted fairy isle, and the allusions are to Greek and Roman literature. Even the supposedly Irish fairies in Yeats's early poems, such as 'Cranberry Fruit' and 'Mousetail' in 'A Lover's Quarrel among the Fairies', demonstrate how much he needed a living folk tradition to bring his poetry to life. Yeats soon realised that both he and Shelley had worked within a literary vacuum : 'Shakespeare and Keats had the folk-lore of their own day, while Shelley had but mythology; and a mythology which had been passing for long through literary minds without any new inflow from living tradition loses all the incalculable instructive and convincing quality of the popular traditions.'[1]

Ireland and its literary traditions rescued Yeats from the imitative romanticism of his early work. Once he decided English literature was in its death throes, he turned to Irish literary tradition and declared: 'England is old and her poets must scrape up the crumbs of an almost finished banquet, but Ireland has still full tables. . . . [and] no lack of subjects, for the literature of Ireland is still young, and on all sides of this road is Celtic tradition and Celtic passion crying for singers to give them voice.'[2] Yeats's articles and letters of the 1880s and 1890s are filled with his now famous declarations of his identity as an 'Irish' writer: 'With Irish literature and Irish thought alone have I to do.'[3] 'There is no great literature without nationality, no great nationality without literature.'[4] An Irish subject matter was indeed much more effective for his purposes and much less hackneyed than the traditions available to him in English literature. Moreover, Ireland, not India or Arcadia, was the antidote for nineteenth-century England: 'The flood-gates of materialism are only half-open among us as yet here in Ireland; perhaps the new age may close them before the tide is quite upon us.'[5] Yeats came to believe that the finite world of nineteenth-century materialism was not the 'real' world; reality was to be found among the Irish peasants and their legends: 'I am very religious, and deprived by Huxley and Tyndall, whom I detested, of the simple-minded religion of my childhood, I had made a new religion, almost an infallible church of poetic tradition, of a fardel of stories, and of personages, and of emotions, inseparable from their first expression, passed on from generation to generation.'[6] Once Yeats realised that in Shelley's poetry and in his own early work there had been a lack of 'geographical and historical reality', of 'the testimony of the ordinary senses',[7] Irish folklore—the legends and the beliefs of a most 'un-English' people, grounded in geographical and historical realities, and yet in communication with the supernatural world of fairies —seemed to offer him a subject matter ideally suited to the theme of temporal realities confronting the supernatural. Yeats wrote of Irish folklore, 'Here at last is a universe where all is large and intense enough to almost satisfy the emotions of man. Certainly such stories are not a criticism of life but rather an extension . . .'[8] Here was a subject matter Yeats believed capable of conveying the themes which he had failed to bring to life in his early verse dramas and lyrics.

Yeats's choice of a literary tradition which originated in and was based upon the life of the Irish peasantry was more radical than one realises when viewing the Literary Renaissance in retrospect. Moreover, his choice was also more complex than his own memories of his early career admit. As early as his explanatory note, 'The Legendary and Mythological Foundation of the Plays and Poems', to the collected edition of his poetry (1907), Yeats began to gloss over the significance of his early intense involvement in Irish folklore, to claim that ancient Irish literature had been his earliest and continuing source of inspiration and to emphasise Lady Gregory's influence on his use of traditional Irish literature.

The whole question of whether or not to use Irish literary materials was a controversial issue in the 1880s. For centuries the character of the Irish people, and consequently their literature and culture, had been objects of derision in English eyes. England's ban on the teaching of Irish, through which it hoped to destroy the last remnants of Irish culture in nineteenth-century Ireland, was typical of the English attitude toward Irish culture. Although Matthew Arnold, in a series of lectures entitled *On the Study of Celtic Literature* (1867), had called for the study of ancient Celtic literature, both Welsh and Irish, the more popular notion of Irish culture was decidedly different. The English historian James A. Froude, in *The English in Ireland in the Eighteenth Century* (1872–1874), described the twelfth-century Irish as 'scarcely better than a mob of armed savages' whose religion had degenerated into superstition and no longer 'served as a check' upon their 'most ferocious passions' which were 'treachery, thirst for blood, unbridled licentiousness, and inveterate detestation of order and rule'.[9] Froude's history implied that England had not been very successful in civilising the Irish during the centuries since the Norman invasion of Ireland. In Froude's description of the nineteenth-century Irish the ferociousness was gone, but there was little to be taken seriously or admired: 'Light-hearted, humorous, imaginative, susceptible through the entire range of

feeling, from the profoundest pathos to the most playful jest, if
they possess some real virtues they possess the counterfeits of a
hundred more.'[10] According to Froude, 'their epic poetry is
ridiculous bombast' and the Irish had 'no secular history, for
as a nation they have done nothing which posterity will not
be anxious to forget. . . .'[11]

In his early articles Yeats mentioned Froude a number of
times and was, of course, familiar with Froude's characterisation
of the Irish and their literature. Contrary to Froude's opinion
of Irish epic poetry as 'ridiculous bombast', Yeats extolled the
ancient sagas as heroic and tragic and praised them for illustrat-
ing the passionate Celtic character which Froude had con-
demned. However, even as late as 1900, Yeats's elevated notion
of ancient Irish literature as a repository of idealism and
imagination was far from accepted, even in Ireland. Both
Douglas Hyde and John M. Synge encountered prejudice against
Irish language, literature, and culture at Trinity College, Dublin.
Not surprisingly then, in 1900, Robert Atkinson, a noted English
philologist who was a professor at Trinity, a member of the
Royal Irish Academy and an authority on Middle Irish manu-
scripts, offered the following estimation of early Irish literature:

> It has scarcely been touched by the movement of the great
> literature; it is the untrained popular feeling. Therefore it is
> almost intolerably low in tone—I do not mean naughty, but
> low; and every now and then, when the circumstance
> occasions it, it goes down lower than low . . . and my aston-
> ishment is that through the whole range of Irish literature
> that I have read (and I have read an enormous range of it),
> the smallness of the element of idealism is most notice-
> able. . . . And as there is very little idealism there is very little
> imagination. . . . The Irish tales as a rule are devoid of it
> fundamentally.[12]

The oral legends of the nineteenth-century Irish peasantry
had fared no better in scholarly and popular opinion than had
ancient Irish literature. Irish folklore was considered to be the
debased superstitions of an ignorant peasantry. When oral folk-
lore had been collected during the nineteenth century, the pur-
pose had usually been the nostalgic preservation of antiquities

which the collector had loved as a child. Various nineteenth-century British committees had deplored Irish folklore as 'nonsensical' and 'foolish'.[13] But generally Irish folklore had been ignored as literature because it belonged to the Irish peasant who had been continually characterised in fiction and in many folklore collections as a sentimental, superstitious buffoon. Although in the late nineteenth century there had been a scholarly interest in the translation of ancient Irish manuscripts and in the collection of oral folklore, the emphasis in both endeavours had been international. Irish legends provided data for comparative philologists and mythologists. Folklore materials collected from Irish oral tradition had been scientifically categorised with similar items from other countries in journals such as *The Folklore Journal* which the Folklore Society of London had begun publishing in 1878. Irish legends, whether from ancient myth or from nineteenth-century folklore, had been valued neither for being Irish nor for being imaginative literature. Even Alfred Nutt in *Studies on the Legend of the Holy Grail with Especial Reference to the Hypothesis of Its Celtic Origin* (1888) valued Irish myth as the most archaic and most abundant tradition of legend extant in Europe and not as an imaginative and still vital creative tradition: 'As a whole Welsh literature is late, meagre, and has kept little that is archaic. The study of Irish promises far better results. Of all the races of modern Europe the Irish have the most considerable and the most archaic mass of pre-Christian traditions.'[14]

Considering the attitudes concerning traditional Irish literature —both ancient and contemporary—in the late nineteenth century, John O'Leary's influence on the young Yeats was especially significant. Only one of Yeats's early 'Irish' works, the tale 'Michael Clancy, the Great Dhoul, and Death', possibly predates O'Leary's influence. In a letter to Standish O'Grady in 1898 Yeats claimed that 'When I was about eighteen I came upon a Connaught folk tale of a tinker and Death and the Devil' and began a long poem about a tinker, 'that kind of jeering cheating Irishman called "a melodious lying Irishman" in another folk tale' and planned 'to bring him through many typical places and adventures' but soon 'gave up my epic and wrote this little tale instead.'[15] If one relies on Yeats's memory and his word, generally not wholly reliable sources, he encountered the Sligo legend in 1883 and wrote his version of it prior to meeting O'Leary in 1885.

Yeats met O'Leary when O'Leary returned to Dublin after five years imprisonment in England and thirteen years of political exile in France. O'Leary had been convicted by an English court for his part in an armed uprising against England in 1867. Before his conviction O'Leary had been the editor of a Fenian newspaper for which he had always tried to evaluate contributions on their literary as well as propagandistic merits. Throughout his life Yeats acknowledged his great debt to O'Leary's extensive knowledge of Irish literature and his houseful of Irish books. In 1889 Yeats wrote, 'The material for many a song and ballad has come from Mr John O'Leary's fine collection of Irish books—the best I know. The whole house is full of them. One expects to find them bulging out the windows.'[16] Yeats acknowledged in 'A General Introduction for My Work' (1937):

> It was through the old Fenian leader John O'Leary I found my theme. His long imprisonment, his longer banishment, his magnificent head, his scholarship, his pride, his integrity . . . had drawn around him a group of young men; I was but eighteen or nineteen and had already, under the influence of *The Faerie Queene* and *The Sad Shepherd*, written a pastoral play, and under that of Shelley's *Prometheus Unbound* two plays, one staged somewhere in the Caucasus, the other in a crater of the moon; and I knew myself to be vague and incoherent. He gave me the poems of Thomas Davis, said they were not good poetry but had changed his life when a young man, spoke of other poets associated with Davis and *The Nation* newspaper, probably lent me their books.[17]

Yeats had spent much of his childhood in Sligo, a seacoast town in the West of Ireland, listening to his mother's family and their servants telling legends of Irish fairies and local events. Such legends were among his fondest childhood memories; however, he did not consider them as serious literary materials until, through O'Leary's encouragement, he began reading nineteenth-century Anglo-Irish literature.

John O'Leary's Inaugural Address to the Young Ireland Society in 1885 had been entitled 'Young Ireland: The Old and

the New', and had stressed the continuity of the new Young
Ireland Society which O'Leary had just formed with the 'Young
Ireland' poets of the 1840s. O'Leary believed that the great
wave of literary activity fostered by the 'Young Ireland' Party
of the 1840s 'gave us, indeed, not all our literature, nor, even
in a purely literary sense, the better part of it, but may be said
to have absolutely given nearly all that part of it which can in
any definite sense be called national', and 'brought a soul back
into Eire' after centuries of English persecution.[18] Thus, Yeats's
first involvement with an Irish literary tradition was with the
poetry of the 'Young Ireland' movement who took patriotic
themes from Irish history and set them to popular verse. The
'Young Irelanders' came together in 1842 to help Daniel
O'Connell's movement to repeal the Act of Union. This Act
in 1800 had dissolved the Irish parliament in Dublin and put
Ireland under the direct authority of Westminster. In October
1842, its leaders had founded the *Nation* newspaper in order to
popularise their political beliefs; the poetry written by members
of the 'Young Ireland' movement such as Thomas Davis and pub-
lished in the *Nation* thus existed as political propaganda first, and
as literature second. 'The Prospectus of the "Nation" ' declared :

> The necessities of the country seem to demand a journal able to
> aid and organise the new movements going on amongst us; to
> make their growth deeper and their fruit more 'racy of the
> soil;' and above all, to direct the popular mind and the sym-
> pathies of the educated men of all parties to the great end
> of Nationality. . . . Nationality is the first great object—a
> Nationality which will not only raise our people from their
> poverty, by securing them the blessings of a Domestic Legis-
> lation, but inflame and purify them with a lofty and heroic
> love of country.[19]

The following excerpt from an article 'Irish Verdict Against
England', 10 December 1842, indicates the *Nation's* ultra-
nationalistic stance : 'The first step to nationality is the open
and deliberate recognition of it by the People themselves. Once
the Irish People declare the disconnexion of themselves, their
feeling, and interests from the men, feelings and interests of
England, they are in march for freedom. . . . We are not English
—let us thank God for it.'

The poetry of the *Nation* usually depicted Ireland's relation-
ship with England in melodramatic and bombastic rhetoric. The
following is an excerpt from a poem by Daniel O'Connell, 'An
Historical Memoir on Ireland and the Irish, Native and Saxon',
published in the *Nation* on 25 February 1843 :

> But onward ! The Green banner rearing,
>   Go flesh every sword to the hilt :
> On *our* side is VIRTUE & ERIN—
>   On *theirs* is Saxon and guilt.

'My Land' by Thomas Davis, the most popular of the 'Young
Ireland' poets, was not much better :

> She is a rich and rare land;
>   Oh ! she's a fresh and fair land,
> She is a dear and rare land—
>   This native land of mine.
>
> No men than hers are braver—
>   Her women's hearts ne'er waver;
> I'd freely die to save her,
>   And think my lot divine.
>
> She's not a dull or cold land;
>   No ! she's a warm and bold land—
> Oh ! she's a true and old land—
>   This native land of mine.[20]

One must credit the influence of O'Leary's fervour for Davis's
poetry, and O'Leary's and Yeats's ignorance of Irish poetry for
Yeats's praise of 'Young Ireland' poetry as representative of an
Irish literary tradition and his summary dismissal of the poetry
of Thomas Moore as not being truly Irish. Moore, the only other
nineteenth-century Irish poet whose popularity equalled that
of Davis and the Young Irelanders, had written English verse
for old Irish melodies in his extremely popular series of *Irish
Melodies* (1807–1834). Yeats claimed that Moore's Irish genius
had been ruined by English literary conventions : Moore had
'quenched an admirable Celtic lyricism in an artificial glitter
learned from the eighteenth century', and, in Yeats's opinion,
Moore's '*Irish Melodies* are to most cultivated ears but excellent
drawingroom songs, pretty with a prettiness which is contraband

of Parnassus.'[21] Seán Lucy has recently credited Moore with using metrical patterns from Irish poetry in some of his lyrics in *Irish Melodies*, the influence of which Yeats himself probably absorbed.[22] While Yeats never fully or consciously appreciated the Irish dimensions of Moore's poetry, Yeats eventually qualified his early praise of Thomas Davis and disclaimed his original enthusiasm for the 'Young Ireland' poets. Yeats said of them in retrospect that, although he had enthusiastically read Shelley and Spenser and modelled much of his own early work on their poetry, 'yet I do not think Shelley or Spenser ever moved me as did these poets. . . . I knew in my heart that most of them wrote badly, and yet such romance clung about them, such a desire for Irish poetry was in all our minds, that I kept saying, not only to others but to myself, that most of them wrote well, or all but well.'[23]

Yeats eventually claimed only the politically neutral subjects of the Young Irelanders : 'When I saw John O'Leary first, every young Catholic man who had intellectual ambition fed his imagination with the poetry of Young Ireland; and the verses of even the least known of its poets were expounded with a devout ardour at Young Ireland Societies and the like, and their birth-days celebrated. The school of writers I belonged to tried to found itself on much of the subject-matter of this poetry.'[24] Yeats wrote two poems in the tradition of 'Young Ireland' political progaganda, 'The Two Titans' (1886) and 'How Ferencz Renyi Kept Silent' (1887), both of which implicitly condemned England's repression of Ireland. However, the fact that Yeats never included either of these poems in collections of his work in 1889 or later indicates his growing disenchant-ment with the use of poetry for political propaganda. Yeats used his critical reviews and articles of the late 1880s and early 1890s to define a more truly Irish popular ballad tradition. In his series of four articles on 'Irish National Literature' in 1895, Yeats dismissed 'that interesting, unsatisfying, pathetic move-ment which we call in Ireland "the poetry of Young Ireland" ' as an unsuccessful branch of a larger nineteenth-century ballad tradition based on translations from the Irish and begun by Jeremiah Joseph Callanan 'while Moore's sentimental trivialities were in their first fame'.[25]

Yeats's own involvement with the poetry of 'Young Ireland'

had been more literary than political from almost the beginning.
His contributions to *Poems and Ballads of Young Ireland* (1888)
—an anthology described in the dedicatory poem to John
O'Leary as 'Strains that have little chance to live/With those
that Davis' clarion blew'—illustrate that Yeats was using Davis'
general Irish subject matter but not with political implications.
The subjects of Yeats's four contributions to the anthology were
politically neutral. Significantly, each of Yeats's poems was based
on some aspect of Irish folklore. One was based on a folk
memory, another on a folk legend, and another on a folk song:
'The Stolen Child' told of the abduction of a human child by
Irish fairies; 'The Meditation of the Old Fisherman' is the sup-
posed reminiscence of an old Irish peasant about his child-
hood; 'King Goll' depicts the madness of an ancient Irish king;
and 'Love Song' is a love lyric based upon an old Irish song.
None of these poems by Yeats either lamented Ireland's past
woes under English rule or referred to contemporary political
issues. Such poems were in decided contrast to other ballads in
the collection such as Douglas Hyde's 'Marching Song of the
Gaelic Athletes':

> We, the numerous men of Eire,
>   Born beneath her pleasant skies,
> To our gatherings in our mountains,
>   In our thousands we arise.
> See the weapons on our shoulders,
>   Neither gun nor pike we bear,
> But should Ireland call upon us,
>   Ireland soon should find them there.[26]

A comparison of this poem with any one of Hyde's translations
of Irish poems and songs in his *Love Songs of Connacht* (1893)
shows that Irish folk traditions would provide a far better poetic
inspiration to Hyde as well as to Yeats.

The folkloristic content of the poems which Yeats contributed
to *Poems and Ballads of Young Ireland* points to another aspect
of John O'Leary's literary influence on Yeats which has often
been overshadowed by the emphasis on Yeats's reaction to the
'Young Ireland' tradition in critical studies of his work. As
Marcus Bourke, John O'Leary's biographer has pointed out,
Yeats discovered 'the great store of Irish legend and fairy lore'

in O'Leary's 'magnificent collection of Irish books'.[27] This conclusion is true enough, if one qualifies it with Yeats's childhood interest in Sligo folklore and credits O'Leary with inspiring him to consider materials from Irish folklore as a serious literary subject matter.

A controversy in the *Freeman's Journal* in 1886 concerning the 'Best Hundred Irish Books' demonstrates how revolutionary O'Leary and his literary disciples were in championing Irish folklore as an important literary tradition in the late 1880s. 'Historicus', the author of the essay 'Best Hundred Irish Books', defined an 'Irish' book as 'about Ireland or the Irish'. Although there were many nineteenth-century books and periodicals containing ancient Irish tales and contemporary Irish folklore, Historicus mentioned only Patrick Weston Joyce's *Old Celtic Romances* (1879). Joyce's 'translations', based on manuscripts rather than oral traditions, actually freely rewrote the old tales according to English literary conventions. Historicus praised the book because of the Irish history it contained. The tales about ancient Ireland were obviously without literary or imaginative value to Historicus, and the beliefs and legends of the nineteenth-century peasantry were beneath his notice and without literary, or even historical, significance. Not surprisingly, Historicus mentions in the second instalment of the essay that he had received a letter from John O'Leary questioning some of Historicus's choices. He praised O'Leary for 'his vast knowledge of Irish books', saying he wished that O'Leary had undertaken the selection in the first place because there were 'not three men in Ireland who could draw up a better list of books'.[28] Letters from other readers also questioned Historicus's list, especially his emphasis on historical works and his neglect of fictional works. But while many recommended titles from nineteenth-century Irish fiction, few suggested Irish folklore. Richard Garnett suggested that Irish legends be published for children; Alfred Webb recommended Thomas Crofton Croker's *Fairy Legends and Traditions of the South of Ireland* as a 'Romance'. Only O'Leary and two of his literary disciples, George Sigerson and Justin McCarthy, lamented the neglect of ancient Irish legends and contemporary Irish folklore and cited books and journals dealing with it. Other recommendations by O'Leary, such as John Mitchel's *Jail Journal* and Jonah Barrington's *Personal Sketches of His Own Times*, would be singled out by Yeats for special praise in his own articles during the next decade.

O'Leary's influential support for the traditional literature of the Irish peasantry was also apparent in the early issues of the *Dublin University Review*, a new literary magazine begun in 1885 and edited by T. W. Rolleston, one of O'Leary's most devoted literary disciples. The August 1885 issue contained an article by Justin McCarthy arguing that every Irishman should become familiar with Irish legends. The September 1885 issue published a folk tale collected by John Todhunter. The October 1885 issue included Douglas Hyde's essay 'The Unpublished Songs of Ireland' which argued that the poems sung by the peasantry had a spontaneity and passion lacking in the refined poetry of the older bardic tradition. The September issue also had contained Yeats's wholly un-Irish poem, 'The Seeker'.

However, the influence of John O'Leary's high opinion of traditional Irish literature soon was apparent in Yeats's work. His earliest article was about the ancient Irish hero, Finn, and his two earliest surviving prose pieces were about Samuel Ferguson's translations of the ancient Irish sagas. In the late 1880s Yeats also identified and propagandised two areas of literary significance within nineteenth-century folklore : he praised folk ballads and songs and wrote poems imitating them, and he edited Irish fairy legends and folk tales and wrote poetry based on them. Yeats opened one of his early articles, 'Popular Poetry of Ireland', which he wrote in 1887 but which was not published until 1889, by distinguishing between the militant poetry of 'Young Ireland' and a larger ballad tradition based on Irish folk tradition. He obviously preferred the latter : 'Behind Ireland fierce and militant, is Ireland poetic, passionate, remembering, idyllic, fanciful, and always patriotic. With this second Ireland only have I to do in this article, and what it writes and what it reads. I have here a row of little blue-paper-poem-books —a whole ballad literature as foreign from all modern English ways as though it were of farthest Iceland and not of neighbouring Ireland. . . .'[29] Yeats went on to praise the translations of traditional Irish songs and ballads by Jeremiah Callanan, Edward Walsh, James Clarence Mangan and Samuel Ferguson. Yeats considered their translations and adaptations of oral nineteenth-century poems sung by the peasantry as a tradition distinct from translations of manuscript versions of ancient Irish literature by Charlotte Brooke and Samuel Ferguson, and as much better than earlier attempts to translate peasant poems and songs into English.

Charlotte Brooke, in her *Reliques of Irish Poetry: Consisting of Heroic Poems, Odes, Elegies, and Songs, translated into English Verse* (1789), had translated ancient Irish poetry into heroic couplets and described the ancient heroes in terms of English chivalry and knighthood. The translators whom James Hardiman employed to translate eighteenth- and nineteenth-century poems and songs for *Irish Ministrelsy, or the Bardic Remains of Ireland with English Poetical Translations* (1831) were equally unsuccessful. Robert O'Driscoll has aptly summed up the failure of both collections :

> Charlotte Brooke and the Hardiman translators imposed on their Irish originals the metrical patterns and conventional language of the English poetry of their time . . . despite their realisation of the need to preserve the spirit of the poems they were translating, and the repeated assertion of their attempts to do so, they cloaked the simple, homely thoughts of the originals in an effete, balanced eighteenth-century language, and fitted the alien metrical patterns of the Irish to tight and inflexible English metres. . . . The failure of Charlotte Brooke and the Hardiman translators was partly a matter of technique, partly a matter of knowledge. The customs, manners of society, and techniques of poetry that lay behind the Irish originals were unknown to an English civilisation.[30]

Recent scholarship has corroborated Yeats's judgment that Callanan, Walsh, Mangan and Ferguson indeed succeeded in rendering something of the real spirit and rhythm of Irish poetry into English. Yeats considered J. J. Callanan (1795–1825) as the first translator who was true to his Irish originals. Callanan, by turns a clerical student, a medical student, a soldier and a teacher, spent most of his life wandering about the Irish countryside collecting poems and legends from the peasantry. Callanan published only two works : *The Recluse of Inchidony* (1830) and *Poems* (1861). The first was a long Byronic poem in Spenserian stanzas which Yeats chose to ignore. The second was a collection of translations from the Irish upon which Callanan's high reputation as a translator deserves to be based. A twentieth-century editor of nineteenth-century Irish poetry reached a conclusion similar to Yeats's, that 'Callanan was the first to transmute not only the verbal meaning but also the rhythms, something of the emotional charge, and the alien spirit of the poems into English.'[31] Edward Walsh (1805–1850), a scholar and schoolmaster who was an authority on Irish folklore, published legends and poems in the *Nation* and other Irish periodicals as well as two collections of translations from Irish oral tradition: *Reliques of Irish Poetry* (1844) and *Irish Popular Songs* (1847). Both Callanan and Walsh were intimately familiar with the peasantry and were fluent Irish speakers. Their translations thus represented a poetic achievement which Yeats, who had had little first-hand experience of the peasantry and who did not understand Irish, could admire but not emulate. The subject matter of traditional Irish literature was much easier to assimilate and use than the metre and other stylistic complexities of Irish poetry. Nevertheless, as Colin Meir had pointed out in his excellent study, *The Ballads and Songs of W. B. Yeats: The Anglo-Irish Heritage in Subject and Style* (1974), the translations by Callanan and Walsh ultimately had a far-reaching influence on the style of Yeats's own poetry. In the meantime Callanan and Walsh provided Yeats with an example of how the oral traditions of the peasantry could offer an effective poetic subject matter.

Yeats was also deeply attracted to the 'translations' of James Clarence Mangan (1803–49). Mangan knew relatively little Irish so his 'translations' are actually adaptations based on prose translations by others. Although in 1886 Yeats admired the folk ballad for being concerned with story rather than with character and passion, and as much as Yeats condemned the 'sad soliloquies of nineteenth-century egoism', his early articles reflect his fascination with the deeply personal and passionate note so characteristic of Mangan's poetry. Although Yeats included Mangan in his article on 'Popular Ballad Poetry of Ireland', Mangan's highly personal approach to Irish poems and songs was not one which Yeats was prepared to adopt in the late 1880s. But, as with Callanan and Walsh, Mangan's poetry was an example for Yeats of the poetic possibilities of subjects from the oral traditions of the peasantry, and features of Mangan's style eventually surfaced in Yeats's own poetry.

Samuel Ferguson and William Allingham were the two most effective Irish poetic models for Yeats in the late 1880s. The poetry of Ferguson and Allingham offered an Irish subject matter whose vitality, simplicity and universality contrasted favourably with the hollow sophistication and obscure egoism he disliked in English literary tradition, and with the empty rhetoric and moralisation he rejected in 'Young Ireland' poetry. Yeats's early articles about Ferguson and Allingham present their work as representative of two distinct kinds of Irish subject matter: the manuscript tradition about the ancient Irish heroes and the oral folklore of the contemporary peasantry. Ferguson had written poems based upon both subjects, Allingham only upon the latter. Yeats emphasised the poems which Ferguson had based on ancient manuscript traditions rather than those Ferguson had based on subjects and songs from nineteenth-century folklore. For example, in 1894 when Yeats wrote his introductory survey of nineteenth-century Irish poetry in English for his *Book of Irish Verse* (1895), he characterised Ferguson's and Allingham's subjects as follows: 'Ferguson selecting his subjects from the traditions of the Bardic age, and Allingham from those of his native Ballyshannon.'[32]

Samuel Ferguson (1810–86), who had been born into an upper-middle-class Protestant family in Belfast, practised law for thirty years and upon his retirement became Deputy Keeper at the Dublin Record Office. After learning Irish he published a number of poems and books on Irish antiquarian and historical subjects. The majority of Ferguson's poems were written about ancient Irish heroes; others were based on contemporary folklore. Yeats used his prose articles to propagandise Ferguson's use of ancient heroic legends because Ferguson's depiction of the ancient heroes was an ideal antidote to the nineteenth-century English stereotype of the Irish character as that of a sentimental, superstitious buffoon. Although in his prose Yeats emphasised Ferguson's use of ancient Irish literature, Ferguson's poems based on poems and topics from nineteenth-century folklore had a significant effect on Yeats's poetic practice. Colin Meir and Robert O'Driscoll have each shown how both early and late poems by Yeats echo the rhythms and style of Ferguson's translations of Irish poems and songs.[33] The subject matter of

Ferguson's poems about Irish fairy lore also inspired Yeats. AE once told Austin Clarke that Ferguson's 'The Fairy Thorn' had 'fascinated' both Yeats and AE and 'was indeed the real origin of the Celtic Twilight'.[34] Yeats responded to the ballad's style and the folklore it contained and quoted it in its entirety in his earliest article about Ferguson, 'The Poetry of Sir Samuel Ferguson—I', published on 9 October 1886, even though the article's thesis was that Ferguson's restoration of the tales and heroes of ancient Ireland was of greater literary significance than his poetry derived from nineteenth-century ballads and folklore.

While Yeats praised Ferguson's use of ancient Irish myth, in actuality such materials were of little interest and of little use to him in the 1880s and 1890s. Ancient Irish myths available to Yeats in scholarly translations and in popularisations were equally unsatisfactory. The impetus for the translation of some of the numerous old manuscripts of Irish heroic sagas had come from Johann Caspar Zeuss's *Grammatica Celtica* (1853), which had shown that the Irish and Welsh languages were part of the same great Indo-European group of languages from which Latin and Greek had come. Ancient Irish manuscripts had thus been given a new prestige that made them seem worth translating, although only a small portion had actually been translated by the 1880s. The translation and studies which Zeuss had inspired had not lost their dry, philological form by the time Yeats began looking for an Irish subject matter. Articles by Celticists in journals such as the *Revue Celtique* treated the ancient Irish myths more as problems of semantics than as imaginative literature. Most articles in the *Revue Celtique* were written in French, a language which Yeats barely knew in the late 1880s. Other treatments of ancient Irish myth available to Yeats provided materials for Irish historians rather than for Irish literature. In *Lectures on the Manuscript Materials of Ancient Irish History* (1861), Eugene O'Curry had listed and briefly described the manuscripts available to the Irish historian and archaeologist; he had not told the stories contained in the manuscripts. Years later Yeats recalled his response to O'Curry's work: 'His unarranged and uninterpreted history defeated my boyish indolence.'[35]

On the other hand, nineteenth-century popularisers of ancient Ireland had arranged and interpreted their materials until comic caricature, sentimentality, moralisation, and a false sublimity almost overwhelmed the myths. Yeats's enthusiastic early articles on Samuel Ferguson's poems about ancient Irish heroes convey what Yeats hoped to find in such popularisations of ancient Ireland rather than their real nature. Significant discrepancies are apparent when Ferguson's poems are compared with Yeats's comments. Yeats chose to ignore the scholarly and antiquarian aspects of Ferguson's work, and Ferguson's many slighting references to the vulgarity and exaggerations of the old legends. The poems convey a vague, shadowy grandeur much more than the heroic passions which Yeats claimed to have found in them. Yeats's emphasis on the 'strange' and 'fantastic' and 'passionate' elements in Ferguson's poetry is a more accurate reflection of Yeats's own attitudes concerning what such poetry about ancient Ireland should be than of Ferguson's work. Ferguson had described his epic poem *Congal* as an account of 'the expiring effort of the Pagan and Bardic party in Ireland', but Yeats, in his earliest articles about Ferguson, emphasised the vitality and energy of the poem.[36] Yeats praised the 'continual' introduction of the supernatural into the poem; however, the encounter between Congal and the prophesying hag which Yeats described is the only such incident in the poem and is quite brief. In a similar vein, Yeats considered Ferguson's 'Conary' and 'Deirdre' as his best poems about ancient Ireland. However, 'Conary' had more Irish folk and fairy lore in it than any of Ferguson's other heroic poems. Although Ferguson had based his 'Deirdre' on a manuscript source, the ancient tale of Deirdre had remained a living oral tradition among the peasantry. The qualities which Yeats admired the most in Ferguson's heroic poems—the supernatural, the grotesque, the weird—abounded in Irish folklore, which was much more readily available to Yeats than the stories of the heroes in the old manuscripts were.

Ancient Irish gods had often become human heroes, and occasionally mock-heroic giants, in peasant tradition. For example, William Carleton's tale, 'A Legend of Knockmany', which Yeats included in his first anthology of Irish folklore, *Fairy and Folk Tales of the Irish Peasantry* (1888), could never have satisfied Yeats's need for a serious Irish subject matter. In Carleton's tale Finn and Cuchulain are mock-heroically portrayed as giants—Finn uses the trunk of a huge fir tree as a walking stick and when a neighbour wanted to borrow some butter, Finn's wife handily threw a piece 'about the weight of a couple dozen mill-stones' across a valley four miles wide. The plot turns on broad comedy and trickery. When Cuchulain arrives at Finn's pleasant Irish cottage, Finn pretends to be a baby in order to unnerve Cuchulain. In Carleton's story, Cuchulain's stature depends on the strength of his magic finger; by 1903 when Yeats began writing his series of plays about Cuchulain, he would portray Cuchulain as the embodiment of tragic passion and heroic energy.

Other literary popularisations of Irish myth available to Yeats in the 1880s represented an approach completely different from Carleton's comic treatment, but one that attempted a false sublimity which even Yeats, no matter how much he wanted to convey the seriousness of Irish literary materials, could not accept. In *Old Celtic Romances* (1879), Patrick Weston Joyce had bowdlerised unacceptable passages and embellished his materials with English literary conventions. His brother, Robert Dwyer Joyce, wrote poems which frequently altered the ancient Irish tales almost beyond recognition—calling Cuchulain and the other heroes 'knights', and inventing episodes imitative of medieval romance. Although in later years Yeats praised Standish James O'Grady's *History of Ireland Vol. I: The Heroic Period* (1878) and *Vol. II: Cuchulain and His Contemporaries* (1880), O'Grady's style, which reminded Yeats of Carlyle's, and O'Grady's treatment of the ancient heroes, which was often reminiscent of the Victorian domestic novel, had actually not appealed to Yeats in the 1880s. Standish J. O'Grady (1846–1928) might have remained a typical member of the Protestant and Unionist Irish upper class and believed that Irish history and tradition were beneath his notice had he not happened upon Sylvester O'Halloran's history of Ireland, the first history of his country he had ever read although he had been educated at Trinity College Dublin. O'Grady was impressed with O'Halloran's rational, scholarly and impassioned approach to his materials. Soon deep in his own research on the subject, O'Grady was amazed at Ireland's rich store of heroic literature and in 1878 began to write his own 'history' of Ireland which he published at his own expense because there was no contemporary market for such subjects. In O'Grady's view, ancient literature was filled with 'a noble moral tone,' 'breathes sublimity', and contained numerous incidents of 'chivalry' and others which 'inculcated chastity'.[37] O'Grady deleted or transformed passages which did otherwise. The proud, aggressive Maeve became a delicate fainting heroine out of a nineteenth-century novel. O'Grady preceded his chapters with excerpts from Milton, Keats, and classical writers. He argued for the 'general historical credibility' of the tales and deplored the presence of marvellous and extravagant episodes —illustrating two attitudes about ancient Ireland which Yeats vehemently opposed. Yeats's description in 1937 of his dissatisfaction with the translations of Standish J. O'Grady's cousin, Standish Hayes O'Grady, in *Silva Gaedelica* (1892) sums up his literary evaluation of both men: 'He worked at the British Museum compiling their Gaelic catalogue and translating our heroic tales in an eighteenth-century frenzy; his heroine "fractured her heart", his hero "ascended to the apex of the eminence" and there "vibrated his javelin", and afterwards took ship upon "colossal ocean's superficies".'[38]

Such translations and popularisations obviously did not encourage Yeats's early enthusiasm for the literary possibilities of Irish myth. Even if Yeats had found the Ferguson translations entirely suitable, his achievement was, like that of Callanan and Walsh, based on a knowledge of Irish which Yeats lacked. So, like O'Grady who did not know Irish, Yeats would have had to rely for materials upon dry, scholarly translations which have been described recently by O'Grady's biographer as 'wretched' and in 'virtual chaos'.[39] Ferguson's and O'Grady's literary purposes were also somewhat different from Yeats's at the time Yeats began using an Irish subject matter. Their ambition had been to raise ancient Irish history to a dignified level, to recast Irish heroic subjects in the lofty dignity of the Homeric epics. Yeats agreed that the status of Irish literature and the Irish character needed to be elevated; however, he felt that his own verse needed simplicity rather than lofty dignity. In 1888, after completing 'The Wanderings of Oisin', a long poem set in Irish heroic times, Yeats felt that his own poetry had been 'sluggish, incoherent, and inarticulate' and that in order to 'simplify' it, he needed 'the landscape of familiar nature substituted for the landscapes of art'.[40] The Irish poems which Yeats valued the least were 'literary', having 'more of the study, less of the earth'

B

in them.[41] Irish folklore was close to the earth and had nothing
of the study about it. Yeats's conclusion, cited earlier, that
Shelley's poetry had had a 'mythology' but lacked 'folk-lore' and
suffered for that deficiency because 'a mythology which had
been passing for long through literary mind without any new in-
flow from living tradition loses all the incalculable instructive
and convincing quality of popular traditions' is especially signi-
ficant in this regard. Irish folklore was a living tradition to be
found among the peasants in the Irish countryside, and not,
like the ancient Irish sagas, a dry, confused body of materials
found only in philological and historical studies if one did not
read Irish. Moreover, Irish folklore was considered by Yeats
and many others at the time to be a living continuation of the
same Irish folk mind which had produced the Irish heroic sagas
of the past. Sophie Bryant argued in *Celtic Ireland* (1889), a
book which Yeats reviewed favourably in 1890, that there was
more ancient belief in peasant lore than in ancient bardic tales.
According to Yeats, the Irish peasant lived in a world where
little had changed since Adam and Eve, especially in the West
of Ireland where 'the second century is nearer than the nine-
teenth, and a pagan memory is more of a power than any
modern feeling.'[42] Thus, when Yeats began to use an Irish
subject matter in his own poetry of the 1880s, the oral traditions
of the peasantry had a more immediate influence on his work
than the manuscript tradition of ancient Irish myth did.

Yeats's own conception of Irish myth in the late 1880s did
not satisfy his need for a serious, vital Irish subject matter. In
1886 Yeats wrote, 'The old heroes were as simple as children
who had never been to school.'[43] The edition of selected trans-
lations of old Irish epics which Yeats considered doing in 1888
never materialised. Yeats's early poetic uses of Irish myth were
few, and presented the Irish heroes in a state of decline rather
than as embodiments of the passionate energy which he later
identified with them. In Yeats's first collection of poetry, *The
Wanderings of Oisin and other Poems* (1889), the majority of
the poems on Irish subjects have to do with Irish fairies or
peasants; ancient Ireland is the subject of only two poems, 'The
Wanderings of Oisin' and 'King Goll'. At first glance, 'The
Wanderings of Oisin', written in 1887 and 1888, appears to
be the retelling of an ancient Irish legend. However, Irish myth

provides little more than names, places and atmosphere. Tales and ballads about Ossian and St Patrick had remained one of the few subjects from ancient myth popular among the peasantry, and Yeats based his poem on recent traditions rather than on ancient manuscript sources. Yeats considerably altered the plot, which he loosely based upon an eighteenth-century Irish poem attributed to Michael Comyn, translated in the fourth volume of the *Transactions of the Ossianic Society* (1859). Because Comyn had based his poem on eighteenth-century oral traditions, the Council of the Ossianic Society preceded the poem with the announcement that it did not hold itself responsible for the 'authenticity' or the 'antiquity' of the poem which was of 'recent' origin. According to Daniel Corkery, when Comyn wrote his version 'every Gaelic mind in Ireland' already possessed some version of the legend of Oisin but 'Comyn's Lay', as it was popularly called, was soon being sung throughout Ireland.[44] Even the structure of the Yeats poem was derived from contemporary tradition. Yeats wrote to the editor of the *Spectator* on 29 July 1889 that the three-island structure was 'wholly my own, having no further root in tradition than the Irish peasant's notion that Tir-n-an-oge (The Country of the Young) is made up of three phantom islands'. Yeats's description of Oisin as going with a 'fairy bride' to 'fairyland' in his discussion of the poem in his 'Notes' to *The Countess Kathleen and Various Legends and Lyrics* in 1892 also emphasises the poem's relationship to contemporary fairy lore. Moreover, all of Yeats's comments, in the 1880s and in later life, indicate that he considered the poem more of an allegory filled with private meanings than a poem about ancient Ireland.

In so far as 'The Wanderings of Oisin' is concerned with ancient Ireland, it laments the dwindling of heroic possibility and the disappearance of the ancient Irish heroes. As printed in Yeats's first collection of poetry, *The Wanderings of Oisin and Other Poems* (1889), the poem implies there is no longer any place where a hero such as Oisin can fulfil his heroic nature. When the poem opens, the Fenians have just suffered their important defeat at Gabra, Oisin longs for this world while with Niamh, and Christian Ireland subdues Oisin at the end. His first fiery declaration that he will rejoin the Fenians who will 'rise . . . exultant' is transformed by Patrick's sermonis-

ing into Oisin's final self-pitying speech about rejoining the
Fenians which makes no mention of the Fenians rising again :

> Ah me! to be old without succour, a show unto children, a
> stain,
> Without laughter, a coughing, alone with remembrance and
> fear,
> All emptied of purple hours as a beggar's cloak in the rain,
> As a grass seed crushed by a pebble, as a wolf sucked under
> a weir.

King Goll's self-description in the same collection of poems is
no more energetic :

> I ruled and ruled my life within,
>   Peace-making, mild, a kingly boy.

In his twentieth-century revisions of the poem Yeats removed
most references to King Goll's placidity and ineffectualness, such
as passages about his 'serene and mild' rule and his 'gracious,
gentle' temperament.

Yeats's only other poems about ancient Ireland prior to the
late 1890s, by which time his conception of Irish myth had
changed considerably, were 'Fergus and the Druid' and 'The
Death of Cuchullin' which were both included in *The Countess
Kathleen and Various Legends and Lyrics* (1892). The majority
of poems in this collection were based on the folklore and life of
the Irish peasantry. In 'Fergus and the Druid' a shape-changing
druid fulfils the request of the ancient Irish king to possess
'dreaming wisdom'. As printed in 1892, Fergus's description of
the result—'But now I have grown nothing, being all,/And the
whole world weighs down upon my/heart'—epitomises the same
languid melancholy which had characterised King Goll. The
lyric 'Who Goes With Fergus?' in the same collection merely
alludes to the ancient Irish hero of that name.

Of Yeats's four early poems about ancient Ireland, only in
'The Death of Cuchullin' does the re-telling of an incident from
Irish myth seem to be his main concern. But in his note to the
poem Yeats made clear that he had modelled it upon an oral
legend still current in Ireland and recorded in Jeremiah Curtin's
Myths and Folk-Lore of Ireland (1890), rather than upon the
version of Cuchulain's death found in ancient 'bardic' literature.[45]

The contrast between Yeats's version of 'The Death of Cuchullin' in 1892 and the final, greatly revised version of the poem, 'Cuchulain's Fight with the Sea' (1923), illustrates the development which Yeats's early attitudes about Irish myth underwent before it would eventually succeed Irish folklore and peasant life as his major Irish subject matter. The change in the title indicates how energetic defiance replaced the passivity of the earlier version. 'The Death of Cuchullin', as printed in *The Countess Kathleen*, concluded with the lines :

> In three days time he stood up with a moan,
> And he went down to the long sands alone,
> For four days warred he with the bitter tide,
> And the waves flowed above him and he died.

'Cuchulain's Fight with the Sea' concludes with the lines :

> Cuchulain stirred,
> Stared on the horses of the sea, and heard
> The cars of battle and his own name cried,
> And fought with the invulnerable tide.

Yeats's dramatic and fictional treatments of ancient Ireland in the 1880s and 1890s also indicate that Irish myth provided more atmosphere than substance to his first attempts to use it. Although the names of the hero, Forgael, and the heroine, Dectora, in Yeats's play *The Shadowy Waters* are taken from ancient Irish literature, the plot of the play is Yeats's own creation. In 1907 Yeats admitted that *The Shadowy Waters* had 'a good deal of incidental Irish folklore . . . but [is] not founded on any particular story'.[46] The heroine was nameless until the manuscript version of 1894. In Standish O'Grady's *History of Ireland* Dectora was the name of Cuchulain's mother, and Emer, Cuchulain's wife, was the daughter of Forgael, but Yeats took only the names from O'Grady's work. *The Shadowy Waters* demonstrates that in the 1880s Yeats was more familiar with Shelley's questing-heroes than with the voyages of Bran and other ancient Irish heroes. As in 'The Wanderings of Oisin', ancient Ireland was not Yeats's main concern. According to the editors of the early manuscripts of *The Shadowy Waters*, Yeats conceived of the play from the first as one in which visionary and more mundane personal experience would be integrated into a quasi-mythological framework, he used Irish mythology as a source of details to fill out the structure of the early versions, and he was sometimes reluctant to particularise the characters by identifying them with specific personages in ancient Irish myth.[47]

When Yeats wrote 'Dhoya' he was more concerned with presenting his tale as a legend still current around Sligo than with reproducing an ancient Irish tale. The basic situation of a man who marries a fairy bride and then loses her to a fairy husband in a chess game derives from an old Irish tale in *The Book of the Dun Cow*. In all four English versions of the tale, which had appeared by 1887 when Yeats finished 'Dhoya', the mortal is named King Eochaid, the bride, Edain, and her husband, Midhir. Although Yeats used these names in his later poem, 'The Two Kings' (1913), he purposely left the fairy husband and wife in 'Dhoya' nameless. Dhoya, whom Yeats said had been named after a deep pool in Sligo Bay, is portrayed as 'a man of giant stature and of giant strength', a figure more characteristic of a nineteenth-century folk tale than like the ancient Irish king in the original tale. Yeats alludes to Diarmid and Grania only in reference to specific places around Sligo. Yeats's conclusion to the tale also reinforces this sense of 'Dhoya' as a current local legend: 'Sometimes the cotters on the mountains of Donegal hear on windy nights a sudden sound of horses' hoofs, and say to each other, "There goes Dhoya." And at the same hour men say if any be abroad in the valleys they see a huge shadow rushing along the mountain.'[48]

Thus, Yeats's writings in the late 1880s and early 1890s reflected a limited use and conception of the subject matter of ancient Irish myth and indicate that he used the life and beliefs of the nineteenth-century Irish peasant much more frequently. For a time in the late 1880s folk ballads based on local folklore seemed to promise Yeats a way of simplifying his poetry and bringing it back down to earth. Yeats spent much of the spring and summer of 1887 trying to write folk ballads using the poetry of William Allingham (1824–1889) as both a positive and negative example. Allingham, the son of a well-to-do Protestant merchant, had been born in Ballyshannon, a seacoast village in the West of Ireland just north of Sligo, where Yeats had spent so much of his boyhood. Yeats was especially enthusiastic about two of Allingham's subjects : his use of Irish fairy lore and his celebration of his native Ballyshannon. Yeats hoped to do for his beloved Sligo what Allingham had done for Bally-shannon. Yeats used Sligo legends in several of his early ballads : 'A Legend' (1888) describes the origin of a drowned city supposed to lie under Lough Gill near Sligo and 'The Fairy Pedant' (1887) is based on the fairy lore of the Sligo peasants.

Critics of Yeats's poetry have generally agreed that Yeats's early attempts at ballad writing were unsuccessful. Dwight Eddins has said that Yeats's ballad writing in the late 1880s 'was essentially a mistaken path so far as it attempted to meet the "people" upon their own linguistic and conceptual grounds', and that it was characterised by 'uncharacteristic triteness' and 'poverty of thought'.[49] Richard Ellmann has explained this failure by the fact that Yeats was probably still confusing an artificial literary ballad with the true folk ballad, neither of which he completely understood.[50] Georges-Denis Zimmerman, an authority on Irish ballads, has concluded that Yeats actually knew 'very little' about ballads and oral poetry in general in the late 1880s.[51] Yeats himself gave a similar explanation for the literary shortcomings of his early ballads. In an essay entitled 'What is "Popular Poetry"?' (1901), Yeats explained that when he first approached nineteenth-century Irish poetry he had rejected the Young Irelanders for having written nothing but 'political opinions' and had turned instead to the ballad poets who wrote 'about the beliefs of the people like Allingham, or about the old legends like Ferguson', but that he had eventually realised that this was a 'middle class' literary tradition, and that to write true folk ballad one had to know and understand the Irish peasants themselves and hear their stories from them.[52]

Yeats's articles in the late 1880s and 1890s had also reflected a growing disenchantment with the literary conventions of the nineteenth-century Irish poets and his own realisation that he needed to get to know the Irish peasant. Yeats criticised Allingham for not really having known the Irish peasant and for not taking his character seriously : 'The people of Ireland seem to Mr Allingham graceful, witty, picturesque, benevolent, everything but a people to be taken seriously. This want of sympathy with the national life and history has limited his vision . . . has thinned his blood.'[53] Allingham had actually written most of his poems about Ireland after he left Ireland for England in 1863, and he had always hoped to become the Irish Tennyson and be 'essentially and entirely English'.[54] Yeats concluded in 1891 that Allingham had never succeeded in 'feeling Ireland as a whole; from writing of the joys and sorrows of the Irish people, as Davis, and Ferguson, and Mangan have done, and from stirring our blood with great emotions', and had lacked a 'sense of the great unities—the revelations of man to man, and all to the serious life of the world'.[55] However, Yeats never lost his belief that Allingham's subject matter, the life and beliefs of the country people in the West of Ireland, was in tune with the great unities, the great mysteries of life. Yeats declared in his article 'The Message of the Folk-lorist' (1893) that there was no human passion 'that cannot find fit type or symbol in the legends of the peasantry'.[56]

For a time the tradition of the Irish folk ballad had seemed the answer to the din and bombast of 'Young Ireland' but, as John Frayne has pointed out, Yeats was too self-consciously searching for a subtler, deeper tone than that found in these poets to be completely satisfied with poetry such as Allingham's.[57] Ultimately Yeats rejected much that he had found in the 'Young Ireland' poetry of the 1840s and in the nineteenth-century Irish ballad tradition, especially their rhetoric and artificial literary mannerisms, but he never rejected the subject matter which they left to him—the Irish peasant and his legends —though his concept of them changed greatly in the course of his career. Yeats himself summed up his indissolvable relation with nineteenth-century Irish poetry in his poem 'To Ireland in the Coming Times' (1892):

> Know, that I would accounted be
> True brother of a company
> That sang, to sweeten Ireland's wrong,
> Ballad and story, rann and song;
> Nor be I any less of them,
>   . . . .
> Nor may I less be counted one
> With Davis, Mangan, Ferguson, . . .

Yeats's response to criticisms of his arrogance in placing himself in such eminent poetic company is significant: 'I did not in the least intend the lines to claim equality of eminence, nor does the context bear out such a reading, but only community in the treatment of Irish subjects after an Irish fashion.'[58] If Yeats rejected the style of the Young Irelanders and of Allingham, and if he could not achieve the style of Irish speakers like Callanan, Walsh and Ferguson who had direct access to Irish tradition, he nevertheless chose to inherit their Irish subject matter, the ancient and contemporary traditional literature of Ireland, and their quest to express uniquely Irish literary and cultural experiences. Callanan, Walsh and Ferguson, and even Davis and Allingham had collected the folklore of the peasantry.[59] So when Yeats realised that nineteenth-century 'Irish' ballad writers had written in an artificial, middle-class tradition rather than in a living folk tradition, he set out to know the Irish peasantry for himself by reading the folklore collected among them earlier in the century and going out among them and collecting their folklore. Austin Clarke has aptly summed up the influence of a living folk tradition on Yeats and the other writers of the Irish Literary Revival: 'When Keats turned to Greek mythology, he went to Lemprière's Classical Dictionary; our poets went out of doors.'[60] Or, as Yeats himself recalled in his essay 'What is "Popular Poetry"?', after he had 'read bad translations from the Irish' in Dublin libraries, and after he had concluded that most nineteenth-century Irish 'popular poetry' was an artificial middle-class literary tradition, he had gone 'at last down into Connacht to sit by turf fires'.[61]

B*

Yeats and Irish Folklore:
The Nineteenth-Century Tradition

Yeats's childhood years in Sligo had introduced him to the peasantry and folklore of Ireland. Richard Ellmann has described Yeats's mother, Susan Pollexfen Yeats: 'She had few opinions about anything, but liked best of all to exchange ghost and fairy stories with some fisherman's wife in the kitchen. Sensitive and deep-feeling but undemonstrative, she always considered her birthplace, the romantic country of Sligo, the most beautiful place in the world, and she passed on the feeling to her children.'[1] William Murphy, in his study of the Yeats family and the Pollexfens of Sligo, argues that by 1881 when Yeats was sixteen, the Yeats children's 'souls had been shaped, and it was Sligo that shaped them'.[2] Yeats's sister, Lily, recalled that in Sligo, 'The servants played a big part in our lives. They were so friendly and wise and knew so intimately angels, saints, banshees, and fairies.'[3] In his *Autobiography* Yeats fondly recalled the folklore he had heard in Sligo as a child: 'Indeed, so many stories did I hear . . . that the world seemed full of monsters and marvels.'[4]

In the late 1880s Yeats's personal interests, not just the demands of his literary nationalism and his professional needs as a poet, rekindled his enthusiasm for the Irish folklore which he had heard from his mother's family and their servants in Sligo. The ghost and fairy stories which Yeats had heard as a child provided a background for his enthusiastic study of the occult in the late 1880s. When Yeats enrolled at the Metropolitan School of Art in Dublin in May 1884, he met George Russell, later known as AE, in whom he found a confederate even more determined than himself in his opposition to nineteenth-century materialism. Together they began to study psychical and occult phenomena, European magic and mysticism, and Eastern religion as alternatives to the scientific, materialistic and rationalistic explanations of the universe so popular in late nineteenth-century England.

Yeats simultaneously began to study a relatively new area of the occult called Theosophy.[5] Its founder, Madame Blavatsky, discounted current theories of evolution and had argued in her first book, *Isis Unveiled* (1877), that ancient man, rather than having been an ape, had been in touch with spiritual realities and had possessed a secret wisdom now known only to an ancient brotherhood in Tibet. Some of these secret doctrines were now to be transmitted to the world through Madame Blavatsky's Theosophical Society. A. P. Sinett, a wealthy English editor who had lived in India, had been convinced by the phenomena —letters dropping from nowhere, mysterious raps, tinklings of an astral bell—which Madame Blavatsky had demonstrated, and he recorded all these phenomena in his book entitled *The Occult World*. In 1885 Yeats was greatly excited by Sinett's second book, *Esoteric Buddhism*, which provided a doctrinal exegesis for magical phenomena. But Yeats's enthusiasm was soon qualified when an investigation conducted by The Society for Psychical Research, a group well-disposed towards occult phenomena, revealed secret panels and other tricks which Madame Blavatsky had supposedly used. Yeats hesitated about becoming a Theosophist, but when his family moved to London in 1887 he began to visit Madame Blavatsky who had recently founded a Theosophical Lodge in London. Yeats was never completely convinced of Madame Blavatsky's occult powers, but in 1888, eager to prove that occult phenomena were possible, he joined the newly formed 'Esoteric Section' of Madame Blavatsky's group which was conducting experiments in magic and the occult. However, no miracles occurred, doubts arose in the minds of other members, and in 1890 when Madame Blavatsky asked Yeats to resign he complied. A few months later he joined the Hermetic Students of the Golden Dawn, a society whose beliefs were similar to those of the Theosophists. But instead of giving Yeats theories as the Theosophists had done, the Golden Dawn gave him the opportunity and methods for constant experiment with the occult.

Yeats's experiments in the occult coincided with his deepening commitment to Irish literary nationalism. His interest in

the occult and his activities as a literary nationalist were recip-
rocal in many respects. In the late 1880s Yeats combined his
occult and literary activities—a necessity if he was not to
violate his own criticisms against non-Irish subject matter—
and Irish folklore provided the link between the two activities.
Yeats's early playlets had depicted man attempting to make
contact with spiritual realities and beings: occultism and folk-
lore mirrored a similar pursuit. Theosophy accepted and in-
corporated ghosts and fairies into their system of belief. Colonel
Henry Olcott, one of the founders of The Theosophical Society
of America, had come to Dublin in the late 1880s to examine
Irish fairy lore from a Theosophical perspective.

Yeats linked his occultism and his literary nationalism through-
out his life. He dedicated his anthology of Irish folklore, *Fairy
and Folk Tales of the Irish Peasantry* (1888), 'To My Mystical
Friend G. R.'—George Russell, his companion in occult studies.
In an article entitled 'Irish Fairies, Ghosts, Witches, Etc' which
appeared in the Theosophical magazine *Lucifer* in 1889 Yeats
asserted that the occultist was as much of an authority on fairies
as the folklorist: 'It has occurred to me that it would be
interesting if some spiritualist or occultist would try to explain
the various curious and intricate spiritualistic beliefs of the
peasants. When reading Irish folk-lore, or listening to Irish
peasants telling their tales of magic and fairyism and witchcraft,
more and more one is convinced that some clue there must be.
Even if it is all dreaming, why have they dreamed this particular
dream? Clearly the occultist should have his say as well as the
folklorist.'[6] In the article which followed Yeats used Theo-
sophical beliefs to explain fairy lore drawn from numerous
nineteenth-century collections of Irish folklore. In a letter to
John O'Leary in 1889 Yeats described Madame Blavatsky as
being 'like an old peasant woman'.[7] In an article entitled
'Invoking the Irish Fairies' in the *Irish Theosophist* in 1892,
Yeats described how he and a fellow member of the Golden
Dawn had invoked the Irish fairies and succeeded in summoning
them.[8] John O'Leary strongly disapproved of Yeats's involve-
ment with the occult; Yeats's answer to O'Leary's objections in
1892 indicates that Yeats regarded his occult and literary pur-
suits as reciprocal:

Now as to Magic. It is surely absurd to hold me 'weak' or otherwise because I chose to persist in a study which I decided deliberately 4 or 5 years ago to make next to my poetry the most important pursuit of my life. . . . The probable explanation however of your somewhat testy postcard is that you were out at Bedford Park & heard my father discoursing about my magical pursuits out of the immense depths of his ignorance as to everything that I am doing and thinking. If I had not made magic my constant study I could not have written a single word of my Blake book nor would 'The Countess Kathleen' have ever come to exist. The mystical life is the centre of all that I do & all that I think & all that I write. It holds to my work the same relation that the philosophy of Godwin held to the work of Shelley & I have all-ways considered myself a voice of what I believe to be a greater renascence—the revolt of the soul against the intellect now beginning in the world.[9]

In his essay entitled 'Magic' (1901) Yeats wrote : 'Magical traditions will someday be studied as a part of folklore.'[10] Later, in his introduction to *A Vision* (1925), Yeats wrote that in the late 1880s he had considered the occult as 'an enlargement of the folklore of the villages'.[11] In 1937 Yeats recalled that when Lady Gregory had asked him to annotate her collection of Irish folklore, *Visions and Beliefs in the West of Ireland* (1920), he 'began an investigation of contemporary spiritualism . . . that I might understand what she had taken down in Galway'.[12]

In the late 1880s the folk beliefs of the Irish peasantry, a group in close contact with earthly realities as well, provided an answer to O'Leary's criticism that Yeats was veering too far from everyday reality in his occult pursuits. Conversely, Yeats could argue that the spiritism of the Irish peasant contained the truth about nature and man which was not to be found in nineteenth-century rationalism. Yeats thus turned to Irish folklore for a subject matter purely Irish in nature, as a means of 'simplifying' his poetry by substituting the 'landscape of familiar nature' for the 'landscapes of art', and in the hope of finding universal patterns and proof of the existence of spiritual beings.

In order to understand Yeats's expectations concerning Irish folklore, it is necessary to view them within the context of nineteenth-century intellectual and literary history, and not as an idiosyncratic offshoot of Yeats's occult and nationalist interests. An examination of the development of folklore studies in the nineteenth-century as an international, British and Irish phenomenon is a necessary introduction to Yeats's complex and occasionally contradictory attitudes about the use of Irish folklore in his private life, in his poetry and articles and in the two anthologies of Irish folklore which he edited, *Fairy and Folk Tales of the Irish Peasantry* (1888) and *Irish Fairy Tales* (1892).

Nineteenth-century folklore studies reflected numerous and often contradictory intellectual movements. Folklore had come into being as a separate academic discipline in England during the nineteenth century only to decline at the turn of the twentieth century. In the Epilogue to his history of nineteenth-century British folklore studies, Richard M. Dorson concludes that it was the eclecticism of British folklore studies which brought about the decline: 'Where once the vitality of the folklore movement had extended into many adjacent areas and captivated specialists in a host of subjects—philology, archaeology, anthropology, Celtic studies, Scandinavian studies, zoology, the classics, the history of religions, psychical research, law, medicine, political institutions, in fact the cultures and literatures of the world—now other concepts and approaches invaded the diminishing boundaries of the province of folklore.'[13] The eclectic nature of the folklore movement made it a perfect medium for Yeats's complex literary and occult interests in the 1880s and 1890s.

Prior to the late eighteenth century, the folklore of the British Isles had attracted little attention or admiration. From the Renaissance through the eighteenth century, classical mythology enjoyed a vogue in English literature, while rural British themes were generally treated as classical pastorals, as references to Irish mythology had been in Edmund Spenser's *The Faerie Queene*. The Arcadian setting of Yeats's own early playlet, *The Island of Statues. An Arcadian Faery Tale*, was typical of the English pastoral.

Samuel Johnson's account of his tour of Scotland with Boswell, *A Journey to the Western Islands of Scotland* (1775), typifies the eighteenth century's intellectual scorn for the rude peasantry of the Celtic areas of the British Isles. Johnson repeatedly refers to the Highlands and rural districts of Scotland as 'regions of ignorance' and to the inhabitants as 'savages'. Although Scottish oral traditions had died out with the bards, according to Johnson, not much had been lost for the Gaelic language of Scotland was 'the rude speech of a barbarous people, who had few thoughts to express, and were content, as they conceived grossly, to be grossly understood'.[14] Johnson scoffed at the 'superstitions' of the Scottish peasantry such as their belief in 'Second Sight' : 'It is a breach of the common order of things, without any visible reason or perceptible benefit. It is ascribed only to a people very little enlightened; and among them, for the most part, to the mean and the ignorant.'[15] However, throughout the book, the reader senses Johnson's extreme curiosity to hear Scottish legends and 'superstitions', and his disappointment that he found so few.

Johnson's curiosity about Scottish folklore and willingness to believe did not extend to James MacPherson's *Ossian* which Johnson repeatedly denounced as a forgery. Here again Johnson's reaction typifies that of eighteenth-century England. MacPherson's poem experienced a great vogue in Europe, only to be condemned in England as a forgery, with no appreciation of the poem's value as an imaginative creation in its own right. Considering its emphasis on the supernatural and the exotic, it is surprising that MacPherson's Celtic subject matter did not inspire a vogue for Celtic subjects in England. But English Romanticism turned instead to Gothic and Oriental material. Even Thomas Moore, whose popularity rested on writing English verses to old Irish melodies, wrote a long Oriental tale, *Lalla Rookh* (1817). James Clarence Mangan published Arabic, Turkish, and Persian translations. In their enthusiasm for the folk song and the speech of the common man, Wordsworth and Coleridge ignored the Irish and Scottish peasant. The traditional British prejudice against Celtic culture and the lack of Irish folklore available to English writers in the early nineteenth century explain why Celtic materials did not enter into the mainstream of English literature at the beginning of the century. But by the end of the century, scholarly research on Irish antiquities had qualified British biases against Celtic culture, and Irish folklore had become much more available—two reasons why the literary movement known as the Irish Literary

Renaissance was able to succeed among English as well as Irish audiences.

The antiquarianism which had helped foster English Romanticism was also the origin of the great vogue for folklore studies in nineteenth-century England, which in turn generated Irish folklore studies. The quest for antiquities of all kinds had intrigued Englishmen throughout the seventeenth and eighteenth centuries. Most of the antiquarian interest had centred on physical remains in England, but from the beginning, antiquarian studies had also covered the oral traditions and beliefs of the peasantry of Ireland as well as England. William Camden's *Britannia* (1586) included material which Camden had gathered from the oral testimony of the countrypeople and contained a section devoted to 'Manners and Customs of the Ancient Irish'.

Folklore studies in nineteenth-century England were written from varied points of view and engendered diverse reactions: sceptical, moralistic, philological, anthropological, scientific, ethnological, and literary. *Observations on Popular Antiquities* (1777) by John Brand underwent numerous editions during the nineteenth century and enjoyed widespread popularity in England. Brand wrote about witchcraft and fairy lore and supernaturalism as a rationalist and cynic speaking to fellow rationalists. According to Brand, the 'vulgar and provincial customs' which his book described 'may appear foolish to the enlightened understandings of men in the eighteenth century'.[16] Brand's sceptical rationalism was the very force Yeats attempted to combat in his own folklore anthologies. But both Brand and Yeats drew upon the curiosity of a large reading public attracted to the entertainment value of folklore rather than to any editorial commentary which accompanied it.

While the adult reading public of nineteenth-century England usually satisfied its curiosity about witches, fairies, and others creatures of folklore by reading works coloured by the cynical scepticism of editors such as Brand, their children read folklore filled with heavy-handed moralising. Under the influence of the doctrine of utility, editors substituted doctrinaire tracts modelled on popular children's fairy tales for the real thing or injected moral messages into authentic folk tales. For example, George Cruikshank reduced the matter to absurdity by turning 'Cinderella' and 'Jack and the Beanstalk' into temperance tracts.[17] Thackeray and Dickens were among those who, indignant at such tampering, defended the imaginative extravagance of folklore. In 1853 Dickens protested in 'Frauds on the Fairies' in *Household Words*: 'In an utilitarian age, of all times, it is a matter of grave importance that Fairy tales should be respected. . . . To preserve them in their usefulness, they must be as much preserved in their simplicity, and purity, and innocent extravagance, as if they were actual fact. Whosoever alters them to suit his own opinions, whatever they are, is guilty, to our thinking, of an act of presumption, and appropriates to himself what does not belong to him.'[18] In his *Irish Sketch-Book* (1843) Thackeray delighted in the availability of folklore in Ireland and lamented that in England 'the march of knowledge' had 'began to banish Fancy out of the world, and gave us, in place of the old fairy tales . . . such books as "Conversations on Chemistry", "The Little Geologist", "Peter Parley's Tales about the Binomial Theorem", and the like.'[19] Later in the century Yeats too would delight in the extravagant amorality of the fairy creatures and realise the importance of keeping his own private beliefs about the fairies out of his anthologies.

Because of his pose as an Irish literary nationalist writing about purely Irish subjects, Yeats generally chose not to demonstrate his knowledge of the broader spectrum of nineteenth-century folklore studies and their relation to Irish folklore. His knowledge of folklore extended well beyond Irish folklore. As a child he read the Brothers Grimm, Hans Christian Andersen and Walter Scott, and his early letters and articles indicate his familiarity with studies of non-Irish folklore materials. Many of his attitudes about Irish folklore were based upon his knowledge of international developments in the study of folklore. In the early nineteenth century folklore had been studied primarily as an antiquarian curiosity, but by mid-century two scholarly interpretations of folklore and myth had developed: the philological and the anthropological approaches. The philological interpretation of folklore originated in the work of Sir William Jones (1746–1794), a noted Oriental and Classical linguist, the first English scholar to master Sanskrit and an authority on the language, literature, and philosophy of India. In the 1780s his discovery of the affinity between Sanskrit and

Latin and Greek gave impetus to the study of comparative philology. Jones also suggested that the Celtic language 'though blended with a very different idiom, had the same origin with Sanskrit'.[20]

In 1856 Friedrich Max Müller (1823–1900), a comparative philologist who had translated and studied Sanskrit, wrote a lengthy essay entitled 'Comparative Mythology' which revised all previous thinking about the origin of myth by proposing that the key to understanding Aryan traditions, whether the myths of gods or the legends of heroes, was the method of comparative mythology. Müller theorised that all Indo-European peoples once belonged to a common Aryan stock and that after the migration of the European groups from their Indic homeland, the parent language and the mythology it related had splintered into various offshoots. A time came when the original meanings of the names of the Vedic gods were forgotten and survived only in mythical phrases and proverbs of uncertain sense. Stories then developed to explain these phrases, according to Müller, and from this 'disease of language' myths were born. Müller believed that philology could determine the beliefs of ancient man. After applying his philological approach to ancient myths and contemporary folklore, Müller concluded that ancient man had constructed his pantheon around the sun, the dawn and the sky.[21]

This 'solar theory' was carried to lengths far exceeding the etymological boundaries of Max Müller by his most aggressive disciple, George William Cox, who reduced all Aryan myth to the contest between day and night.[22] Yeats was enthusiastic about applications of this 'solar theory' to Irish folklore. In his discussion of 'Authorities on Irish Folklore' at the end of *Irish Fairy Tales* (1892) and elsewhere, Yeats cited David Fitzgerald's contributions to the *Revue Celtique* in the 1880s as one of the three best series of articles on Irish folklore ever written. Fitzgerald had applied Cox's theories to Irish myth and concluded that the characters in ancient Irish myth were personifications of the various powers of nature. But, going to even further extremes than Cox had, Fitzgerald proceeded to identify specific astrological constellations as the origins of various ancient Irish myths.[23] Yeats's praise of Fitzgerald is representative of the anti-scholarly nature of Yeats's use of Irish folklore studies. As a reader of the *Revue Celtique* in the 1880s and 1890s Yeats must have known that Fitzgerald's theories had been considered ridiculous by scholars in the mainstream of Irish studies. In the issue of *Revue Celtique* which followed the one with Fitzgerald's article, Whitley Stokes, a respected authority on Irish myth, had demolished Fitzgerald's arguments and concluded his article with the comment 'But I cannot waste any more time on this farrago of bad Irish, doubtful English, mythological guesswork, and impossible etymology.'[24] But Yeats, who was involved in astrological studies with his uncle George Pollexfen in the 1880s, was fascinated by Fitzgerald's theories and willingly discounted scholarly objections. Yeats would also have been in agreement with Fitzgerald's statement that there was nothing historical about ancient Irish myths except that they came from ancient times. Valuing Irish myths and folklore for their imaginative literary value and their relation to his personal interests such as the occult and astrology, Yeats repeatedly criticised scholars who interpreted Irish mythology and folklore as historical or philological data. But regardless of Yeats's objections to philological and anthropological interpretations of folklore, he was indirectly indebted to scholarship in both areas for much of his theory and usage of Irish folklore. In the twentieth century the solar and lunar symbolism in Yeats's treatment of the Irish mythological figure, Cuchulain, reflected the influence of the solar theory of the philological folklorists.

Yeats's association of Irish folklore with the occult beliefs of the Near East was in the tradition of another philological folklorist, Robert Brown (1844–1902), who had declared that comparative mythology should be expanded to include the religious cults and myths of Arabia, Persia and Egypt. Throughout the nineteenth century several Irish folklorists, all of whose works Yeats read carefully, had already used theories of comparative philology and mythology to suggest parallels between Irish folklore and ancient Near Eastern and Far Eastern myth. In Volume I of *Fairy Legends of the South of Ireland* (1825), Thomas Crofton Croker had pointed out ancient Hindu and Germanic parallels to the Killarney legend of the sleeping hero O'Donoghue.[25] Thomas Keightley, an associate of Croker's, in *The Fairy Mythology* (1829) had explained similarities between Irish legends and those of ancient India and Persia by arguing that Celts, 'Hindoos', and Persians shared a common ancestry.[26]

In 1852 Nicholas O'Kearney had argued that contemporary
Irish oral traditions which indentified the Irish goddess Aine
with the moon derived from ancient Irish worship of the sun
and moon which in turn had parallels in the Roman worship
of Diana and the Egyptian worship of Isis.²⁷ In 1853 Sir
William Wilde mentioned parallels between contemporary Irish
folklore and Hindu and Assyrian traditions.²⁸ Later in the
century his wife, Lady Wilde, expanded his 'theories' consider-
ably, arguing in the *Dublin University Magazine* in 1877 that
the 'fairy mythology' of Ireland was of Persian origin.²⁹ In
Ancient Legends, Mystic Charms and Superstitions of Ireland
(1887) and *Ancient Cures, Charms and Usages of Ireland*
(1890) she cited philological evidence of the relationship be-
tween the Irish language and Sanskrit for her argument that
Irish fairy legends represented a primitive worship of mystic beings
which had originated in ancient India and arrived in ancient
Ireland via Egypt and Greece and Celtic Spain. Such arguments
by Irish folklorists obviously convinced Yeats that contemporary
Irish fairy lore was obviously of as much occult and symbolic
significance as ancient Irish myth. Yet because he feared to
alienate readers he kept his occult beliefs out of the folklore
anthologies he edited and most of his early articles.

Although Yeats had denounced 'scientific folklorists' who
were 'on the gad after . . . the primitive religion of mankind' in
his Introduction to *Fairy and Folk Tales of the Irish Peasantry*
(1888), a few months later he was expounding John Rhys's and
Henri D'Arbois de Jubainville's theories about the relationship
between Greek and Celtic mythology and the relation of both to
contemporary Irish fairy lore. Both men had used the methods
of comparative philology and mythology to examine Celtic
mythology: Rhys in his *Lectures on the Origin and Growth of
Religion as Illustrated by Celtic Heathendom* (1888) and Jubain-
ville in *Le Cycle Mythologique Irlandais et la Mythologie
Celtique* (1884). Yeats's knowledge of Jubainville's work was
probably based on Alfred Nutt's lengthy review of the book
in the *Folklore Journal* in 1884.

Yeats was also indirectly indebted to the theories of the
anthropological folklorists who disagreed with the theories offered
by philological folklorists. Anthropological folklorists sought to
replace philology with ethnology by attempting to create a

science devoted to reconstructing the world view of pre-historic man from the contemporary lore of peasants of various countries. But whereas the majority of anthropological folklorists considered the irrational beliefs and practices of the peasantry as the remains of a low and savage level of human culture, Yeats believed that the folklore of the Irish countryside preserved remnants of ancient secret doctrines, the wisdom of which was desperately needed by a materialistic modern world. Yeats's occult interpretation of anthropological folklore studies was not unprecedented. During the 1880s Andrew Lang (1844–1912), an authority on anthropological folklore studies and a populariser of contemporary folklore, had become deeply involved in the psychic and spiritualistic aspects of folklore and had sought to identify genuine patterns of psychic experience in recurring folk tales. In *Isis Unveiled* (1877) Madame Blavatsky had attributed the similarity in the fundamental beliefs of all religions to the existence of a secret doctrine which was their common parent. But she claimed that this ancient wisdom was preserved in a secret oral tradition rather than in the old written texts being studied by philological and anthropological folklorists. Yeats too would prefer current oral traditions rather than old written accounts of myth. His preference for oral Irish folklore was also in the tradition of Alfred Nutt (1856–1912), a noted Celtic folklorist who had objected to the general belief that nineteenth-century oral tradition represented a debased and shrunken mythology. Nutt claimed that medieval Irish manuscripts were themselves derived from a worthy and poetic oral folk tradition which was still current in the oral traditions of the nineteenth-century Irish peasant. Nutt argued in his Postscript to Douglas Hyde's *Beside the Fire: A Collection of Irish Gaelic Folk Stories* (1890) that the oral traditions of the peasants had remained in fuller sympathy with the lore of Irish antiquity than had the manuscript traditions of the cultured Irish bards. Twentieth-century scholarship on Irish literary traditions, such as Gerard Murphy's *Saga and Myth in Ancient Ireland* (1955), generally corroborated Nutt's argument that early Irish sagas had their roots in an ancient oral tradition. However, Nutt's theories concerning the contemporary peasantry's links with ancient Ireland have not been received as enthusiastically by recent scholars as they were by Yeats and others in the late nineteenth century.

Nineteenth-century scholarship on folklore, whether anthropological or philological, had generally been written from an international perspective. Even Alfred Nutt, who had continually asserted the distinctive quality of Gaelic folklore, had valued it primarily for its illumination of other national mythologies. Yeats's search for ancient occult wisdom in Irish folklore derived from this universal approach to folklore. His literary use of Irish folklore as a purely national rather than international phenomenon must, however, be understood in terms of other aspects of nineteenth-century folklore studies. Nationalistic concerns had been implicitly connected with the collection of folklore from the beginning. Jacob and Wilhelm Grimm's *Household Tales*, which had appeared in 1823 and 1826 and had given tremendous impetus to the collection of oral folklore, had been collected and published out of the patriotic desire to preserve German traditions during the French occupation of Germany. In English literature Sir Walter Scott (1771–1832), in his three-volume collection of Scottish folklore entitled *Minstrelsy of the Scottish Border: Consisting of Historical and Romantic Ballads, Collected in the Southern Counties of Scotland, with a few of Modern Date, Founded upon Local Tradition* (1803), had already treated the customs and beliefs of the Scottish border as examples of a unique Scottish national character distinct from the English. Scott's interest in Scottish folklore in this collection was primarily that of an antiquarian —he emphasised that he had collected his material as a youth, that the Scottish border's unique manners and customs were rapidly dissolving into those of England, and often cited old manuscripts and books rather than current oral tradition as his source. But although Scott's interest in folklore derived from the same source—antiquarianism—as scientific folklore studies, his imaginative, literary use of folklore to express national character represented an approach to folklore distinct from the scientific collection and interpretation of folklore by philologists, comparative mythologists and anthropologists. Although Scott discussed the traditions of the Scottish border primarily as antiquarian curiosities, his defence of the imaginative interest of Scottish local legends, albeit somewhat apologetic in tone, marked the beginning of a literary use of folklore which would culminate in the work of Yeats and his fellow

Irish writers at the end of the century.

After acquiring the broad knowledge of Scottish folklore which he had displayed in *Minstrelsy of the Scottish Border* and in which he had mingled Border lore and literary invention, Scott utilised his knowledge of folklore in his poetry and fiction, especially in *The Lay of the Last Minstrel* (1805) and his Waverley novels. Scott bolstered these novels with long prefaces and copious notes for which he ransacked old chronicles and records and consulted with Scottish peasants. In his 'Postscript' to *Waverley* (1814), he declared that 'for the purpose of preserving some idea of the ancient manners of which I have witnessed the almost total extinction, I have embodied in imaginary scenes and ascribed to fictitious characters, a part of the incidents which I have received from those who were actors in them. Indeed, the most romantic parts of this narrative are precisely those which have a foundation in fact.'[30] Scott's combination of historical, romantic background with real people living out credible, recognisable lives instead of the fantastic Gothic tales that had previously been offered as historical novels, took the nineteenth-century reading public by storm. Coleman O. Parsons, in an analysis of Scott's literary use of Scottish folklore entitled *Witchcraft and Demonology in Scott's Fiction* (1964), has summarised Scott's achievement as follows: 'Scott rarely intends the weird merely to startle or to entertain. Instead, he avails himself of materials appropriate to time, place, and people in order to convey a sense of the past. . . . In long and short Scottish narratives, Sir Walter encompasses the great range of native superstitious belief and sharpens understanding of a tumultuous national past through its legendary fears.'[31] But Scott's innovative use of folklore as a means of depicting national character should also be noted. In his 'Postscript' to *Waverley* he said, 'It has been my object to describe these persons, not by caricature and exaggerated use of national dialect, but by their habits, manners, and feelings.'[32]

While Yeats the occultist was influenced by the scientific folklorists' view of folklore as a universal phenomenon, Yeats the literary nationalist edited and wrote folklore in the tradition of Scott and the nineteenth-century Irish literary folklorists whom Scott's work had inspired. In his *Autobiography* Yeats recalled his father reading aloud to him from Scott's works and his own reading of Scott as a boy. Numerous remarks in his essays, articles and letters also indicate his familiarity with Scott's works. Yeats was undoubtedly influenced by Scott's literary use of Scottish folklore to illustrate Scottish character. However, while Scott's perspective was usually that of an anti-quarian, Yeats would emphasise that Irish folklore was still a vital tradition among the Irish peasantry. Both Scott and Yeats wavered between scepticism and belief concerning the spiritual phenomena of Scottish and Irish folklore, but, while Scott became more and more sceptical—his *Letters on Demon-ology and Witchcraft* (1830) explain why 'the Vulgar and the Ignorant' still believed in the old, irrational superstitions—Yeats never attempted to explain away Irish folklore by rationalistic arguments. And, whereas Scott asserted that Celtic superstitions were not uniquely Celtic but had been derived from different sources—Classical, Gothic, Germanic, Scandinavian—Yeats gen-erally treated Irish folklore as a purely Irish phenomenon illustrative of Irish character.

Nevertheless, Yeats's literary nationalism was definitely in the tradition of Scott and the Irish folklorists whom Scott's works had inspired. Scott himself had claimed in the 'Postscript' to *Waverley* that he had been inspired by Maria Edgeworth's fictional portraits of the Irish peasant. In the course of the nine-teenth century Scott's work had in turn inspired Irish folklorists in whose work true folklore was often coloured by or indistin-guishable from fiction. Scott's own novels indicate how blurred the distinction between folklore and fiction was to become. Richard Dorson has pointed out that, although the oral tales collected by Jacob and Wilhelm Grimm had been in striking contrast to the imaginative revision such tales had undergone in literary works from Ovid through Boccaccio, as the Grimms' tales became popular and prompted similar publications, col-lectors and editors, instead of refining the Grimms' empirical techniques for accurately recording spoken texts, assumed in-creasing freedom with the narratives by 'inserting phrases and developing character portrayals, with the intent of clarifying the story line and bringing forth the inner expression of the peasant soul. From this convention but a short step was needed to the doctrine that a collector could rewrite oral fiction in his own style.'[33] Although folklorists inspired by Scott often confused folklore and fiction, Scott himself was somewhat aware of the distinction. He took liberties with folklore in his fiction, but generally stayed close to his sources in his introductions and notes. The distinction between folklore and fiction was more blurred in the collections of Irish folklore which had been published in the nineteenth century, and which Yeats drew upon for materials for his two anthologies of Irish folklore.

Irish folklore researches had originated with the antiquarian interests of Thomas Crofton Croker (1798–1854). Croker was born in Cork and at sixteen, after little formal schooling, was apprenticed to a Cork firm of Quaker merchants. Between 1812 and 1815 he rambled about the South and West of Ireland collecting the songs and legends of the peasantry. In 1818 he moved to London where he worked as a clerk in the Admiralty but he frequently returned to Ireland to collect folklore. He sent nearly forty airs from peasant songs to Thomas Moore for his *Irish Melodies* and later published a collection entitled *Popular Songs of Ireland* (1839). But Croker's chief fame as a folklorist rests on his collecting and editing of 'legends'.

Folklorists distinguish three distinct genres of traditional narrative : (1) Myths—tales laid in a world supposed to have preceded the present order which tell of sacred beings and semi-divine heroes and of the origins of all things and are thus originally connected with religious beliefs and practices. Such narratives once existed in oral form in ancient Ireland; they are contained in medieval manuscripts and continued to exist in a fragmented form as oral folklore among the peasantry throughout the nineteenth century. (2) Legends—localised accounts of an extraordinary, possibly supernatural happening believed to have occurred among actual people in the historical past. Legends are frequently anecdotal in form and are much less structured then either myths or folktales. Irish fairy lore and local traditions, the major interest of both Croker and Yeats, would be categorised as legends. (3) Folktales—strictly fictional narratives set in an unspecified time and place with stereotyped characters, a happy ending and, in contrast to legends, relatively standardised in structure and style.[34] During the nineteenth century what folklorists today label 'folktales' were generally referred to as 'märchen' or 'household tales' (Yeats's usual term for such tales); both terms were derived from the title of the famous folk-

tale collection of Jacob and Wilhelm Grimm, *Kinder- und Haus-
märchen*, 'Children's and Household Tales'. Such märchen had
been published in the hundreds of chapbooks which circulated
in the hundreds of thousands all over Ireland in the late eight-
eenth and early nineteenth centuries. Such published folktales
soon passed over into oral tradition on which their written chap-
book form frequently exercised significant influence.

   Although Irish folktales in chapbook form and translations of
hero tales from ancient Irish mythology had both appeared in
the eighteenth century, Croker was the first to collect and pub-
lish Irish legends. The title of Croker's *Researches in the South
of Ireland, Illustrative of the Scenery, Architectural Remains,
and the Manners and Superstitions of the Peasantry* (1824)
indicates its topographical as well as legendary interest. The
collection, based on notes he had made during several walking
tours in the South of Ireland between 1812 and 1822, con-
tained a wide assortment of materials : detailed descriptions of
places; local and national history; fairy lore and folk customs;
discussions of national character and literature. Croker's intro-
ductory comments included an admirable sense that a collector
of oral traditions should report his materials accurately : 'The
labours of the antiquary are here of infinite service; and from
the undigested stores which his investigation and research have
amassed, it is for others to select and apply.'[35] Unfortunately
Croker himself would 'digest' and thus transform his materials
in future collections. Yet it is unfair to judge Croker only by the
precise collection methods of twentieth-century folklorists. For
his time Croker had a remarkable appreciation of Irish folk-
lore as 'a literary record' and as an illustration of 'national
character'. Many of Croker's other judgments were typical of
his times as well as indicative of why he chose the beliefs and
customs of the peasantry rather than their songs or their tales
of ancient Ireland as the major subject of his later collections :
peasant songs too frequently voiced 'the most positive treason';
the 'romantic tales' about Ossian and other heroes of the ancient
Fianna which Croker found recorded in oral and manuscript
tradition in every village were abundant but, concluded Croker,
had 'a great poverty of fancy and sameness of incident in them'
and so it was 'an idle "amor patriae" to suppose that Irish
literature or history can suffer, even by the total loss of the

legendary records of an age of ignorance and superstition'. On the other hand, peasant beliefs and customs, which Croker believed closely resembled those of Elizabethan England, were 'harmless superstitions which the mind lingers on with pleasure rather than disgust'.[36]

Croker's *Fairy Legends and Traditions of the South of Ireland* (1825), the first collection of oral legends ever assembled in the British Isles, appeared anonymously because, although Croker was responsible for the majority of the materials, he had lost his original manuscript and friends who were familiar with the legends helped him to rewrite it.[37] The collection was so popular that his publisher sent him back to Ireland to collect materials for a sequel, and a second series (dedicated to Sir Walter Scott) and a third series (dedicated to Dr Wilhelm Grimm) were published in 1828. The Brothers Grimm had translated the first volume into German within a year, a French edition came out within three years, and the work was re-issued in England throughout the century. The Brothers Grimm and Walter Scott began an enthusiastic correspondence with Croker after the publication of *Fairy Legends*. Croker later edited further collections of Irish folklore but none of his later works, such as *The Legends of the Lakes: or, Sayings and Doings at Killarney* (1829) or *The Keen of the South of Ireland: as Illustrative of Irish Political and Domestic History, Manners, Music, and Superstitions* (1844), ever came close to the popularity and significance of *Fairy Legends*.

Croker's editorial introductions and notes to the *Fairy Legends* convey a rationalistic, light-hearted, patronising attitude toward his materials. In his 'Preface' to Part II (1828) Croker declared he 'deeply lamented' that the 'popular superstitions of Ireland' still existed among the peasantry and that 'such delusions . . . retard the progress of their civilization', citing examples of the abuses of Irish fairy lore, among them the verdict of 'not guilty' which had been handed down at the Tralee Assizes in July 1826 in the case of a child who, because she could neither stand nor speak, had been drowned by persons attempting to rid her of the fairy they believed had possessed her. Croker concluded his first volume as follows :

The Shefro, the Banshee, and the other creatures of imagination who bear them company now take their farewell of the reader. As knowledge advances, they recede and vanish, as the mists of the valley melt into the air beneath the beams of the morning sun. When rational education shall be diffused among the misguided peasantry of Ireland, the belief in such supernatural beings must disappear in that country, as it has done in England. . . . And now, gentle reader, permit the 'tiny folk', at parting to address thee in the words of their British kindred, after their revels through 'the Midsummer Night's Dream' :

> If we shadows have offended,
> Think but this (and all is mended),
> That you have but slumber'd here
> While these visions did appear :
> And this weak and idle theme
> No more yielding but a dream.[38]

This Shakespearian allusion is typical of Croker's attempt in all three volumes of the *Fairy Legends* to place Irish folklore in the context of English literature and international folklore studies. For example, at the end of a story entitled 'Fairies or No Fairies', Croker appended a Latin poem by Joseph Addison on the origin of the fairies, and excerpts from a poem by Alexander Pope introduced the section entitled 'Legends of the Pooka' in the first volume. In the dedicatory poem to the first volume, Croker consciously placed his collection in the graceful, light-hearted tradition of eighteenth-century English poetry about the fairies: 'Thee, Lady, would I lead through Fairy land/. . . . A land of dreams, with air-built castles piled.' In addition to numerous allusions to English literature, Croker's explanatory 'Notes', which were filled with references to the international analogues of the Irish tales he had collected, demonstrated his wide reading in folklore and antiquarian scholarship. Although Croker usually gave detailed accounts of the Irish families and places associated with his tales, he was obviously unconcerned with presenting his tales as uniquely Irish.

Croker presented the tales he had collected among the Irish peasantry as irrational, antiquarian curiosities, and used them as materials for fiction. The *Fairy Legends* reflected a dichotomy between folklore and fiction reminiscent of Scott: while the tales themselves had been transformed into highly fictionalised narratives, Croker's 'Notes' after each story included a wealth of unadorned information about local legends and customs. Croker took oral legends which by their very nature were short and anecdotal in form and rewrote them into literary narratives filled with descriptions of scenery and with humorous dialogue in the manner of Anglo-Irish fiction. Croker's alterations will be specified in the next chapter when Yeats's editorial emendations to the materials from *Fairy Legends* are considered. Croker's basic materials, however, were authentic. For example, three fairy legends collected in County Kerry in 1951 by Richard Dorson matched fairy legends first collected by Croker in 1825, a proof of his basic trustworthiness.[39] Moreover, despite the fictional liberties Croker took with his materials in *Fairy Legends*, the methods and attitudes he displayed in his later work, *The Keen of the South of Ireland*, even prefigured the methodology of twentieth-century folklorists: he gave detailed descriptions of his informants and the contexts in which he collected his materials and apologetically recalled that in 1813 he had had 'the bad taste . . . to refine upon some keens and embellish others'.[40]

When Douglas Hyde, the pre-eminent Irish folklorist of the late nineteenth century, reviewed his predecessors' accomplishments in his 'Preface' to *Beside the Fire: A Collection of Irish Gaelic Folk Stories* (1890) he declared that Croker's *Fairy Legends* had 'led the way . . . all others have but followed in his footsteps'. Hyde appreciated the literary merits of Croker's graceful and witty style—'his light style, his pleasant parallels from classical and foreign literature, and his delightful annotations'—but decried Croker's 'weak point' as a folklorist, his having been 'too often his own original' which was also 'the defect of all who have followed him'.[41]

Yeats acknowledged Croker as the originator of Irish folklore collections and used almost twice as many stories from Croker as from any other nineteenth-century Irish collector in his own two anthologies of Irish folklore. However, as will be demonstrated in the next chapter, Yeats's use of Irish folklore differed from Croker's in many respects and Yeats made some revisions in the materials from Croker which he anthologised. While Croker lamented that the 'delusions' of the Irish peasantry still existed,

Yeats rejoiced that Irish folklore was still a living tradition. Whereas Croker patronised and rationalised Irish 'superstitions', Yeats strove to take them seriously and delighted in their extravagant imagination. While Croker presented Irish folklore in terms of English literature and international studies in folklore, Yeats presented his materials as a peculiarly Irish tradition.

Irish literary periodicals provided a major outlet for the publication of Irish folklore for about forty years after Croker's collections of the 1820s. Yeats's introductions, notes, and lists of 'Authorities on Irish Folk-Lore' in his two anthologies indicate that he had read widely in nineteenth-century Irish periodical literature, and he used materials from these periodicals in his anthologies. John Power's descriptive bibliography of Irish periodicals, *List of Irish Periodical Publications (Chiefly Literary) from 1729 to the Present Time* (1886) illustrates that journals published in Ireland during the eighteenth and nineteenth centuries had generally been short-lived and had been modelled upon English originals in format and subject matter. In the eighteenth century some Irish periodicals were piracies of London magazines. In the nineteenth century, Irish folklore and fiction and articles on Irish subjects began to be included in Irish periodicals, and a few periodicals were entirely devoted to Irish literature and antiquities. Usually what passed for Irish folklore was actually in the tradition of 'literary folklore' begun by Croker: the tales and beliefs which the authors chose to retell at length as supposedly authentic peasant legends were rewritten by the author to conform to nineteenth-century standards of fiction. Such 'peasant legends' were presented in the framework of essays filled with many unelaborated examples of the beliefs and tales of the peasantry and skeptical, patronising comments by the author. No effort was made to preserve the oral tales and traditions of the peasantry in their original form. For example, in an anonymous article entitled 'The Sheoge' (the Irish term for changeling) which was the third in a series of articles on the 'Legends and Tales of the Queen's County Peasantry' in the *Dublin University Magazine* of 1839, the author matter-of-factly related many interesting examples and events connected with the 'wild and absurd superstitions' about changelings current in his native village and then proceeded to tell a tale which began as follows:

Close by the fine old castle of Gurtnaclea, there lived, some seventy or eighty years ago, a wealthy scullogue, or small farmer, named Pat M'Mahon. He was married at an early age to a blooming girl of the village, and in due time became the joyful father of a fine little girl, which, after his pretty wife, he named Maria. Pat and his wife were extremely fond of the little Maria, and no wonder, for in the country round there was not so fine, so rosy-cheeked, or so healthy-looking a child; and then, she was of such a lively, playful disposition, and so quiet and engaging, that she was the favourite of every one who saw her; and many an old hag of the neighbourhood, as she gazed on the beautiful features of the lovely child, shook her head, and muttered an orison, which, in the language of Sir Walter Scott,

　　Although the holiest names were there
　　Had more of blasphemy than prayer,
for the future safety and well-being of the cherubic girl.[42]

In all elements except plot, the story which follows is indistinguishable from nineteenth-century popular fiction. Ironically, the author of the article just cited claimed that he was an Irish peasant—'born and reared in an Irish cabin, and educated in an Irish hedge school'—writing about the real peasants of Ireland in order to counter the 'demi-savages' and 'caricatures' of nineteenth-century Anglo-Irish fiction 'in which the creations of fancy were substituted for "things as they are"'.[43] The author was indeed a peasant. He was John Keegan (1809–1849), a self-educated peasant who contributed poems and fictionalised legends to the *Nation*, the *Irish Penny Journal*, and the *Dublin University Magazine*. But the only glimmer of the real Irish peasant is in the unelaborated beliefs recounted in the paragraphs preceding the story.

Keegan was obviously writing in the tradition of Croker. He commented that he was attempting to show that the beliefs and practices of the Irish peasantry about changelings were 'much more inhuman and barbarous than one would be led to imagine from reading' Crofton Croker.[44] Keegan's materials were much less humorous than Croker's and usually quite morbid. Yeats used selections from this series of articles in his first folklore anthology, *Fairy and Folk Tales of the Irish Peasantry*, partly to offset the humorous tone of materials from Croker and Samuel Lover. However, Keegan's general attitudes about Irish folklore were basically the same as Croker's, and typical of the condescending skepticism with which folklorists in nineteenth-century periodicals generally regarded their materials. Keegan repeatedly referred to the beliefs and customs of the Irish peasantry as 'wild and absurd superstition' whose 'effects are ridiculously conspicuous in the powerful, and, I may add, degrading influence it has on the moral and social habits' of the Irish.[45]

The anonymous contributor of a series of articles entitled 'Superstitions of the Irish Peasantry' in the *Dublin and London Magazine* of 1825 used the same format that Scott, Croker and Keegan had: the combination of unelaborated folklore items, fictionalised tales, and editorial comment. The rationalistic approach of his introductory paragraph to the series was also in the tradition of Scott and Croker:

> It is a singular fact, in the history of the human mind, that man will embrace any doctrine, however absurd, rather than continue in doubt; for nothing can be more irritating than a novel or strange effect without any assignable cause. Hence superstition is the consequence of imperfect knowledge; for when men, in the infancy of sciences, were unable to account, on natural principles, for the daily phenomena which took place around them, they attributed what they could not comprehend to the agency of aerial beings, whom their imagination invested with peculiar powers, both good and evil.[46]

This anonymous contributor to the *Dublin and London Magazine* of 1825, the source for one of the legends Yeats anthologised, did not share Keegan's belief that Irish folklore was degrading, but said instead: 'Unlike the popular tales of the northern nations, there is in them nothing revolting to humanity; nothing to absolutely terrify or alarm; nothing but what a simple peasantry might believe without injury to themselves, or mischief to others; while, at the same time, they are not the less amusing, and to minds not vitiated by a depraved taste for the horrible, they will, I fancy, be far more acceptable.'[47] This last point—the value of Irish folklore as popular entertainment—was agreed upon by all Irish folklorists no matter how much they condemned Irish folklore as irrational and absurd.

What distinguished Keegan and this anonymous folklorist from Crofton Croker is that they both present Irish folklore as a phenomenon still very much alive in the Irish countryside; their articles contained more unadulterated folklore materials; and they lacked Croker's continual citation of international analogues—three reasons which probably explain why Yeats recommended their articles. Moreover, like Croker, they treated Irish folklore as illustrative of Irish character.

The popularity of Croker's *Fairy Legends* and the nineteenth-century reading public's desire to know the 'real' Irish peasant encouraged many Irish novelists to write tales based on the life and legends of the peasantry. Such fiction, rather than having revealed what Daniel Corkery was later to call 'the hidden Ireland', too frequently disguised the life and folklore of the peasantry with propaganda, humour, melodrama or the trappings of the English novel. Nevertheless, Yeats used the least fiction-alised folklore materials from two such fiction writers, William Carleton and Samuel Lover, in his two folklore anthologies.

William Carleton (1794–1869), a peasant from Country Tyrone whose parents were Gaelic speakers famous for their knowledge of traditional tales and songs, based his novels and tales on the peasant life he knew so well. Although Yeats believed that Carleton's famous series entitled *Traits and Stories of the Irish Peasantry* (1830–1833) marked the beginning of modern Irish literature, he selected materials for his folklore anthologies from Carleton's most folkloristic collection, *Tales and Sketches, Illustrating the Character, Usages, Trad-itions, Sports and Pastimes of the Irish Peasantry* (1845). Carleton's introductory remarks for each collection reflect the fictional bent of the first work and the more accurate record of peasant traditions he achieved in the second : in his 'Preface' to the first series of *Traits and Stories* he said he had given fictitious names and localities to actual incidents; in his 'Preface' to *Tales and Sketches* he said the names, people, and places were all real, although he apologised for such materials—'unpretend-ing as they are, in a literary point of view'.[48] Not surprisingly, twentieth-century folklore collected in County Tyrone contains motifs which parallel material in Carleton's fiction. Although

c

Samuel Lover (1797–1868) is known primarily as a novelist, his first major work was two series of tales derived from oral tradition, *Legends and Stories of Ireland* (1831, 1834). If one removes the humour and condescension of Lover's treatment of his materials, as Yeats did in selecting and editing Lover's tales, a core of real folklore remains.

Such fictionalised folklore and periodical articles were the major outlet for the publication of Irish folklore after Croker until the 1860s when Patrick Kennedy began publishing collections of legends and folk tales, some of which he had published earlier in the *Dublin University Magazine* and other periodicals. Patrick Kennedy (1801–1873), who had been born a peasant and lived among the peasantry of County Wexford until he was twenty, was a major figure in the publication of nineteenth-century Irish folklore. He was a schoolmaster in County Wexford and later in Dublin until he opened a book shop in Dublin in 1839. He was widely read in English and French literature but Irish folklore was his chief interest. In 1851 he wrote the editor of the *Wexford Independent*: 'Do not you and I and others still retain many of the traditions and legends of our native place? In the present transition state of our country they are likely to be lost, and will it not be doing some service to preserve them, however imperfectly?'[49] Kennedy's zeal as an antiquarian and his sentimental attachment to the oral traditions he had experienced as a boy generated six collections. His first collection, *Legends of Mount Leinster* (1855), published under his pseudonym 'Harry Whitney', contained nine sketches, four of which were stories supposedly told at the fireside of a Wexford farmhouse. Besides the tales, whose settings ranged from the days of Brian Boru through the Penal times, Kennedy provided a careful picture of local life which became his hallmark. However, the influence of Croker and Carleton was apparent in Kennedy's handling of his materials in *The Banks of the Boro* (1867) and *Evenings in the Duffrey* (1869). The books told the story of a hero named Edward O'Brien whose adventures Kennedy claimed were based on the actual lives and love affairs of two of his former schoolmates. Kennedy managed to weave many tales, legends and ballads as well as a wealth of information about local customs and traditions into the plot.

Kennedy's remaining three collections were his least fictional and most significant collections. *Legendary Fictions of the Irish Celts* (1866) is Kennedy's major collection and encompasses the entire range of Irish oral narrative. Part I, 'Household Stories', contained folktales (märchen); Part II, 'Legends of the "Good People" ', presented fairy legends; Part III, 'Witchcraft, Sorcery, Ghosts, and Fetches', considered legends about supernatural beings besides the fairies; Part IV, 'Ossianic and Other Early Legends', presented contemporary oral traditions derived from ancient myth; Part V, 'Legends of Celtic Saints', explored legends about the miraculous wonders credited to the saints which had once been attached to ancient gods and goddesses. Kennedy's collection thus distinguished between folktale, legend and myth, the major generic categories of folk narrative defined by twentieth-century folklorists. Kennedy's final two collections also maintained such distinctions: *The Fireside Stories of Ireland* (1870) was composed of folktales while *The Bardic Stories of Ireland* (1871) retold ancient myths and historical legends.

Kennedy's categorisation of his materials into three distinct genres highlights the international nature of folktales and the more uniquely national identity of legends and myths. In his 'Preface' and 'Notes' to his collection of folktales, *Fireside Stories*, and in his opening remarks to the 'Household Stories' section of *Legendary Fictions*, Kennedy emphasised that such tales were common to most countries in Europe and Asia. The stereotyped characters and events of such tales could indeed be told anywhere. On the other hand, Kennedy's legends of Irish fairies and heroes were unmistakably Irish. The significance of the narrative distinctions in Irish oral tradition was not lost on Yeats who filled his own anthologies with legends and only added folktales when a printer's mix-up necessitated his adding new materials.

Kennedy's collections were all based on his firsthand observations and recollections of peasant life. His chief oral informants were his godmother, whose own oral source had been a wandering pedlar, and the local faggot cutter. In his running commentary between his tales he frequently described his other informants in some detail. Kennedy's tales and legends have few of the literary mannerisms from nineteenth-century fiction which

abounded in Croker's and most Irish folklorists' materials, and
are thus much closer to the original idiom and structure of the
oral traditions of the English-speaking peasantry of Ireland.
However, Kennedy did manipulate his materials, but for moral
not literary effect. His commercial success as a bookseller had
been hindered by his refusal to deal in books which he con-
sidered objectionable, and the Hibernian Temperance Asso-
ciation met at his home for many years.[50] Kennedy's moral
positions also influenced his editorial practices. In his 'Preface'
to *Legendary Fictions*, he deplored 'the exciting and demoral-
ising pictures of unmitigated wickedness abounding in modern
fiction' so readily available to young people, and hoped to offset
its influence with the innocent pleasures of the tales he had
'collected and narrated'.[51] In his 'Preface' to *The Fireside
Stories*, Kennedy noted that, in addition to corrupting modern
youth, modern fiction had 'given a death-blow to the oral
literature of the fireside', and he said, 'I hope the present col-
lection may give pleasure to many a young and unsophisticated
reader, and revive healthy and pleasant recollections of early
life in the hearts and minds of those advanced in years.'[52] He
admitted that he had bowdlerised his tales, 'I have endeavoured
to present them in a form suitable for the perusal of both sexes
and all ages,' but he claimed that 'no changes have been made
. . . except where decency required', and that although he had
omitted many 'scenes of blood and cruelty', good was generally
victorious over evil in Irish folklore anyway.[53] Interestingly, the
Reverend Stephen Brown in *Ireland in Fiction: A Guide to
Irish Novels, Tales, Romances and Folklore* (1915) labels all of
Kennedy's collections as 'suitable' or 'healthy' for young readers
with the exception of *Legendary Fictions*, Kennedy's most sig-
nificant and accurate collection which Brown calls 'hardly suit-
able for children'.[54]

Despite the moral improvements Kennedy had wrought on his
materials, Yeats preferred him and especially his *Legendary
Fictions* to Croker. In his 'Introduction' to *Fairy and Folk
Tales*, Yeats praised Kennedy for having had 'far less literary
faculty' than Croker, who had transformed the Irish country-
side into a 'humorist's Arcadia', and for having been 'wonder-
fully accurate, giving often the very words the stories were told
in'.[55] Kennedy's contemporaries had also praised his authentic

record of peasant life and lore. The *Irish Times* editorial which eulogised Kennedy in 1873 noted the lack of successful 'literary' characterisation in his works, but declared that Kennedy's 'social pictures of the farming and labouring class are photographs rather than works of art. . . . He has bequeathed to us a record of Irish country life before the Famine of '46, more faithful and minute and more impressive on the memory than Lord Devon's Commission, or any other Blue Book.'[56]

Kennedy's contemporary in the publication of Irish folklore, the Reverend Canon John O'Hanlon (1821–1905), shared his zeal for preserving in print the 'antiquities' of the Irish countryside but lacked his ability to publish folklore in a relatively unadulterated form. O'Hanlon, who was born in Ireland and lived for many years in the US before returning to Ireland, is most famous for his nine-volume *Lives of the Irish Saints* and *The Irish Emigrants Guide to the United States*. O'Hanlon published two works 'derived' from Irish folklore in 1870 under his pen name of 'Lageniensis'. *Irish Folk-Lore: Traditions and Superstitions of the Country: with Humorous Tales,* based mainly on manuscript sources and previous collections of Irish folklore, contained materials coloured by O'Hanlon's literary style, verbose theories and allusions to classical and English literature. He transformed local legends gathered mainly from oral sources into rhyming verse in *Legend Lays of Ireland*. A few lines from O'Hanlon's poem, 'The Beanshee Beetlers', based on 'A Legend of Lough Gill', present an interesting contrast to the poetry Yeats was eventually to write about Lough Gill scenery and lore :

> By blue Lough Gill at even-tide
> The *beanshee* beetlers troop beside
> Smooth, stilly waters, circling wide,
>   And oft beguile
> Their hours of toil with shrill refrain,
> Wafting faint echoes o'er the main,
> When voices blend in wildest strain
>   From Fairy Isle.

The note following this poem was three times as long as the entire poem and filled with undiluted folklore. Each of the

thirty-six poems in the collection were followed by such exten-
sive notes about local history and folklore. O'Hanlon's notes
and his 'Preface', which surveyed and discussed most previous
Irish folklore published in book and periodical form, demon-
strate a broad background in Irish folklore. But he had no
appreciation for either the content or style of Irish folklore
in its original form. He considered legends and beliefs to be
'absurd and irreligious notions' caused by 'disordered intellect,
imperfect knowledge and neglected education'; he believed that
such antiquarian curiosities could only hope to appeal to
readers if transformed into English poetry, chatty essays, or
humorous tales.[57] Not surprisingly, Yeats did not include any
separate selection from O'Hanlon's collections in either of his own
anthologies of Irish folklore, but he cited O'Hanlon as an authority
on Irish folklore in both anthologies. Much of the material in
Yeats's introductions and notes in both anthologies is obviously
derived from information he gleaned from reading O'Hanlon.

The common practice of obvious but unacknowledged bor-
rowing by folklorists from earlier collectors by both Yeats and
most of his predecessors raises the issue of plagiarism. But such
a question is ultimately irrelevant when applied to nineteenth-
century folklorists. Plagiarism is generally defined today as an
unacknowledged use of words or ideas derived from an existing
source. For nineteenth-century folklorists the 'existing source'
was frequently the published collections of their predecessors.
Both Patrick Kennedy and John O'Hanlon took information
from Crofton Croker's notes to his *Fairy Legends*; O'Hanlon
borrowed from Kennedy's *Legendary Fictions*; Yeats appro-
priated information from all three men. Yet behind the folklore
in published collections stretched centuries of anonymous oral
traditions—traditions which had belonged to millions and which
continued to be passed on orally throughout Ireland well past
the publication date of any single published collection. Once
published, such folklore did not necessarily belong to an editor
who had collected rather than created it. His literary version
belonged to him but not the folklore on which it was based.
Oral traditions often passed into printed versions in chapbooks
or in collections which frequently had a far-reaching influence
on succeeding oral tradition. For example, Seamus Delargy has
pointed out that a tale, 'The Black Thief and the Knight of

the Glen', originally printed in the chapbook *The Royal Hibernian Tales* published sometime before 1825, generated at least nineteen versions in oral tradition because, from 1941, the Irish Folklore Commission had catalogued nineteen versions collected from oral tradition and there were probably at least as many more uncatalogued.[58] To their credit, Yeats and most of his predecessors generally only borrowed information from each other. Although Yeats's bibliographic data about the sources of tales and poems in his folklore anthologies were far from complete or entirely accurate, he usually gave the name of the author for a selection which was not anonymous. Such had not always been the case in the nineteenth-century publishing history of Irish folklore. Four tales originally printed in Croker's *Fairy Legends* in 1825 reappeared verbatim in the anonymous collection *Ancient Irish Tales, A Collection of the Stories Told by the Peasantry in the Winter Evenings* (1829) with no mention of Croker. Croker's 'Daniel O'Rourke' was retitled 'The Wonderful Adventures of Daniel O'Rourke and the Eagle', his 'The Legend of Knockgrafton' became 'Lusmore and the Fairies', his 'Legend of Bottle Hill' became 'Mick Purcell and the Fairy'; only 'Flory Cantillon's Funeral' retained Croker's title. Croker's notes were not reprinted, but otherwise the tales, three of which Yeats reprinted citing Croker in 1888, matched Croker's versions completely. Moreover, Yeats's use of information in his introductions and notes similar to that in his predecessors' collections was just as likely drawn from the same oral traditions his predecessors had mined for their materials. Even when Yeats's wording parallels theirs suspiciously, his sense that folklore was ultimately anonymous and the property of past, present and future generations of tradition bearers excuses him from charges of 'plagiarism'. Yeats's response, in a letter to the editor of the *Academy* of 16 March 1892, to accusations about the similarity of his poem 'The Ballad of Father Gilligan' to another literary ballad exemplifies Yeats's attitude to folklore : he said that he and the other poet had both heard the tale from the same oral source and that 'I have never claimed the story as mine, but—have given full credit where it is due, namely, to its inventors, the peasantry of Castleisland, Kerry . . . even if I had seen Tristram St Martin's ballad before writing mine, and had never heard the story apart from the ballad, I should none the less have considered myself perfectly justified in taking a legend that belonged to neither of us, but to the Irish people.'[59]

When Yeats published his first anthology of folklore in 1888 he preferred the work of Lady Wilde to that of any previous collector of Irish folklore. Jane Francesca Elgee, Lady Wilde (1826–1896), who under the pseudonym 'Speranza' had contributed to the *Nation* between 1845 and 1848, was the wife of Sir William Wilde (1815–1876), a Dublin physician and occultist who was a famous populariser of current research on Irish antiquities. Sir William Wilde's interest in Irish folklore had begun during his childhood in the West of Ireland. Wilde had combined authentic oral traditions with his extensive knowledge of manuscript sources and his rambling commentary on Irish history and the rapid and unfortunate disappearance of the Irish language and antiquities from the countryside to produce *Irish Popular Superstitions* (1853), the first collection to tap the rich oral traditions of Mayo and Galway. His collection methods were unique if not notorious. George Bernard Shaw claimed that Wilde, whose love affairs and other supposed escapades became legends in their own right, had left a 'family' in every farmhouse he visited in Ireland. Yeats, who knew Lady Wilde personally, described her version of how her husband collected folklore :

> From these remote parts [of the west of Ireland] Sir William Wilde collected a vast bulk of tales and spells and proverbs. In addition to the peasants he regularly employed to glean the stubble of tradition for him, he got many things from patients at his Dublin hospital; for when grateful patients would offer to send him geese or eggs or butter, he would bargain for a fragment of folk-lore instead. He threw all his gatherings into a big box, and thence it is that Lady Wilde has quarried the materials of her new book.'[60]

After her husband's death, Lady Wilde drew upon the large and heterogeneous body of Irish folklore he had collected to write *Ancient Legends, Mystic Charms and Superstitions of Ireland* (1887) and *Ancient Cures, Charms and Usages of Ireland* (1890).

Thomas Flanagan, a twentieth-century authority on the nine-teenth-century Irish novel, has called Lady Wilde 'one of the silliest women who ever set pen to paper'.[61] Although Lady Wilde's two collections of Irish folklore contain many ridiculous authorial comments—e.g., she proposes that the Irish in America pool their resources and buy Ireland from England—they un-doubtedly contain a wealth of information on the beliefs and customs of the Irish countryside. Douglas Hyde, whose own collections were outstanding from both a literary and scholarly standpoint, said that he regretted that Lady Wilde had not annotated her sources and kept her own ideas separate from her materials, but he praised her two collections as 'a wonderful and copious record of folk-lore and folk-customs'.[62] Lady Wilde's collections contained a jumbled mass of materials—tales, pro-verbs, customs—and Yeats mined them for the veritable treasures of Irish folklore they were, taking entire stories as well as details and examples for his introductions to the various sections of *Fairy and Folk Tales* (1888).

Lady Wilde's seriousness about the content and the literary possibilities of Irish folklore, and the small amount of literary elaboration in her collections obviously appealed to Yeats. She remarked of one of the tales she included in *Ancient Legends*: 'The idea that underlies the story is very subtle and tragic, Calderon or Goethe might have founded a drama on it; and Browning's genius would find a fitting subject in this contrast between the pride of the audacious, self-reliant sceptic in the hour of his triumph and the moral agony that precedes his punishment and death.'[63] Her statements about the relationship between folklore and the occult—although Yeats never mentions them—must have been welcomed by Yeats as support for his own theories. According to Lady Wilde, 'the mythology of a people reveals their relation to a spiritual and invisible world,' and she began her second anthology with the following state-ment:

All nations and races from the earliest time have held the intuitive belief that mystic beings were always around them, influencing, though unseen, every action of life, and all the forces of nature. They felt the presence of a spirit in the winds, and the waves, and the swaying branches of the forest
c*

trees, and in the primal elements of all that exists. . . . Thus
to the primitive races of mankind the unseen world of mystery
was a vital and vivid reality; the great over-soul of the visible,
holding a mystic and psychic relation to humanity, and ruling
it through the instrumentality of beings who had strange
powers either for good or evil over human lives and actions.[64]

Although Lady Wilde recognised that Irish folklore closely
resembled the ancient legends of other nations, she argued that
the imagination of the Irish peasant alone still dwelt in the
ancient mystical realm because Ireland had been completely
separate from European thought and culture for centuries. The
ethnological theories of Lady Wilde, which she had learned
from her husband, offered Yeats a rationalisation for treating
Irish folklore as a uniquely Irish cultural phenomenon rather
than using the international perspective he was familiar with
in Croker, Kennedy and journals such as the *Revue Celtique*
and *The Folklore Journal*.

Although Yeats implicitly agreed with Lady Wilde's nation-
alistic interpretation of Irish folklore, he drew upon her col-
lections primarily for their folklore materials rather than Lady
Wilde's views. Yeats ignored the extremes of her political and
ethnological nationalism, as well as her lavish praise of the
Young Ireland movement of the 1840s of which she had been
a part. This is typical of Yeats's use of his predecessors in the
collection of Irish folklore: he took only the folklore materials
which appealed to his imagination, generally the most extra-
vagant and inexplicable, and ignored editorial commentary.

Yeats's enthusiasm for an Irish folklorist named Letitia
McClintock illustrates a growing appreciation of idiomatic
accuracy and a presentation unmarred by authorial theories
and superficial literary effects. Yeats praised Letitia McClintock,
a relatively unknown Donegal folklorist, for using the Anglo-
Irish dialect of Ulster to achieve an even greater idiomatic
accuracy and success in recording Irish folklore than Patrick
Kennedy had. The stories recounted in the two matter-of-
fact articles by Letitia McClintock from which Yeats drew
selections let the peasant speak for himself, without literary
elaboration which even Kennedy's collections had not been
completely without. Nor did Miss McClintock's articles reflect

any propagandistic biases—moral or political.

The nature and extent of Yeats's use of Miss McClintock's materials illustrates his great admiration for her work as well as how rare her idiomatic accuracy and lack of fictional elaboration were among Irish folklorists. During the 1870s and 1880s she had published 'Folk-Lore of the County Donegal', *Dublin University Magazine* (November 1876); 'Folk-Lore of the County Donegal: Fairy Tales', *Dublin University Magazine* (February 1877); 'Folk-Lore in the County Donegal', *All The Year Round*, 24 (10 April 1880); 'Ulster Folk-Lore', *All The Year Round*, 25 (10 September 1881); 'Fairy Legends of the County Donegal', *All The Year Round*, 28 (21 January 1882); 'Legends of the County Donegal', *All The Year Round*, 42 (2 June 1888)—(a reprint of first three-quarters of first article listed). From the two articles in the *Dublin University Magazine* Yeats used what appeared as five separate stories by Letitia McClintock in *Fairy and Folk Tales* (1888). All five stories were actually just short conversational anecdotes, which Yeats had removed and given separate titles, from her two articles— two from 1876 and three from 1877.

In addition to obviously being attracted to Miss McClintock's technical handling of Irish folklore, Yeats must also have been drawn to her attitudes about folklore. She believed that the materials she was relating demonstrated human interaction with 'the world of spirits—that mysterious world, lying, it may be somewhere near us' which preoccupied 'peasant, student, and spiritualist' alike.[65] The serious tone of her articles was never patronising and she never attempted to rationalise the tales she told. Moreover, she presented her materials as a living and uniquely Irish tradition which she had observed all around her in County Donegal. Yeats chose to ignore, or perhaps he did not know, that Miss McClintock had transformed the Irish countryside with Victorian literary conventions in her anti-Land League novel, *A Boycotted Household* (1880). She also published several romantic stories based on Irish and non-Irish topics and on the occult.

The nationalism inherent in much of the Irish folklore published during the nineteenth century and which was rampant in Lady Wilde's collections culminated in the work of Douglas Hyde (1860–1949), the most important of all the folklorists

Ireland has ever produced. Hyde's parents were English-speaking Protestants, and he had been born in the West of Ireland where his father was a clergyman. In 1873 Hyde was sent to a boarding school in Dublin but after a few weeks returned home to convalesce from the measles and did not return to school. He received a good education at home, especially in languages, and developed an avid interest in Irish during these years which proved to be the determining force in his life.[66] In 1874 Hyde began a series of diaries composed in both Irish and English which record how eagerly he began learning Irish and collecting the oral songs and tales of the local countrypeople. Hyde took the entrance examination for Trinity College, Dublin in June 1880, and placed seventh out of a hundred candidates. His personal library at the time included over one hundred books written in Irish, twenty-four books mainly in English but on Irish subjects and eighteen Irish manuscripts—an extraordinary collection for a young man of twenty who had never had a formal lesson in Irish language or literature about to enter a university which was a bastion of prejudice against Irish language and culture. Hyde perfunctorily fulfilled his formal studies at Trinity, first in divinity and then in law, reserving his real enthusiasm for his continuing efforts to teach himself Irish and to learn as much as possible about Irish culture. His early booklists indicate that by 1888 he had read almost all Gaelic poetry in print and a considerable amount in manuscript. Hyde received an LL.D. in 1888 but the prizes he won while at Trinity—the Vice-Chancellor's Prize for English verse in 1885, for prose in 1886, and both prizes in 1887—demonstrate that his genius and enthusiasm were for language and literature rather than for law.

Hyde had begun writing poetry in Irish and English in 1877 and between 1879 and 1883 he published original poems in Irish in *The Irishman* and *The Shamrock* under the pseudonym 'An Craoibhin Aoibhinn', The Pleasant Little Branch. The Fenianism he had absorbed in Roscommon and expressed in his early poetry and diaries was transformed into a cultural nationalism in Dublin during the 1880s. He was an active member of the Contemporary Club which Charles Oldham had founded in 1885. Its weekly meetings were a lively forum of debate about politics and literature among John O'Leary, W. B. Yeats, George Sigerson, T. W. Rolleston and others who became the leaders of the literary revival. John O'Leary inspired Yeats to devote himself to producing a distinctively Irish literature written in English, but Hyde's devotion to the preservation of Irish language and culture made it inevitable that his nationalism would be modelled on that of George Sigerson who had succeeded James Clarence Mangan as translator of the Irish poems in John O'Daly's *Poets and Poetry of Munster* (Second Series, 1860). Hyde devoted his life and his considerable talents as a poet, a folklorist and a scholar to the restoration of Irish which he considered to be above and more important than the divisive revolutionary nationalism. Nevertheless, Hyde's collection and translation of Irish oral traditions had a profound effect on Yeats and his literary movement, and Hyde's avowedly unpolitical propagandising on behalf of Irish inevitably influenced Irish political events.

Hyde proclaimed his linguistic nationalism in an essay entitled 'A Plea for the Irish Language' in Charles Oldham's *Dublin University Review* in August 1885. Hyde's own knowledge of Irish oral tradition is apparent in the notes and three stories translated from the Irish which he contributed to Yeats's *Fairy and Folk Tales of the Irish Peasantry* (1888). In the same year Hyde contributed six poems in English to the anthology of the emerging literary revival, *Poems and Ballads of Young Ireland*. But his main interest continued to be Irish and his first book, *Leabhar Sgéulaigheachta* (1889), a collection of folktales, rhymes and riddles, was the first of its kind ever to be published in Irish. In *Beside the Fire: A Collection of Irish Gaelic Folk Stories* (1890) Hyde presented English translations of about half the folktales in his first book together with six other traditional folktales in the original Irish with English translations. *Beside the Fire* is a landmark in Irish folklore studies and in Irish literary history. Numerous collections of Irish legends and folktales in English had been published throughout the nineteenth century, but Hyde was the first to present the exact language, names and various localities of his informants. The 'Index of Incidents' which he included at the end anticipated the use of motifs by twentieth-century folklorists. Hyde's forty-page preface reviewed the entire tradition of Irish folklore, presenting a scholarly evaluation of its significance and evaluating earlier collectors who had tampered with

the substance and idiom of their originals. Hyde's own trans-
lations represented the first attempt to render Irish folklore in
a true Anglo-Irish idiom. Hyde's prose bore little resemblance to
the imaginary and ludicrous English of the stage-Irishman and
the artificial literary style of his predecessors in the publication
of Irish folklore. The poetic possibilities of this Anglo-Irish idiom
were even more apparent in Hyde's translations of folk poetry,
the 'Songs of Connacht', which began to appear in serial form
in the *Nation* in 1890. The fourth chapter of these songs, pub-
lished in *The Weekly Freeman* in 1892 and early 1893 and in
book form as the *Love Songs of Connacht* (1893), was a poetic
and scholarly achievement and had immense literary significance.
Hyde published the originals with translations to preserve them
from oblivion and to aid students of Irish. He translated most
of the poems twice. The first version, a free translation, repro-
duced the rhythm of the Irish verse; the second version, given
as a footnote, was a literal translation. Ironically, Hyde's achieve-
ment as a translator and a poet in the *Love Songs of Connacht*
frustrated his own goal for it furnished Yeats, Synge, and Lady
Gregory with Irish themes in a beautiful idiom which made
an Irish literature in English seem all the more possible.

Hyde assumed the presidency of the new National Literary
Society in 1891. His inaugural address, 'The Necessity for De-
Anglicising Ireland', was his most famous and influential lecture.
It marked the beginning of an organised effort not only to pre-
serve but to revive Irish language and culture. In 1893, largely
as a result of Hyde's energetic propaganda on behalf of the
language, the Gaelic League was founded with Hyde as its
President. The two aims of the Gaelic League, at its founding
a cultural rather than a political organisation, were to revive
Irish as the national language and to create a modern Irish
literature. The Gaelic League was an immensely popular move-
ment which attracted and inspired many literary as well as
revolutionary nationalists. Hyde managed to keep the League
from becoming politicised until 1915 when its constitution was
amended to declare that its aim would be the realisation of 'a
free, Gaelic-speaking Ireland'. Hyde resigned immediately from
the presidency and from the Gaelic League. Nevertheless the
political implications of Hyde's movement had been immense
from the very beginning. Dominic Daly has summed up

Hyde's significance: 'Although the actual course of events was not what he would have chosen, his ideology was the mainspring that set these events in motion. It was he who created the ground-swell on which the Volunteer movement was launched; his students and disciples were the officers and men of the insurrection. With the zeal of a convert he opened the eyes of Irish men and women to the source of their identity as a nation.'[67] When the new Irish Constitution was adopted in 1938 it was fitting that Douglas Hyde was elected unopposed as the first President of the Republic of Ireland.

Hyde's *Literary History of Ireland, From Earliest Times to the Present Day* (1899) had defined 'Irish literature 'as 'literature produced by the Irish-speaking Irish' and did not even consider the various traditions of Irish literature written in English which Yeats attempted to define and popularise in the 1880s and 1890s. While Yeats often criticised Hyde's enthusiasm for reviving Irish, his involvement in Irish politics and his definition of Irish literature as that produced by the Irish-speaking Irish, he shared Hyde's literary nationalism and his great admiration for Hyde's work with Irish folklore influenced many of his own attitudes about folklore. But Hyde's insistence on scholarly accuracy went well beyond the admiration for idiomatic accuracy which Yeats had shown in the 'Introduction' to *Fairy and Folk Tales*. In his 'Preface' to *Beside the Fire* Hyde said that nineteenth-century attempts to gather Irish folklore 'though interesting from a literary point of view, are not always successes from a scientific one'; he criticised Croker and Kennedy for altering the form and content of their originals and regretted that 'the chief interest in too many of our folk-tales lies in their individual treatment of the skeletons of various Gaelic stories obtained through English mediums', and that previous Irish folklorists had not attempted to give the exact language, names and various localities of their informants.[68] In his 'Introduction' to *Fairy and Folk Tales*, Yeats had also distinguished between the highly literary tradition of Irish folklore and the scientific tradition of international folklore studies but his conclusions, at that time, were different from Hyde's:

The various collectors of Irish folk-lore have, from our point of view, one great merit, and from the point of view of others, one great fault. They have made their work literature rather than science, and told us of the Irish peasantry rather than of the primitive religion of mankind, or whatever else the folk-lorists are on the gad after. To be considered scientists they should have tabulated all their tales in forms like grocers bills—item the fairy king, item the queen. Instead they have caught the very voice of the people, the very pulse of life.[69]

Yeats's great admiration for Hyde's translations gradually lessened his own bias against scholarly accuracy, partly because the materials which Hyde collected from the Irish-speaking peasantry contained plenty of imaginative extravagance and needed no literary embellishments to make them interesting. In 1888 Yeats wrote to Katharine Tynan : 'Hyde is the best of all Irish folklorists. His style is perfect—so sincere and simple—so little literary.'[70] The content, idiom and handling of Irish folklore in Hyde's work, as in the following excerpt from the tale entitled 'Trunk-Without-Head' in *Beside the Fire*, illustrate Yeats's taste perfectly :

> Donal went to bed agin; but he was not long there till there walked in two men, carrying a coffin. They left it down on the floor, and they walked out. 'I don't know who's in the coffin, or whether it's for us it's meant', said Donal; 'I'll go till I see.' He gave a leap out, raised the board of the coffin, and found a dead man in it. 'By my conscience, it's the cold place you have,' says Donal; 'if you were able to rise up, and sit at the fire, you would be better.' The dead man rose up and warmed himself. Then said Donal, 'the bed is wide enough for three.' Donal went in the middle, the poor man next to the wall, and the dead man on the outside. It was not long until the dead man began bruising Donal, and Donal bruising in on the poor man, until he was all as one as dead, and he had to give a leap out through the window, and to leave Donal and the dead man there.

Likewise, the idiom and the inexplicable content of the following passage, the conclusion to 'Neil O'Carree', is unlike anything quoted from Croker and other 'literary folklorists' elsewhere in this chapter :

Neil went, drawing towards home. Not far did he walk till

his share of cattle and his nag met him. He went home and the whole with him. There is not a single day since that himself and his wife are not thriving on it.

I got the ford, they the stepping stones. They were drowned and I came safe.[71]

Yeats reviewed *Beside the Fire* in 1891 and presumed to judge the accuracy of Hyde's translations :

Dr Hyde's volume is the best written of any. He has caught and faithfully reproduced the peasant idiom and phrase. In becoming scientifically accurate he has not ceased to be a man of letters. . . . The Gaelic is printed side by side with the English, so that the substantial accuracy of his versions can always be tested. The result is many pages in which you can hear in imagination the very voice of the sennachie, and almost smell the smoke of his turf fire.[72]

Yeats's admiration for Hyde's idiomatic and scholarly accuracy qualified his own earlier view. In 1888 when he had called Lady Wilde's *Ancient Legends* the best collection since Croker, he pointed out that Hyde had not yet published any collection. In 1890, when Yeats reviewed Lady Wilde's second collection, *Ancient Cures, Charms and Usages of Ireland*, he criticised her for seldom specifying the district where a tradition was collected and for never indicating the date a tale was collected : 'I heartily wish they had been better and more scientifically treated. . . .'[73]

Yeats's own anthology of 1888 had been criticised by Percy Myles, in his review of Lady Wilde's *Ancient Cures* in the *Academy* of 27 September 1890, for having shown the same anti-scientific bias as Lady Wilde's collections. Referring to Yeats's statement in his 'Introduction' to *Fairy and Folk Tales* that he preferred literary to scientific folklore, Myles remarks, 'the editor goes out of his way to gibe at the honest folk-lorist who tells what he had actually heard, not what he thinks he might have heard, or what he thinks his audience would like to hear.'[74] Myles was not being fair to Yeats because Yeats had actually praised idiomatic accuracy in the same 'Introduction' and had merely condemned overly dry, scientific treatments of folklore. Moreover, as will be shown in the next chapter, Yeats continually omitted the most literary stories from his own an-

thology and deleted the most literary passages from the stories
he did include. Yeats's reply to Myles summarised Yeats's seem-
ingly contradictory attitudes about poetry and science in folklore :

> He [Mr Myles] misunderstands, however, what I said about
> scientific folk-lorists in the Introduction. I do not want the
> fairy-tale gatherer to tell us 'what he thinks he might have
> heard, or what he thinks his audience would like to hear'. But
> I deeply regret when I find that some folk-lorist is merely
> scientific, and lacks the needful subtle imaginative sympathy
> to tell his stories well. There are innumerable little turns of
> expression and quaint phrases that in the mouth of a peasant
> give half the meaning, and often the whole charm. The man
> of science is too often a person who has exchanged his soul for
> a formula; and when he captures a folk-tale, nothing remains
> with him for all his trouble but a wretched lifeless thing with
> the down rubbed off and a pin thrust through its once living
> body. I object to the 'honest folk-lorist', not because his ver-
> sions are accurate, but because they are inaccurate, or rather
> incomplete. What lover of Celtic lore has not been filled with
> a sacred rage when he came upon some exquisite story, dear
> to him from childhood, written out in newspaper English and
> called science? To me, the ideal folk-lorist is Mr Douglas
> Hyde. A tale told by him is quite as accurate as any 'scientific'
> person's rendering; but in dialect and so forth he is careful
> to give us the most quaint, or poetical, or humorous version
> he has heard. I am inclined to think also that some concen-
> tration and elaboration of dialect is justified, if only it does not
> touch the fundamentals of the story. It is but a fair equivalent
> for the gesture and voice of the peasant tale-teller.[75]

This blend of scholar and poet in Hyde was what always
appealed to Yeats, but as Hyde directed his attention more
and more to politics and the movement for the revival of the
Irish language in the 1890s, Yeats complained that Hyde the
nationalist and scholar was completely eclipsing Hyde the poet
and taleteller. In *The Story of Early Gaelic Literature* (1895)
Hyde took sides in the debate as to whether Irish folklore was
'legend coloured by history' or 'history coloured by legend' and
chose the latter. Yeats's review of Hyde's book indicated that
Yeats had chosen the former :

Dr Hyde throws in his lot with those who hold them [Irish legends] historical in the main; and this choice seems to an obstinate upholder of the other theory but a part of one capital defect of his criticism. He is so anxious to convince his little groups of enthusiasts of the historical importance of the early Irish writings, of the value to modern learning of the fragments of ancient customs that are mixed up with their romance, that he occasionally seems to forget the noble fantasy and passionate drama which is their crowning glory.[76]

Yeats declared in the 'Introduction' to his *Book of Irish Verse* in 1895 that 'Dr Hyde is, before all else, a translator and scholar.'[77] Many years later, in 1934, Yeats wrote that Hyde and his followers 'sought the peasant' while Yeats and his associates 'sought the peasant's imagination'.[78] In his *Autobiography* Yeats wrote that Douglas Hyde 'was to create a great popular movement, far more important in its practical results than any movement I could have made, no matter what my luck, but, being neither quarrelsome nor vain, he will not be angry if I say—for the sake of those that come after us—that I mourn for the "greatest folk-loreist [sic] who ever lived", and for the great poet who died in his youth.'[79]

As early as 1895 Yeats had concluded that Lady Wilde and Douglas Hyde represented two distinct and irreconcilable traditions in Irish folklore: 'Lady Wilde's *Ancient Legends* is the most imaginative collection of Irish folk-lore, but should be read with Dr Hyde's more accurate and scholarly *Beside the Fire*. Lady Wilde tells her stories in the ordinary language of literature, but Dr Hyde, with a truer instinct, is so careful to catch the manner of the peasant story-tellers that, on the rare occasions when he fails to take down the exact words, he writes out the story in Gaelic, and then translates it into English.'[80] For awhile Hyde had represented to Yeats the possibility of combining the accuracy of a scholar with the imagination of a poet, but Yeats, who lacked Hyde's facility with the Irish language and the Irish peasantry, never succeeded in reconciling his admiration for the idiomatic accuracy which resulted from the scientific collection of folklore, with his own intention to use Irish folklore as the basis for imaginative literary creation.

3

The Folklore Anthologies:
Fairy and Folk Tales of The Irish Peasantry and *Irish Fairy Tales*

Nineteenth-century scholarly studies of folklore, including ancient Irish myth, had been philological or historical in their emphases, whereas, prior to Douglas Hyde, the mannerisms of popular fiction had been superimposed on collections of Irish folklore. Yeats's two anthologies of Irish folklore, *Fairy and Folk Tales of the Irish Peasantry* (1888) and *Irish Fairy Tales* (1892), reflect his search for an imaginative yet authentic depiction of Irish folklore which avoided the extremes of a ponderous scientific air on the one hand and a bogus stage-Irish literary charm on the other. Yeats's hope for a more serious and vital tone than he had found in the artificial literary ballads of the nineteenth century is also mirrored in his two folklore anthologies. But it was a hope that Irish folklore, a tradition of ultimately irreconcilable extremes, would not fulfill.

Although Yeats tried to simplify Irish folklore of the elaborate literary effects imposed on it by Croker and his followers, his imaginative needs as an artist ultimately could not accept the scholarly accuracy of Douglas Hyde which had replaced the tradition of Croker. Yeats turned more and more to the life and character of Irish peasants and heroes for his subjects once he realised the non-human fairies could never possess the human passions and tragic themes he wanted in his works. When frustrated by his attempts to resolve the conflicting demands of the imagination of the artist and the accuracy of the folklorist, Yeats would eventually turn to another area of Irish subject matter—ancient Irish myth—for the energy, the imaginative extravagance and the remnants of ancient occult wisdom he had once hoped to find in the beliefs and legends of the nineteenth-century Irish peasantry.

Yeats's letters of 1887 and 1888 explain the genesis and formation of *Fairy and Folk Tales of the Irish Peasantry* (1888). It originally was to have been an edition of Croker's *Fairy Legends* for the series entitled 'Camelot Classics' which Ernest Rhys was publishing. In July 1887, Yeats wrote to John O'Leary, 'I have been asked to edit an Irish or other volume in the Camelot Classics and have thought of Croker's *Irish Fairy Tales* but fear the copyright has not lapsed—could you suggest me some book?' In August 1887, Yeats had written to Katharine Tynan that he might edit Croker's *Fairy Legends* for Rhys, but in February 1888, he wrote to her that 'Rhys has written from America asking me to bring out in the Camelot series a book of selected Folklore.'[1]

Yeats's *Fairy and Folk Tales* has been described as a 'hasty compilation'.[2] But actually a great deal of time and effort went into it. Yeats knew as early as February 1888 that it was to be an anthology of selected folklore, and in early June he wrote to Katharine Tynan that he had already extracted tales from various nineteenth-century Irish folklore collections. A letter dated 5 July 1888 to Father Matthew Russell, the editor of the *Irish Monthly*, outlining the progress of the anthology and requesting advice about additional materials, indicates that a great deal of research and planning had already gone into the organisation and compilation of the anthology.[3] And although it was supposed to have been completed by the end of July, Yeats was still working feverishly on it into September.

Nor had he begun the project without a great deal of background. Yeats's familiarity with Irish folklore had begun during his childhood, and during the summer of 1887 he had collected folklore around Sligo for use in articles. In the fall of 1887 he wrote to Katharine Tynan, 'with old yarns, mainly fairy yarns collected round about here, I have filled two note-books. . . .' In February 1888, he wrote to Katharine Tynan: 'I have written a long article, nearly fifty manuscript pages long on Folklore.'[4] Yeats, as we know, was familiar with international as well as Irish folklore.

According to his letters, Yeats began preparing his anthology by extracting tales from such standard collections as those by Croker and Kennedy, as well as selecting William Carleton's tales based on the beliefs and legends of the Irish peasantry. Soon afterwards he acquired a copy of Lady Wilde's *Ancient Legends*.

Yeats continually wrote to John O'Leary, Katharine Tynan, Father Russell, and others for advice on potential materials. He seemed anxious to include material from as many authors and sources as possible. He examined numerous nineteenth-century Irish periodicals for materials and was proud of including relatively unknown folklorists such as Letitia McClintock and previously unpublished materials, such as some original translations by Douglas Hyde. Yeats included stories from folklore collectors such as Croker, Kennedy, Hyde, McClintock, Nicholas O'Kearney and anonymous contributors to Irish periodicals; and from fiction writers such as William Carleton, Samuel Lover, Mrs Crow, and Mr and Mrs S. C. Hall. Although Yeats did include materials by authors known for writing fiction rather than folklore, his selections from such authors maintained a distinction between folklore and fiction. None of the six tales by William Carleton which Yeats used are from Carleton's famous series entitled *Traits and Stories of the Irish Peasantry* (1830–1833); all were selected from among the least fictionalised stories in Carleton's more folkloric *Tales and Sketches, Illustrating the Character, Usages, Traditions, Sports, and Pastimes of the Irish Peasantry* (1845). Tales by other fiction writers are in a decided minority—two by Samuel Lover and one by Mrs Crow —all three of which are essentially descriptions of the supernatural beliefs of the Irish, rather than fictionalised tales based upon their life and character. Although Mr and Mrs S. C. Hall primarily wrote fiction, Yeats used nothing from it, but took an example of Irish folklore from their three-volume non-fiction survey of Ireland, *Ireland: Its Scenery, Character, Etc.* (1846).

In addition to selecting materials from Irish folklorists and fiction writers, Yeats also used some of the numerous county histories and surveys which had been published in Ireland during the nineteenth century. The three such works which Yeats drew upon for materials—Samuel M'Skimin's *The History and Antiquities of the County and Town of Carrickfergus, from the Earliest Records to the Present Time* (1832), W. G. Wood-Martin's *History of Sligo County and Town, from the Earliest Ages to the Close of the Reign of Queen Elizabeth* (1882) and William Shaw Mason's three-volume *Statistical Account or Parochial Survey of Ireland, drawn up from the communications of the Clergy* (1814)—contained as much legend and folklore as historical fact and reflected the century's growing interest in Irish folklore. M'Skimin's *History* was filled with the legends and superstitions of the Irish countryside; Wood-Martin's *History* contained a long section on 'Prehistoric and Legendary' Sligo and his other chapters, such as the one on 'Topography', were filled with legendary materials; Mason's *Statistical Account* quoted lengthy, detailed accounts of the beliefs and customs of the Irish peasants which had been sent in by clergymen from all over Ireland. A comparison of these three works with other Irish county histories and surveys published in the eighteenth and nineteenth centuries indicates that Yeats's sources contained much more folklore and were much less scientifically and historically orientated. For example, Wood-Martin entitled the first chapter in his *History of Sligo* 'Prehistoric or Legendary' and thus left its historical authenticity open to question. Wood-Martin's entire book is filled with legends associated with places throughout County Sligo rather than factual data. Such contemporary oral legends often linked Sligo with Ireland's legendary ancient past. One legend about Lough Gill claimed it was named after Gill, one of the nine beautiful daughters of the ancient Irish sea god, Mananan Mac Lir. Wood-Martin declared matter-of-factly that Hy-Brazil, the ancient Irish happy otherworld, had been sighted off the coast of Sligo in 1885. Wood-Martin's statement that the Annals of the Four Masters had referred to the island of Inishfree in Lough Gill as a thirteenth-century island fortress would have enhanced its significance for Yeats. Yeats evidently recalled Wood-Martin's reference to Inishfree as 'heathery island' when he explained that the line referring to 'noon a purple glow' in his poem 'The Lake Isle of Inishfree' alluded to the local name 'Heather Island'. Wood-Martin's interpretations of Irish legends would also have appealed to the young Yeats. According to Wood-Martin 'The Celtic mind is essentially eastern in character.'[5]

In contrast, the county histories which Yeats did not use presented the factual rather than legendary history of Ireland. James M'Parlan's *Statistical Survey of the County of Mayo* (1802) mentioned the beliefs of Mayo peasants in a brief summary fashion, and Charles Smith's three histories of County Waterford, County Cork and County Kerry, recounted the history and described the topography of the three counties and cited population and other statistics without mentioning any of the beliefs and customs of the Irish inhabitants.

Topographical and historical surveys of Ireland which had been written since the Norman invasion of Ireland had generally included popular legends and beliefs of the Irish. None was more fantastic than *Topography of Ireland, and the History of the Conquest of Ireland* which was written in the twelfth century by Giraldus Cambrensis who had continually introduced popular tales and beliefs into his work for the interesting and curious pictures they gave of the life and character of the twelfth-century Irish. Yeats used an edition of Giraldus which had been published in 1863 as a source of information for the introductions to the various sections of his first anthology of Irish folklore. Never mentioning the extraordinary credulity which is apparent in the *Topography*, Yeats selected the most extraordinary and outlandish details it contained, such as the ability of the ancient Irish to change into wolves, the absence of martyrs in Ireland until the English came, and the tale of how a fire arrow stabilised a disappearing phantom island.

Yeats began his Introduction with a quotation from Richard Corbet's seventeenth-century ballad entitled 'The Fairies' Farewell' which lamented the disappearance of the fairies from England. In order to demonstrate the continued vitality of Irish fairies and the suitability of Irish folklore as material for poetry, Yeats included poems about the fairies by William Allingham, Samuel Ferguson, J. J. Callanan, Edward Walsh, James C. Mangan, and Ellen O'Leary in his anthology. This was a definite departure from earlier anthologies of Irish folklore which had quoted only from English poetry about the fairies. Such a practice was unsatisfactory to Yeats who remarked in his Introduction: 'Several specimens of our fairy poetry are given. It is more like the fairy poetry of Scotland than of England. The personages of English fairy literature are merely, in most cases, mortals beautifully masquerading. Nobody ever believed in such fairies. They are romantic bubbles from Provence. Nobody ever laid new milk on their doorsteps for them.' Yeats emphasised that Irish folklore was still a living tradition in the Irish countryside in contrast to the sceptical rationalism rampant elsewhere. Visionaries abounded in the Irish countryside and even the Irish sceptic was different from English sceptics. Yeats described meeting an

Irish 'Sceptic' who claimed he did not believe in ghosts—'There are no such things at all'—or in the fire of hell—'that's only invented to give the priests and parsons something to do'—but who did believe in the fairies and said, 'They stand to reason.'[6]

Irish tradition offered Yeats three explanations of the origin of the fairies. True to his editorial intention of being as representative and as comprehensive as possible, Yeats presented all three theories and cited evidence for each in his introduction to 'The Trooping Fairies' section : many of the peasantry claimed that the fairies were 'Fallen angels who were not good enough to be saved, nor bad enough to be lost'. The Book of Armagh offered the explanation that the fairies were 'the gods of the earth'—a theory with mystical and occult overtones which must have appealed to Yeats. Arguments by antiquarians that the fairies had once been 'the gods of pagan Ireland' enhanced the ancient and symbolic significance of fairy lore for Yeats. Yeats maintained a pose of editorial objectivity and did not indicate a preference for any of the three theories, although his lengthy note about the 'gods of the earth' implies which explanation he favoured.

Yeats was more definite about how traditional narratives were to be categorised. He recognised three distinct kinds of traditional narrative and intended *Fairy and Folk Tales* to be a collection of legends. He referred to three kinds of traditional Irish narratives in his Introduction : 'bardic tales', 'folk tales', and 'fairy legends'. These three categories parallel the three categories (myths, folktales and legends) of traditional narrative recognised by folklorists today. When all three kinds of narrative are sometimes subsumed under the general term 'folktale', the term 'märchen' denotes the fictional tales.

Yeats, Douglas Hyde and Alfred Nutt believed that the exploits of the ancient Irish heroes in the 'bardic tales' were based on tales about the gods in ancient Irish myth, and that the manuscript 'bardic tales' were based on medieval oral traditions derived from ancient Irish mythology; thus Yeats's category 'bardic tales' is in some ways the equivalent of 'myth'. However, the ancient myths had generally survived in a legendary form because centuries of oral tradition under the impetus of Christianity had transformed the pagan gods into historical human heroes. Remnants of Cuchulain's and Finn's early god-like qualities might survive in oral legends about them, but the legends presented them as super-human heroes or giants rather than gods. Only two of the fifty-two prose narratives which Yeats included in *Fairy and Folk Tales* could be called 'bardic' : Croker's 'The Legend of O'Donoghue' and O'Kearney's 'The Story of Conn-eda'. But, although the heroes of both stories personify certain god-like attributes, they are presented as the historical heroes of legend. The ancient chieftain O'Donoghue's recurring journeys to and from the otherworld parallel such journeys in ancient Irish mythology. However, in the oral legend which Crofton Croker collected and published, O'Donoghue is considered as an actual human chieftain who lived in County Kerry in ancient times and who had continued to appear to the peasantry over the centuries. Likewise, Conn-eda personifies many attributes of an ancient fertility god, but Nicholas O'Kearney's narrative, which O'Kearney had introduced as a 'legend' transcribed from a contemporary oral version when he published it in Volume II of the *Transactions of the Ossianic Society* (1855), presents Conn-eda as an actual prince who lived in ancient Connacht and whose adventures in the story provide a place name legend explaining the origin of the province's name.[7]

Yeats had originally intended to include only legends in his anthology. In the letters during the months preceding its publication he repeatedly referred to it as being a 'fairy book' or including 'selected fairy tales'. His use of the term 'fairy tale' must be clarified. Today the term is popularly used to refer to tales such as 'Cinderella' which folklorists would label a folktale or märchen. Yeats, however, used the term 'fairy tale' or 'fairy legend' to refer to legends about the fairies and other quasi-supernatural beings like ghosts and witches, and used the term 'household tale' when referring to folktales such as 'Cinderella'. His usage of the term 'household tale' reflects the common nineteenth-century English translation of the title of the Grimms' famous collection of folktales, *Kinder- und Hausmärchen*, 'Children's or Household Tales'. In July of 1888, while preparing his first anthology, Yeats wrote to Father Matthew Russell, 'I hardly know if I will have space to include any of what they call "Household Tales", that is to say stories of the Cinderella kind. I will include some if possible but fear

want of space.'⁸ However, according to a later letter to Katharine
Tynan, a mistake in the publisher's calculations about the fin-
ished length of the book caused him to add folktales as filler:
'I have had a great deal of trouble over the folklore, the pub-
lishers first making me strike out one hundred pages, on the
ground that the book was too long and then, when two-thirds
was in print, add as many pages of fresh matter—because they
had made a wrong calculation, and I had to set to work copy-
ing out and looking over material again, as the pages struck out
had to do with the section already in type.'⁹

The proposed topics for the various sections of his anthology
which Yeats mentioned in his July letter to Father Russell refer
to all of the sections which actually appeared in the anthology
except for the final section, 'Kings, Queens, Princesses, Earls,
Robbers'. This last section, which includes no separate intro-
duction such as Yeats had prepared for the earlier sections, was
obviously hastily tacked on. Two of the eight tales in the final
section, 'The Enchantment of Gearoidh Iarla' and 'The Story
of Conn-eda' are legends. The other six are all folktales: 'Donald
and His Neighbours' and 'The Jackdaw' were folktales from the
chapbook *The Royal Hibernian Tales*, although 'The Jackdaw'
resembled a legend in that it was told as actually having happened
to one Tom Moor who lived on Sackville Street in Dublin. The
materials from Patrick Kennedy which Yeats had used in the
earlier sections were all legends from Kennedy's *Legendary
Fictions of the Irish Celts*, but when Yeats had to add a new
section to *Fairy and Folk Tales* he chose three folktales—'The
Twelve Wild Geese', 'The Lazy Beauty and Her Aunts' and
'The Haughty Princess'—which were all variations on the com-
mon folktale theme of 'poor girl marries rich prince and they
live happily ever after'. 'Munachar and Manachar', a trans-
lation from the Irish by Douglas Hyde, is a cumulative folktale
similar to 'The House that Jack Built'. Yeats's remark at the
end of the tale that 'There is some tale like this in almost every
language', presents it as an international folktale.

Indeed, five of the six Yeats included in the last section can
be assigned 'tale-type' numbers from the system for classifying
the plots of international folktales devised in the twentieth cen-
tury by Antti Aarne and Stith Thompson. According to classi-
fication systems outlined in Aarne-Thompson's *The Types of the*

Folktale (1961) and in Sean O'Sullivan and Reidar Christian-
sen's *The Types of the Irish Folktale* (1963), these tales would
be considered international folktales and would be assigned the
following Aarne-Thompson tale-type numbers: 'The Twelve
Wild Geese' (A-T451), 'The Lazy Beauty and her Aunts'
(A-T501), 'The Haughty Princess' (A-T900), 'Donald and his
Neighbours' (A-T1535), 'The Enchantment of Gearoidh Iarla'
(A-T766). The latter story about Gearoidh Iarla (Earl Gerald)
can be assigned a folktale type number even though it is told
as a legend because the way a story is presented and whom it is
told about and not its plot determines whether it is a myth, a
folktale or a legend. If Earl Gerald's journey to the otherworld
had been told about a god it would be classified as a myth.
If it had been told about a stereotyped hero named Jack who
could have lived anytime and anywhere, it would be classified
as a folktale. But because it was told about a prominent mem-
ber of the Fitzgerald family who lived in sixteenth-century
Kildare, it is a legend.

On the other hand, although seven of the forty-four stories
in the first eight sections of the anthology can be assigned tale-
type numbers because their plots resemble the plots of various
international folktales, the seven stories are actually legends
because they are told as legends. As its title indicates, 'The Legend
of Knockgrafton' (A-T503) retells the gifts-of-the-little-people
plot as a matter-of-fact legend in which a hunchback named
Lusmore who lived in the Galtee Mountains received the gift
of fairy music in exchange for his hump. 'Far Darrig in Donegal'
(A-T2412B) recounts the man-who-had-no-story plot as an actual
encounter between a tinker, Pat Diver, and the fairies in Donegal.
'The Legend of O'Donoghue' (A-T766) and 'Rent-Day' apply
the sleeping-warrior plot to the chieftain O'Donoghue who sup-
posedly was in an enchanted sleep under the lake of Killarney
from which he reappeared periodically. 'The Story of the Little
Bird' (A-T471) recounts the 'bridge-to-the-other-world' plot
which Croker claimed he wrote 'word for word as he heard it
from an old woman at a holy well' who obviously believed it
was true and told it as a religious legend. 'The Three Wishes'
(A-T330) presented the very popular tale of how the blacksmith
outwits the devil in the form of a legend about one Billy Dawson,
the supposed founder of an actual present day town called

Castle Dawson. 'A Legend of Knockmany' (A-T1149) presents the legendary Finn and Cuchulain, now having deteriorated from human heroes into mock-heroic giants, in the children-desire-ogre's-flesh plot.

Thus, in its actual published form, *Fairy and Folk Tales of the Irish Peasantry* was indeed what its title claimed : numerous 'fairy tales' in Yeats's sense of the term—legends about fairies, ghosts, witches, fairy doctors, Tir-na-n-og, saints, priests, the devil and giants—plus several folktales which were added out of necessity rather than choice. The broad scope of legendary topics which Yeats included, the careful introductions he wrote for the earlier sections, and the extensive research he did to locate materials, all suggest that he was attempting to survey and comment upon an entire tradition rather than just to publish whatever materials he had randomly heard or read. After publishing *Fairy and Folk Tales*, Yeats could claim with confidence to have read 'most, if not all, recorded Irish fairy tales.'[10] Because the sources for Yeats's selections, his introductions and notes represent an extensive and relatively unknown literary tradition, and because Yeats did not identify his sources for some materials he included and the bibliographic data he did give is often incomplete or inaccurate, the bibliography of Yeats's sources included in Colin Smythe's new edition of *Fairy and Folk Tales* and *Irish Fairy Tales* is most helpful.[11]

Yeats's careful categorisation of the types of Irish fairies is another indication of the care with which he prepared his materials and of the significance he attempted to give to his materials. While elaborate categorisation had been used in studies of ancient Irish myth, international folklore and occult systems of belief about spiritual creatures, Irish folklore collections had generally not classified the Irish fairies and other creatures in such detail. Patrick Kennedy had separated fairy stories from ghost and witch stories in *Legendary Fictions of the Irish Celts*, but only Crofton Croker had used separate categories for the various kinds of fairies. Daniel Hoffman has claimed that Yeats took his classifications from Croker.[12] However, Yeats's classifications bear little resemblance to the haphazard categories in which Croker had placed his various stories. Croker does not even distinguish between fairy stories and stories about ghosts, witches, and other earthly creatures—a distinction which Yeats borrowed from Patrick Kennedy if anyone. Neither Croker nor Kennedy have introductions to separate groups of stories. Yeats's categories and his carefully prepared introductions indicate a much more serious, intellectual approach than in any previous Irish folklorist.

Yeats's classification of the fairies is based on his distinction between the 'trooping' or sociable fairies and the more malignant 'solitary' fairies, and is not found in any of his predecessors in Irish folklore. Croker had not distinguished or mentioned any such distinction between sociable groups of fairies and singular evil ones in organising his materials. The first volume of his *Fairy Legends* included a section on 'The Shefro', whom Yeats identified as the sociable fairies, and other separate sections on beings whom Yeats categorised as solitary fairies—'The Cluricaune', 'The Banshee', and 'The Phooka'. The second volume of *Fairy Legends* contained a section about 'The Merrow', a sociable group of water fairies, and other sections dealing with the solitary fairies, 'The Dullahan' and 'The Fir-Darrig', as well as a section of 'Treasure Legends' and another about 'Rocks and Stones'. The title of David Rice McAnally's collection of Irish folklore, *Irish Wonders: The Ghosts, Giants, Pookas, Demons, Leprechawns [sic], Banshees, Fairies, Witches, Widows, Old Maids, and other Marvels of the Emerald Isle*, reflects the light-hearted jumble of materials it contained. Yeats's *Fairy and Folk Tales* lists McAnally as an 'authority' on Irish folklore but the only parallel between Yeats's classification and organisation and that in *Irish Wonders* is McAnally's remark in one of his chapters about the fairies that 'Unlike Leprechawns, who are not considered fit associates for reputable fairies, the good people are not solitary, but quite sociable.'[13] Even if this offhand comment suggested Yeats's categories, he significantly expanded the idea. Indeed, Yeats's distinction of good as opposed to bad fairies is more in the tradition of nineteenth-century folklore scholars who viewed myth and folklore as representing elemental battles of light and darkness, or occultists who distinguished between good and evil spirits. Significantly, Yeats also published the classification system for the fairies, which he had used in *Fairy and Folk Tales* and he appended to *Irish Fairy Tales*, as an article in the Theosophical magazine *Lucifer* in 1889. Whatever its genesis, Yeats's classification of the fairies has been accepted as authoritative by later writers. Carolyn White began her *A History of Irish Fairies* (1976) with the statement, 'In Ireland two distinct fairy types exist—the trooping fairies and the solitary fairies.' Like Yeats, she devoted one section of her book to 'the trooping fairies' and another to 'the solitary fairies'. Admittedly, Carolyn White is not a folklorist. However, as eminent a folklorist as Katharine Briggs repeatedly cites Yeats in her definitive study of British fairy lore, *An Encyclopedia of Fairies* (1976).

Yeats's voiced and unvoiced criteria for the selection of materials for *Fairy and Folk Tales* further clarify his position in relation to his predecessors and illustrate his developing attitudes about Irish folklore. He had originally been interested in the visionary and spiritual aspects of Irish folklore, especially fairy lore, but he became more and more concerned with depicting the character of the Irish peasant. As might be expected, Yeats's basic organisational perspective is that of the Irish peasant as visionary. The many stories about the fairies and other spiritual creatures are the most obvious evidence of Yeats's preoccupation with country spiritism. But Yeats believed that folk tales about more earthly creatures such as ghosts and witches also had spiritual significance. In 1891 he wrote, 'In towns the fairy tradition is gone indeed, but even there the supernatural survives in visions and ghost-hauntings.'[14] Even the stories Yeats selected about kings and other purely earth-bound creatures portray a world in which unearthly forces are in control of human destiny and which is filled with inexplicable events like shape-changing, a world in which the imagination of the Irish peasant dwelt even if he did not. Yeats's only stated criterion for selection of materials occurs in the Introduction: 'I have tried to make it representative, as far as so few pages would allow, of every kind of Irish folk-faith.' Because Yeats had expended a great amount of effort locating a variety of sources and materials, the resulting collection indeed represents the entire spectrum of Irish folklore publications prior to Yeats.

Yeats's perspective is pointedly Irish. While Croker had introduced some stories in *Fairy Legends* with excerpts from the poetry of Shakespeare and other English poets, no Irish folklorist prior to Yeats had included poems by Irish poets on subjects from Irish folklore. Yeats selected Irish poems by Ferguson,

Allingham, Griffin, Graves and Mangan from volumes of their poetry which actually contained relatively few poems on Irish subjects. Yeats's lists of 'Authorities on Irish Folk-lore' at the end of both of his folklore anthologies contain only Irish books and journals. Mrs Crow is the only contributor in the two folklore anthologies who is not Irish, but her story recounts a historic Irish legend about Lord Castlereagh. The citation of international analogues had abounded in Croker's and Kennedy's anthologies. Even Lady Wilde had included references to the similarities between ancient Ireland and ancient Hebrew and Egyptian cultures. Although such theories had led Yeats to search for occult phenomena in the Irish countryside, he scrupulously avoided presenting Irish folklore from an international perspective with the exception of some notes contributed by Douglas Hyde. From the beginning Yeats had insisted on viewing Irish folklore and ancient Irish myth as representative of a uniquely Irish tradition and national character, as is demonstrated in the first published prose piece by Yeats which has survived, his article of 1886 on Sir Samuel Ferguson which began: 'In the garden of the world's imagination there are seven great fountains. The seven great cycles of legends—the Indian; the Homeric; the Charlemagnic; the Spanish, circling round the Cid; the Arthurian; the Scandinavian; and the Irish—all differing one from the other, as the people differed who created them. Every one of these cycles is the voice of some race celebrating itself, embalming for ever what it hated and loved.'[15] The Blakean doctrine that the universal was contained in the particular was Yeats's defence against charges of provincialism.

However, Irish birth and residence were not Yeats's only criterion. His letters requesting advice about potential materials indicate that he was searching for tales which would fit into the various categories which he had drawn up. Yeats's omissions of some well-known sources he was quite familiar with also demonstrate some of his editorial standards. He ignored folklore materials in travel books about Ireland by English writers, notably Thackeray's *Irish Sketch-Book*, and did not use materials from Thomas Keightley, an Irishman by birth who resided in Ireland a number of years before going to London. Keightley's *The Fairy Mythology* (1828) and *Tales and Popular Fictions; their Resemblance and Transmission from Country to Country*

(1834) were well-known collections of folklore from various countries which included many Irish and Celtic materials. Yeats knew Keightley's works because he cited statements from them in articles in the late 1880s, in particular Keightley's claim that he had contributed 'The Young Piper' and 'The Soul Cages' and other stories to Croker's *Fairy Legends*, a fact which Croker never denied. But Yeats never mentioned Keightley in either of his anthologies, which did include 'The Young Piper' and 'The Soul Cages', nor did he use any materials from Keightley's own collections. According to Keightley, little worthwhile could be learned from the Irish who, prior to the introduction of Christianity into Ireland, were 'nothing but rude ferocious barbarians and Christianity does not seem to have made them much better. . . .'[16] Yeats could have overlooked Keightley's international perspective and prejudices against the Irish and their folklore. He had overlooked worse and more specific charges against the Irish in Cambrensis. But Keightley's own collections completely lacked something Croker and Cambrensis possessed in abundance : fantastic, inexplicable materials.

While Yeats's stated criterion was to make his first folklore anthology as 'representative' as possible of every kind of 'Irish folk-faith', an equally vital criterion which Yeats never voiced and which is apparent only after examining the materials he omitted in the sources from which he drew is his predilection for weird, inexplicable material. Yeats was not only interested in the peasant as visionary, but in the most extravagant, unexplainable examples of their imaginary and visionary powers. Yeats's appreciation of Irish folklore's imaginative extravagance was a departure from the tradition of previous collectors of Irish folklore who had publicly belittled the extravagance of Irish folklore. Most Irish folklorists would have seconded Patrick Kennedy's apology that, 'These ancient fictions, when thoroughly abandoned to a traditional existence, passing from the mouths of one generation of story-tellers to the ears of their successors . . . have been preserved by the peasantry . . . in the worst taste, grotesque, extravagant. . . .'[17] Whereas Kennedy had tried to omit such materials from his collections, Yeats obviously selected materials on the basis of their imaginative extravagance.

Yeats's early articles illustrate his preference for imaginative extravagance. In the article on Samuel Ferguson, he praised

D

Ferguson because he 'loves to linger on what is strange and fantastic' and cited the most grotesque and supernatural incidents from Ferguson's 'Congal' claiming that such incidents are continually introduced into the poem.[18] Such supernatural and grotesque incidents are not nearly as prevalent in the poem as Yeats claimed. In 1890 he wrote that there were 'two traditions in poetry'—the Arnoldian tradition which viewed poetry 'as a purely human art . . . a criticism of life by subtle and refined thinkers' and the tradition which considered poetry as 'a direct message from the Most High . . . extravagant, exhuberant, mystical'—saying that he preferred the latter.[19] In a review of Douglas Hyde's *Beside the Fire* in 1891, Yeats said that 'the imaginative impulse—the quintessence of life—is our great need from folklore.'[20]

Throughout the late 1880s and early 1890s Yeats repeatedly referred to 'Teig O'Kane and the Corpse', translated from the original Irish by Douglas Hyde, as the 'weirdest' and the 'best' of all Irish folklore.[21] In Hyde's tale, Teig, the wild son of a wealthy farmer, meets a group of 'the good people' while walking in the countryside at night. They drop a corpse at his feet and command him to pick it up. When he refuses, they fasten it irremovably on his back and order him to carry it to five specific burial grounds until he finds a place in one of them in which to bury the corpse, which he must do before sunrise. Driven on by the 'good people', Teig sets out on his quest, during which the corpse on his back speaks to him. When he arrives at the first churchyard, he keeps finding corpses wherever he digs, but finally decides to bury the corpse there even though there is no room. Then the corpses already buried there voice their objections—'one stood up in the grave, and shouted an awful shout.' The presence of 'hundreds and hundreds of ghosts' at the second burial ground prevents Teig from burying the corpse there. At the third churchyard 'something he could not see seized him by the neck, by the hands, and by the feet, and bruised him, and shook him, and choked him, until he was nearly dead; and at last he was lifted up and carried more than one hundred yards from that place, and then thrown down in an old dyke, with the corpse still clinging to him.' Trudging on to the fourth graveyard, Teig is again prevented from burying the corpse on his back, this time by mysterious lightning. He finally buries the corpse at the fifth burial ground just before daybreak. Having walked twenty-six miles with a mysteriously talking corpse on his back, he returns home a changed man. In 1920, Yeats still claimed that 'Teig O'Kane' was 'the best of all in my *Faery and Folk Tales*'.[22]

Examination of Yeats's sources indicates that his other selections, though not always as weird as 'Teig O'Kane', were usually chosen on the basis of their imaginative extravagance. Folklore materials were often quite similar in the various collections which he used, and he invariably chose the most unique and mysterious versions he could find. Yeats chose two of the most inexplicable stories—'The Horned Women' and 'The Black Lamb'—from Lady Wilde's *Ancient Legends*. 'The Horned Women' was preceded by the following sentence which Yeats omitted but which obviously reflected his own preferences: such tales told 'in the Irish vernacular are much more weird and strange, and have much more of old-world colouring than the ordinary fairy tales narrated in English by the people, as may be seen by the following mythical story, translated from the Irish, and which is said to be a thousand years old.'[23] The story tells how twelve mysteriously horned women appeared to an Irish peasant woman one night. Each horned woman had one more horn on her head than the preceding one, the final woman having twelve horns. The peasant woman performs their inexplicable ritualistic commands. After their departure, the 'spirit of the well' gives the woman counter-charms to break the witches' spell. The story concludes with the statement that the mantle left behind by one of the witches has been in the possession of the same family for over five hundred years—a statement of factual proof typical of a legend. Another selection from Lady Wilde, 'The Black Lamb', a short anecdote about how a fairy scalded by a woman reappears and dies as a scalded black lamb several times only to disappear after burial, is also one of the weirdest stories available in *Ancient Legends*. In a similar manner, Yeats cited the strangest details from Lady Wilde's next collection, *Ancient Cures, Charms, and Usages of Ireland* when he reviewed it in 1890. For example, from a section containing generally commonplace cures and charms, Yeats repeated the one Lady Wilde herself called the 'most awful': 'if you love in vain, all you have to do is go to a graveyard at midnight, dig up a corpse, and take a strip of skin off it from head to heel, watch until you catch your mistress sleeping and tie it round her waist, and thereafter she will love you for ever.'[24] The collections of Hyde and Lady Wilde are totally different in attitude and technique, yet Yeats chose the same kind of material from each one.

Yeats's selections from Patrick Kennedy's *Legendary Fictions of the Irish Celts* and *The Fireside Stories of Ireland* reflect the same criterion of imaginative and supernatural extravagance. Yeats used the stories by Kennedy which had the largest amount of contact between man and unearthly creatures, and the weirdest material such as shape-changing and grotesque hags. Even in selecting materials for the least overtly spiritual section, 'Kings, Queens, Princesses, Earls, Robbers', Yeats chose the strangest and most inexplicable folktales. Most of the potential stories in Kennedy's *Fireside Stories* which Yeats rejected for this last section could be described as mundane variations on a 'poor girl marries rich prince' plot. The stories from *Fireside Stories* which Yeats did use had the same basic plot but also contained unearthly creatures and weird events. All the materials which Yeats hurriedly selected for his last section, whether folktales or legends, reflected his interest in the character of the Irish peasant: the stories contained kings and other nobility about whom the peasant fantasised, but none of the simple-minded peasants such as were found in the folktales in Kennedy's *Fireside Stories* which Yeats did not use.

Yeats's selections from Crofton Croker also illustrate his preference for inexplicable and unearthly materials. The first volume of Croker's *Fairy Legends* contained two stories about men who believed devoutly in the fairies and each of whom described his observations of them. In the first story, 'Fairies or no Fairies' which Yeats did not use, the fairies whom the man sees turn out to be a field of mushrooms. In the second story, 'The Confessions of Tom Bourke', not surprisingly the one Yeats uses, Tom Bourke's serious explanation of the mysterious fairies is not shattered by a concluding rationalisation. The fairy in 'Master and Man', another story which Yeats selected from the first volume of *Fairy Legends*, possesses more mysterious, unearthly powers than any other in that volume. In the legends from Croker which Yeats did not select, the Irish peasant is generally depicted as being concerned with the fairies out of materialistic motives; the fairies themselves are presented more as light-hearted sprites than as mysterious, spiritual beings; and the few times that supernatural or weird phenomena occur, they are usually just superfluous embroidery and often quite prosaic. For example, 'The Harvest Dinner', which Yeats does not use, is a long tedious tale about an ordinary dinner which ends with a peasant merely seeing some fairies dancing under a bush, an event which has no relation to the story preceding it.

Yeats included an extremely fantastic story from Croker entitled 'Daniel O'Rourke', a monologue by an old peasant describing how he once dreamt he was swept off the earth by an unearthly eagle and taken to the moon. Once there he talked with the old man in the moon and was then swept off the moon by flying geese who dropped him into the Indian Ocean where he talked with some whales. 'Daniel O'Rourke' indicates that it was the extravagant imagination of the peasant, and not only his visionary powers, which appealed to Yeats. Nevertheless, there were limits to even Yeats's fondness for imagination. The weirdness of his selections was generally not a matter of pure fantasy. 'Teig O'Kane' presented an air of mystery rather than pure fantasy, and at the end of 'Daniel O'Rourke' the fantasy is admitted to have been a dream. Yeats distinguished between imaginative extravagance and ridiculousness. He did not use a Croker story entitled 'The Wonderful Tune' in which fish danced and an Irish peasant went off to marry a beautiful underwater merrow, leaving his mother pondering the question of whether she would one day unknowingly eat her own grandchildren. Yeats's inclusion of tales by William Carleton tempers the fantastic atmosphere of some of his other selections. Although the stories which he selected from Carleton were the weirdest ones available in Carleton's *Tales and Sketches*, and as fantastic as others in Yeats's anthology, they are presented in a much more matter-of-fact tone and manner. Carleton's firsthand accounts and details in the stories themselves provide credibility, which is a definitive characteristic of legends, to the tales. For example, the main character in 'Frank Martin and the Fairies' is described as being 'as sensible, sober, and rational as any other man' and yet his belief in the fairies, with whom he 'maintained the most friendly intimacy, and . . . dialogues', was 'peculiarly strong and immovable'. Moreover, Yeats's deletion of the long prefatory note in which Carleton had mocked 'the absurd doctrine of apparitions' and of Carleton's concluding rationalisation of the events in the story transformed Carleton's fictionalised skeptical tale back into an anecdotal legend which frankly set forth folk beliefs about the fairies. Yeats removed similar rationalising and condescending commentary from Carleton's 'The Fate of Frank M'Kenna'.

Yeats found some materials too 'imaginative' for use in *Fairy and Folk Tales* because he wanted to portray the imagination of the Irish peasant and not the imagination of contemporary authors. Yeats found it impossible to use any story from David McAnally's *Irish Wonders*, although he had gone to considerable trouble to locate a copy. *Irish Wonders* did not present the easily-solved problem of objectionable authorial commentary which could simply be omitted. The materials themselves were unsatisfactory. Whereas Keightley's tales had been too prosaic, McAnally's were too wildly imaginative. In two reviews of *Irish Wonders* in 1889, Yeats admitted there was 'not a dull chapter' in the book, but dismissed it as 'a bubble for circulating libraries' because it was not a faithful and serious record of Irish folklore. In Yeats's judgment McAnally 'dresses up his fine tales in a poor slatternly patchwork of inaccurate dialect and sham picturesqueness', and 'strains to make everything humorous' thus presenting a 'false Ireland of sentiment'.[25] While Yeats repeated a few details from *Irish Wonders* in his introductions and notes in *Fairy and Folk Tales*, he included no separate selection by McAnally.

Yeat's selections from the sources he did use demonstrate a number of other criteria. The following are general characteristics of the materials which Yeats did not choose from the various sources he did draw upon : he rejected any story written to inculcate a moral, such as the stories in Kennedy's *Legendary Fictions* which advocated early baptism or preached the evils of cursing. In a similar vein, he did not use stories by Carleton which contained religious or political propaganda and deleted anti-Catholic references from the stories by Carleton such as 'Moll Roe's Marriage; or, The Pudding Bewitched' which he did use. He rejected any stories concerned with earthly matters only; which took place in countries other than Ireland; and in which the Irish country people were characterised as especially materialistic, gullible, or silly, as in some stories by Carleton and Croker. Yeats often omitted stories told in a mock-serious tone by a patronising narrator, a common quality in many of Croker's stories. In Yeats's opinion, Croker 'was continually guilty of that great sin against art—the sin of rationalism. He tried to take away from his stories the impossibility that makes them dear to us.'[26] Because of his dislike of historical interpretations of Irish folklore, Yeats omitted all legends concerning the early settlement of Ireland—a common type of Irish folklore especially in the various county histories which Yeats used and in Patrick Kennedy's collections.

In addition to the kinds of materials which Yeats omitted outright, his deletions and changes in the materials which he did include in *Fairy and Folk Tales* illustrate that his criteria went well beyond selecting representative Irish folk-faiths. Yeats was not an anthologist who merely selected and arranged materials; he was an editor who freely edited his materials. Authorial commentary and superfluous literary atmosphere which did not support Yeats's presentation of a uniquely Irish subject matter free from stale English literary conventions were omitted. He omitted Lady Wilde's comment about the moral significance of 'The Priest's Soul'. The only notes from Croker's *Fairy Legends* which Yeats used in his own anthology were those of Irish reference. He omitted all of Croker's notes, such as the one following 'The Priest's Supper' in the first volume of the *Fairy Legends*, which cited many international analogues to the Irish tale and quoted 'some playful stanzas in Drayton's very fanciful poem of Nyphidia' in order to remind the reader that Irish tales often 'bring to the mind' literary works by Shakespeare, Spenser and other English poets.[27] Yeats also omitted materials within some Croker stories. He deleted Croker's comment in 'The Brewery of Egg-Shells' that it would be impertinent to explain a changeling since no one is unacquainted with Shakespeare's 'Midsummer Night's Dream' and Spenser's 'Fairy Queen', both of which Croker went on to quote.[28]

Yeats's omission of the following paragraph in the same story reflected his objection to having Irish folklore read like a nineteenth-century sentimental novel : 'Who can tell the feelings of a mother when she looks upon her sleeping child? Why should I therefore endeavour to describe those of Mrs Sullivan at again beholding her long lost boy? The fountains of her heart overflowed with the excess of joy—and she wept!—tears trickled silently down her cheek, nor did she strive to check them—they were tears not of sorrow, but of happiness.'[29] In a similar manner Yeats omitted the following two passages of atmospheric description from two stories he used in *Fairy and Folk Tales*—'A Queen's County Witch' and 'Bewitched Butter' —which he had extracted from the same anonymous article, 'Legends of the Queen's County Peasantry. No II: The Bewitched Butter', in the *Dublin University Magazine* of October 1839:

It was still calm night, and, for the season, extremely dark and gloomy. There was not a single star visible in all the vast expanse of heaven, whilst large masses of dark vapour, which rolled slowly athwart the brow of the silent summer-night sky, almost constantly obscured the waning moon, which at intervals appeared sinking redly on the western horizon. There was a solemn tranquility, too, over the face of nature— not a sound was to be heard, except the monotonous, grating call of the land-rail from the adjacent meadows, or, now and then, the appalling shriek of the screech owl over the ivy-wreathed ruins of Aghavoe Priory, which, a little to the eastward of where the watchers lay, reared its venerable head in grim and isolated grandeur. . . .[30]

He had not gone far when the grey dawn began to appear over the hills, and he amused himself in contemplating the varied lovely scenes presented to the intelligent observer by the splendid breaking of a May-day morning. The western sky was streaked with all the magnificent shades of crimson, blue, and gold, so peculiar to 'rosy May', and the brilliant morning star was shining as refulgently as if it had been created but that very hour. Every thing was hushed in calm repose, except the 'merry lark', as Shakespeare calls her, which poised high in the air, amid the fleecy, gold clouds, poured forth her matin hymn of praise and gratitude to the great Author of the Universe, or the wild, discordant cry of the heather-bleat from the adjacent grasses, or the irregular pattering of the large dew drops, as they fell like globules of liquid silver from the stirless trees at either end of the road.[31]

The Folklore Anthologies 95

Yeats likewise deleted the condescending frame stories which had introduced Lover's 'The White Trout' in *Legends and Stories* and John Todhunter's 'How Thomas Connolly Met the Banshee' in the *Dublin University Magazine*. Once Yeats had removed the sceptical, condescending narrator, his stage-Irish peasant informant and some of the mock-heroic adventures from Lover's 'King O'Toole and St Kevin', it indeed deserved to be given an entirely new title 'King O'Toole and His Goose' because it was essentially an entirely new story. Yeats's objection to the historical reading of Irish folklore explains his omission of a long paragraph concerning the history of the MacCarthy family in Croker's 'The Banshee of the MacCarthy's'.

. Yeats's markings in his personal copy of some of Carleton's works, now at the Kenneth Spencer Research Library of the University of Kansas, indicate that Yeats deleted not only editorial commentary or literary embellishments of which he disapproved, but also passages which detracted from the immediacy of the materials no matter how much he agreed with the content of such passages. Yeats's personal copy of *Barney Brady's Goose; The Hedge School; The Three Tasks, and other Irish Tales* contains his pencilled-in deletion markings in 'Moll Roe's Marriage; or, the Pudding Bewitched'. The version of 'The Pudding Bewitched' included in *Fairy and Folk Tales* corresponds exactly with the sections Yeats had not deleted in his personal copy. Yeats crossed out two pages of essay-like commentary by Carleton about the extravagance of Irish folklore and the strong susceptibility of the Irish character to extremes of emotion—two ideas with which Yeats could not have agreed more, the latter being one of the main ideas Yeats adopted from Carleton as his own. The deleted material also contained a considerable amount of information about the manners and customs of the Irish peasantry which was indeed folklore but not the kind of folklore which interested Yeats in 1888.

Generally, Yeats's omissions and changes improved the literary quality of his materials because he merely deleted passages of unnecessary commentary or literary atmosphere. As a consequence of his editing, his selections became more direct and faster-paced narratives. In most cases, his editing also improved their quality as folklore because the authorial commentary, humour and literary embellishments which had masked actual

D*

oral traditions were removed. Yeats's editorial practices in *Fairy and Folk Tales* thus attest to the keen sense of folklore as it existed in oral tradition which he had acquired during his own oral collecting expeditions. Yeats's selections were also improved by Douglas Hyde's knowledge of Irish which enabled Yeats to correct some of the Irish words in some of the stories.

Other alterations which Yeats made in his source materials changed their nature more radically and did not improve his materials as literature or as folklore. In his 'Introduction' to *Fairy and Folk Tales,* Yeats praised Patrick Kennedy for having 'had something of a genuine belief in the fairies'.[32] However, affectionate scepticism rather than belief is the dominant tone in Kennedy's Introductions, Prefaces, and Notes to his collections. Although Yeats claimed that Kennedy's 'one great advantage' as a folklorist was that he 'believed in his goblins as sincerely as any peasant' in his *Legendary Fictions,* it was in that very collection that Kennedy himself had said that 'could all circumstances connected with the occurrences be ascertained, everything related might probably be referred to natural causes.'[33]

Yeats also radically altered the nature of the pooka. In Irish folklore in general, in all Yeats's specific source materials and in the additional folklore materials he cited as 'Authorities on Irish Folk-lore' at the end of both his anthologies, the pooka is portrayed as nothing more than a mischievous prankster. However, in his introduction to the section entitled 'The Pooka', Yeats presents the pooka as a fearful, malignant creature 'grown monstrous with much solitude' and 'of the race of nightmare', and as a 'wild staring phantom' who 'like all spirits is only half in the world of form'. Even the three pooka stories which follow do not bear out this fearful introduction in the least. In the first story, 'The Piper and the Puca' by Douglas Hyde, the pooka actually helps a foolish piper by taking him to a banshee feast inside Croagh Patrick where the piper is given sense and music and gold, and although the music suddenly turns into screeching geese and the gold into ordinary leaves, the ability to play beautiful music on old pipes remains with the piper. In any event, the pooka does not present the piper with any terrible experience. The pooka who leads Croker's Daniel O'Rourke to the moon provides a fantastic adventure but causes no harm. The 'Kildare Pooka' in Patrick Kennedy's story of that name is merely the spirit of a boy who was a lazy scullion when alive and after death is condemned to wash pots nightly until a human being rewards him for his labours. At the end of the story the human scullion whom he has helped by his nightly labours gives him a reward, the spell is broken and he never returns. Meanwhile, all he has done is cause some harmless clatter from pots and pans while others were sleeping. Nor is any character in any of the three pooka stories even portrayed as feeling much fear towards the pookas they encounter. The fearful tone in Yeats's introduction on the pooka is an obvious attempt to introduce a seriousness and awe into Irish folklore which his materials simply had not provided. Yeats himself admitted in his note to the poem 'Michael Robartes bids His Beloved to be at Peace' in *The Wind Among the Reeds* (1899) that the pookas 'are now mischievous spirits'.

All of Yeats's criteria of selection, including the omissions and alterations in his sources, reflect his attempt to present fairyland as representative of a separate spiritual realm which was to be taken seriously even if it could not be understood. Yeats's desire to present Irish folklore as a serious literary subject matter and not merely as light entertainment or an antiquarian curiosity required that he make his readers take the Irish peasant seriously, a none too easy task since popular writers like Croker and Lover had persisted in presenting the Irish peasant as an object of laughter throughout the century. Yeats pointedly criticised this tradition in his Introduction :

> Croker and Lover, full of the ideas of the harum-scarum Irish gentility, saw everything humorised. The impulse of the Irish literature of their time came from a class that did not—mainly for political reasons—take the populace seriously, and im-agined the country as a humorist's Arcadia; its passion, its gloom, its tragedy, they knew nothing of. What they did was not wholly false; they merely magnified an irresponsible type, found oftenest among boatsmen, car men, and gentlemen's servants, into the type of a whole nation, and created the stage Irishman.[34]

Because their image of Ireland presented at least a part of the Irish character and because their work contained a great deal of Irish folklore, Yeats included material by both Croker and

Lover, thirteen stories from Croker and two from Lover, in *Fairy and Folk Tales.* He chose the least humorous legends in Croker's *Fairy Legends*; and only two of the thirteen from Croker in Yeats's anthology, 'Master and Man' and 'Daniel O'Rourke', contain the humorous 'stage-Irish' peasant. In making his selections from Croker, Yeats carefully omitted such stories as 'Seeing is Believing' in which the main character, an Irish peasant named Felix O'Driscoll, is described as a 'rattling, rollicking, harum-scarum, devil-may-care sort of fellow'.[35] Neither of the two stories which Yeats selected from Lover even contained an Irish peasant. The Irish peasant is humorous in a number of stories in Yeats's collection, but none is as ridiculous as those in the majority of Croker's and Lover's tales which Yeats did not use.

In contrast to Croker and Lover, Yeats sought to present the Irish peasant as characterised by seriousness and tragedy as well as gaiety and humour. Yeats had always admired Irish subject matter for its potential seriousness and tragedy. In 1889 he praised Davis, Mangan and Ferguson at the expense of other nineteenth-century Irish writers who had not taken Ireland seriously: 'Ireland was a metaphor to Moore, to Lever and Lover a merry harlequin, sometimes even pathetic, to be patted and pitied and laughed at so long as he said, "your honour" and presumed nowise to be considered a serious or tragic person. Yet the poetry of the men I write about is above all things tragic and melancholy.'[36] Yeats's descriptions of the Irish peasant in the late 1880s reflected his belief in the depth rather than superficial humour of their character: 'Irish legends and Irish peasant minds, however, have no lack of melancholy. The accidents of Nature supply good store of it to all men, and in their hearts, too, there dwells a sadness still unfathomed. Yet in that sadness there is no gloom, no darkness, no love of the ugly, no moping. The sadness of a people who hold that "contention is better than loneliness", it is half a visionary fatalism.'[37] The Irish peasant and his folklore could provide more than humour: 'Here at last is a universe where all is large and intense enough to almost satisfy the emotions of man. Certainly such stories are not a criticism of life but rather an extension, thereby much more closely resembling Homer than that last phase of "the improving book", a social drama by Henrik Ibsen.

They are an existence and not a thought, and make our world of tea-tables seem but a shabby penumbra.'[38]

In selecting materials for *Fairy and Folk Tales* Yeats preferred stories which reinforced his serious conception of the Irish peasant. In his Introduction Yeats said that although Carleton was primarily known as a humorist, he had selected Carleton's 'ghost stories' in which Carleton had 'a much more serious way with him, for all his humour'. The real-life peasants whom Yeats described and quoted in his Introduction are matter-of-fact and serious about their beliefs and display none of the harum-scarum humour of Lover's and Croker's peasantry.

A brief summary of the materials which Yeats included in the first section of his anthology illustrates his belief that the Irish peasant and his beliefs and his experiences were to be taken seriously rather than laughed at. The section opens with Allingham's poem, 'The Fairies', in which a child dies of sorrow after being stolen by the fairies and returning to find all her friends gone. 'Frank Martin and the Fairies', by William Carleton, tells how the fairies built a coffin on the eve of a child's unexpected death. In Croker's 'The Priest's Supper' the peasant is totally serious about his encounter and discussion with the fairies. Samuel Ferguson's 'The Fairy Well of Lagnanay' emphasises the terror of fairy enchantment and repeats the refrain 'Save us all from fairy thrall.' The mysterious events of Hyde's 'Teig O'Kane' were recounted earlier. In 'Paddy Corcoran's Wife' Carleton recounts how an Irish peasant was fairy struck for seven years because she unknowingly let her children throw dirty water out the door as the fairies were passing it. In Callanan's song, 'Cusheen Loo', a woman longs to be free of fairy enchantment and return to her normal life. In Lover's 'The White Trout: A Legend of Cong', a soldier's whole character is transformed by his encounter with an enchanted fairy trout. In Ferguson's poem, 'The Fairy Thorn', a 'wild terror' is instilled in the characters by the fairies. In Croker's 'The Legend of Knockgrafton', the main character is a peasant who is very serious about his belief in the fairies, who are portrayed as in complete control of his destiny. Letitia McClintock's 'Donegal Fairy' is a matter-of-fact conversation of some peasants about the fairies being good neighbours if treated kindly, but unfriendly when angered. While humour is an element in a number of the stories just mentioned, Yeats's selections are definitely not in the tradition of stage-Irish humour. His entire anthology is a blend of humour and seriousness. Yeats's praise of Douglas Hyde in the Introduction to *Fairy and Folk Tales*—'his work is neither humorous nor mournful; it is simply life'—apparently reflects Yeats's own intention.

During the summer of 1891 Yeats was asked to edit a volume of Irish fairy tales for the Fisher Unwin 'Children's Library' series. The collection of Irish folklore which Yeats compiled, *Irish Fairy Tales* (1892), was not nearly as significant as Yeats's first anthology, *Fairy and Folk Tales* (1888) in terms of scope and Yeats's own involvement in the materials. Yeats was quite active in other literary and national matters at the time and devoted much less time and effort to the compilation of this second anthology, obviously drawing upon the large background he had accumulated in preparing his first collection of Irish folklore. Having already defined and studied the previous tradition of Irish folklore, Yeats was less interested in preparing another collection of other folklorists' materials than in preparing his own collection of the materials he had gathered around Sligo—a project begun during 1891 and which appeared as *The Celtic Twilight. Men and Women, Dhouls and Faeries* in 1893. Moreover, Yeats's great admiration for Douglas Hyde's accomplishments as a folklorist probably lessened his respect and interest concerning previous collections.

The compilation and nature of *Irish Fairy Tales* reflect the fact that it was written for children and Yeats's own waning interest in previous Irish folklore. *Irish Fairy Tales* includes only fourteen tales while there had been sixty-five tales and poems in *Fairy and Folk Tales*. Two of the fourteen tales are folktales : 'The Man Who Never Knew Fear' (A-T326) and 'The Little Weaver of Duleek Gate' (A-T1640). The plots of three other tales can also be assigned Aarne-Thompson tale-type numbers but they are narrated as legends : 'The Rival Kempers' (A-T500), 'A Fairy Enchantment' (A-T2412B), and 'Owney and Owney-na-Peak' (incident from A-T1535). Yeats did not write a separate introduction for each section or any notes at the end of the collection as he had in 1888. Fewer authors are represented and the stories themselves reflect a much lighter tone and attitude than those in the first anthology. The three stories from Crofton Croker are all from among the more humorous stories in *Fairy Legends* which Yeats did not select in 1888. In 'Teigue of the Lee' Yeats allows a long atmospheric passage describing an old mansion to remain, although he edited several of the other tales as he had those in *Fairy and Folk Tales*. The peasants in *Irish Fairy Tales* are generally more serious about worldly success than about the fairies, and the fairies themselves are more human and less mysterious.

Yeats presented *Irish Fairy Tales* as a continuation of *Fairy and Folk Tales of the Irish Peasantry*: 'These two volumes make, I believe, a fairly representative collection of Irish folk tales. . . . I have included no story that has already appeared in my *Fairy and Folk Tales of the Irish Peasantry*.'[39] However, Yeats's own contribution to *Irish Fairy Tales*, 'A Fairy Enchantment', is quite similar to a longer story, 'Far Darrig in Donegal', by Letitia McClintock in *Fairy and Folk Tales* and would share the same tale-type number, A-T2412B. Yeats's own story and his Introduction are the most reminiscent of the matter-of-fact yet mysterious tone which had pervaded the first collection. In the Introduction Yeats describes the beliefs of Biddy Hart, a peasant woman near Sligo who took the fairies quite seriously: 'Her news about the creatures is always quite matter-of-fact and detailed, just as if she dealt with any common occurrence.' The Irish countryside is still presented as an alternative to 'this century of great engines and spinning-jinnies', and the *living* belief of the Irish peasantry is reiterated: 'How firmly she believed in them! how greatly she feared offending them!'

The obviously limited effort which went into the compilation of *Irish Fairy Tales* indicates that the nature of Yeats's interest in Irish folklore had changed. To begin with Yeats had been interested in the literary and occult use of the fairies. His letters of 1888 reflect his belief on his first anthology had been worthwhile because of the poetic materials he had accumulated in the process. In 1888 he wrote to Katharine Tynan concerning the compilation of *Fairy and Folk Tales*: 'It has been a very laborious business, but well worth doing, for all the materials for poetry, if for nothing else. You and I will have to turn some of the stories into poems.'[40] But it turned out that the Irish peasant rather than his fairy lore provided the better subject matter. Several of the poems based on Irish fairy lore which

Yeats had published in *The Wanderings of Oisin and Other Poems* (1889) were never included in later collections of his poetry but can be examined in its variorum edition. Three of the poems demonstrate how Yeats tried unsuccessfully to impose human passions on his fairy characters. In 'The Fairy Pedant' light-hearted fairies, the normal kind, mock the thoughtful, serious fairy who is wasting away because of his pursuit of wisdom. Female fairies in 'A Lover's Quarrel among the Fairies' experience jealousy and the fairies weep when they learn their souls are lost in 'The Priest and the Fairy'. The thoughtfulness, jealousy and sorrow with which Yeats endowed these fairies represent neither folklore nor good poetry. The Irish peasant was fascinated by the fairies precisely because they were neither human nor subject to human passion and tragedy. The fascination and power of fairy lore was based on what the peasantry believed the fairies could do to them. Human passions were trivialised rather than deepened when Yeats injected them into a lore about creatures who were anything but human.

Significantly, the relatively few poems about the fairy which Yeats allowed to remain in later editions of his poetry, such as 'The Stolen Child' (1886) and 'A Faery Song' (1891), present a dramatic confrontation between the human peasantry and a fairy realm characterised by the mystery, enchantment and non-human traits given it in folk tradition. The fairies are the only speakers in 'The Stolen Child' yet their lovely song expresses the child's predicament rather than any passions of their own. Only they judge their life of 'weaving olden dances' as preferable to the incomprehensible sorrow of the human world. Their description of what the child is leaving—'He'll hear no more the lowing/Of the calves on the warm hillside/Or the kettle on the hob/Sing peace into his breast,/Or see the brown mice bob/Round and round the oatmeal-chest'—arouses ambiguous emotions in a reader as to which world is preferable. Can the 'solemn-eyed' child they are leading away be at peace in a world of sheer joy? Oisin, after all, longed to see the Finians and the real world of Ireland again despite his love for Niamh. Likewise, the thematic depth of 'The Wanderings of Oisin' centred on the human passions of Oisin rather than on the fairy lore which the poem contained. The rhetorical question which the fairies who sing 'A Faery Song' pose about their world—'Is anything better, anything better?'—significantly remains unanswered. The only other early poem having anything to do with fairyland in either of Yeats's first two collections of poetry, *The Wanderings of Oisin and Other Poems* and *The Countess Kathleen and Various Legends and Lyrics*, is 'The Man who Dreamed of Fairyland' (1891) which describes the man and his adventures rather than the fairies.

Fairy lore had obviously not been of much poetic value to Yeats. Nor did it prove to be of much dramatic value. The early plays which Yeats derived from the plots of tales he had anthologised in *Fairy and Folk Tales* and *Irish Fairy Tales* were all based on human drama rather than fairy lore. 'The Countess Cathleen' (1892) was based on the story 'The Countess Kathleen O'Shea' in *Fairy and Folk Tales*. 'The Hour-Glass' (1903) was based on the story 'The Priest's Soul' in *Fairy and Folk Tales*. The dramas of the Countess Cathleen and the priest centre on their encounter with the devil and with angels rather than on any encounter with the fairies. 'The King's Threshold' (1904) is based on the story 'Seanchan the Bard and the King of the Cats' in *Irish Fairy Tales*. Yeats's play focuses on the human conflict between Seanchan and King Guaire and does not even mention Seanchan's encounter with the fairy animal 'the King of the Cats' which had been the major conflict in the original tale. 'The Land of Heart's Desire' (1894) is the only play Yeats wrote which is in any sense based on fairy lore. Even in this play the conflict is basically a human one: Mary Bruin's inability to accept the mundane peasant world around her. Whether or not she has died or has been 'taken' by the fairies at the end of the play remains ambiguous. In any event, fairy lore has simply been used as a vehicle for expressing the longings of Mary Bruin's soul.

Nor had Irish fairy lore given Yeats the conclusive proof of occult phenomena he had hoped to find. The contrast between Yeats's Introduction of 1888, which had focused on the nature and existence of the fairies, and his Introduction of 1892, entitled 'An Irish Story-teller', which emphasised the character and imagination of the Irish peasant who believed in the fairies, illustrates that Yeats's interest in Irish folklore had focused more and more on its human elements. The nature of the Irish peasant characters had been a major criterion of selection even in *Fairy and Folk Tales*, and in that first anthology the earthly world of the Irish peasant was almost always presented as preferable to fairyland. Yeats's gradual loss of interest in Irish fairy lore ultimately made his involvement with Irish folklore and Irish literary tradition fuller and more truly representative. Irish fairy lore, while an important part of Irish folklore, was the subject of only a relatively small portion of poetry and prose in Irish literary tradition. Yeats's disenchantment with the occult and literary possibilities of Irish fairy lore enouraged him to explore other aspects of Irish folklore and peasant life, and other genres of Irish literature.

Yeats's compilation of *Fairy and Folk Tales of the Irish Peasantry* marked a stage in his developing use of Irish literary materials—the outgrowth of his interest in literary ballads based on subjects from Irish folklore and the prelude to his interest in the character and life of the Irish peasant. Yeats discovered in Irish folklore a rich, eclectic literary tradition which he could and did use for his own purposes. His criteria of selection and his editorial emendations are those of an editor whose literary taste qualifies the stereotyped image of the early Yeats as an ethereal 'Celtic Twilight' poet. Even commentators who are sympathetic to Yeats can easily misinterpret his purposes and accomplishments in *Fairy and Folk Tales* if they are not familiar with the tradition from which Yeats drew his materials. Kathleen Raine, in an otherwise beautiful and sympathetic introduction to a new edition of *Fairy and Folk Tales* and *Irish Fairy Tales*, argues that Yeats's 'literary admiration' for the fairy lore in the stories he anthologised was based on their 'highly formalised art of story-telling' and their 'idiomatic turns of phrase which arise from the translation, by Gaelic-speakers, from one language to the other'.[41] Only Douglas Hyde's stories could possibly have offered these things to Yeats. His other selections, because of their very nature as legends, could not represent the highly formalised art of story-telling characteristic of other genres in oral Irish narrative. Such formalised telling could only have been apparent in folktales, hero tales or myths—all of which are scarce in the two anthologies. Any narrative elaboration in Yeats's materials was due to the influence of Anglo-Irish fiction on his predecessors and was one of the very features he deleted from his selections as editor. Only the selections he included by Hyde were translations; few of his other sources could speak Irish and so presented their legends—or, in Kennedy's case, folktales—in a literary English in which stage-Irish diction was more common than a true Anglo-Irish idiom. The compilation of the two anthologies was undeniably a valuable literary experience for Yeats, but the literary nature of his materials was actually the very opposite of what Miss Raine presumes.

Other commentators on Yeats and Irish folklore have overestimated the importance of Lady Gregory and John M. Synge. Long before Yeats met Lady Gregory and Synge in the late 1890s, both of whom have too often been regarded as Yeats's main influences in the use of Irish folklore, Yeats had sought out and studied Irish folklore as a means of bringing his poetry down to earth, and as an editor had tried to simplify folklore of elaborate literary conventions and transform it from the light-hearted depiction of a harum-scarum peasantry into a serious literary subject matter. In the process Yeats was influenced by a number of Irish folklorists, in particular Douglas Hyde, before Lady Gregory and Synge even began writing about Irish folklore.

4

From Fairy to Folk:
Representative Irish Tales and
The Celtic Twilight

Although the publication of *Irish Fairy Tales* in 1892 marked the end of Yeats's interest in previously published Irish folklore and his waning enthusiasm for the literary possibilities of fairy lore, he continued to be interested in the literary possibilities of the life and character of the Irish peasant and to be intrigued by the occult implications of Irish fairy lore. The character and life of the Irish peasant had been examined in the greatest detail in nineteenth-century Anglo-Irish fiction, so Yeats began to study this tradition soon after compiling *Fairy and Folk Tales of the Irish Peasantry* in 1888. He selected tales by William Carleton, the Irish peasant who had become the century's most distinguished Irish novelist in the course of writing about the peasantry he knew so well, for *Stories from Carleton* (1889). Two years later Yeats published a two-volume collection, *Representative Irish Tales*, in which he surveyed and interpreted the entire tradition of nineteenth-century Anglo-Irish fiction. All the while he prepared these two anthologies of materials about early nineteenth-century peasant life Yeats continued to explore the life, character and beliefs of the contemporary peasantry for himself. Yeats's work as a collector and recorder of Irish folklore produced *The Celtic Twilight, Men and Women, Dhouls and Fairies* in 1893.

A month before *Stories from Carleton* appeared in August 1889 Yeats was already reading 'all the chief Irish novelists of peasant life' in preparation for compiling *Representative Irish Tales*, although that collection was not published until March 1891.[1] In December 1889 Yeats described his editorial perspective for *Representative Irish Tales*: 'I am trying to make all the stories illustrations of some phase of Irish life, meaning the collection to be a kind of social history.'[2] He declared in his

Introduction to the collection: 'I have made the selection in such a way as to illustrate as far as possible the kind of witness they bear to Irish character.'³ The life and character of the Irish peasantry provided the focus for both *Stories from Carleton* and *Representative Irish Tales*. Yeats selected five stories from William Carleton's five-volume *Traits and Stories of the Irish Peasantry* (1830–1833) for *Stories from Carleton*: 'The Poor Scholar', the story of a young peasant's journey across Ireland in search of a clerical education; 'Tubber Derg; or, the Red Well', the tale of a peasant family's eviction from their farm; 'Wildgoose Lodge', a nightmarish description of the revenge of one group of Irish peasants against a rival faction; 'Shane Fadh's Wedding', the boisterous account of a peasant wedding; and 'The Hedge School', a tale of the village life and secret societies of the Irish peasantry. Yeats used materials from ten Irish fiction writers in *Representative Irish Tales*, which includes the complete text of Maria Edgeworth's *Castle Rackrent*, excerpts from Gerald Griffin's *The Collegians,* Michael Banim's *The Mayor of Wind-Gap*, Charles Lever's *Charles O'Malley* and Charles Kickham's *For the Old Land*, and several tales, including an anonymous one from an Irish chapbook.

The first volume of *Representative Irish Tales* begins with a nine-page Introduction in which Yeats evaluates nineteenth-century Irish fiction writers on the basis of how well they had depicted the Irish peasantry and their life. In addition, Yeats wrote separate introductions on the individual authors which preceded the selections from their fiction. Each of these introductions emphasised the peculiarities of the author's life as much as the nature of his fiction. For example, Yeats ignored Michael Banim's humdrum life and concentrated instead on his brother John's fated love affair—while attending the funeral of his estranged lover, John caught a disease which was eventually fatal. In a similar vein, Yeats pointed out that Charles Lever lived for a time among Canadian Indians and had an affair with an Indian maiden. This focus on the personalities and private lives of the authors, together with the emphasis on Irish character in the selections from their fiction, reflect Yeats's growing interest in personality in literature and in life, which was in contrast to his praise of a few years earlier for the Irish ballad and its 'impersonality'.

The Introduction to *Representative Irish Tales* illustrates Yeats's preference for authors who had been peasants themselves or who had grown up in close contact with the peasantry:

> I notice very distinctly in all Irish literature two different accents—the accent of the gentry, and the less polished accent of the peasantry and those near them; a division roughly into the voice of those who lived lightly and gayly, and those who took man and his fortunes with much seriousness and even at times mournfully. The one has found its most typical embodiment in the tales and novels of Croker, Lover, and Lever, and the other in the ruder but deeper work of Carleton, Kickham, and the two Banims. There is perhaps no other country in the world the style and nature of whose writers have been so completely governed by their birth and social standing.

Yeats considered William Carleton to be the greatest Irish novelist of the century because Carleton was a peasant and wrote of the Irish countryside he knew so well: 'The great thing about Carleton was that he always remained a peasant, hating and loving with his class.'[4]

Yeats's conception of the character of the Irish peasant resembled Carleton's more than that of any other Irish novelist. In the 'Preface to the First Series' (1830) of *Traits and Stories of the Irish Peasantry*, Carleton declared that the author 'disclaims subserviency to any political purpose whatsoever. His desire is neither to distort his countrymen into demons, nor to enshrine them as suffering innocents and saints, but to exhibit them as they really are—warm-hearted, hot-headed, affectionate creatures —the very fittest materials in the world for either the poet or the agitator—capable of great culpability, and of great and energetic goodness—sudden in their passions . . . variable in their temper . . . at times rugged and gloomy . . . often sweet, soft, and gay. . . .'[5] But, whereas Carleton always emphasised the humanity of a peasantry known chiefly for their brutality in the early nineteenth century, Yeats sought a peasantry capable of deep passion and tragedy. In this sense, Yeats's conception of the Irish character owes more to Lady Wilde than it does to Carleton. In an essay on 'Irish Nature' in *Ancient Legends*,

Mystic Charms and Superstitions of Ireland, Lady Wilde described the Irish character thus : 'To believe fanatically, trust implicitly, hope infinitely, and perhaps to revenge implacably—these are the unchanging and ineradicable characteristics of Irish nature. . . . And it is these passionate qualities that make the Celt the great motive force of the world, ever striving against limitations towards some vision of ideal splendour.'[6]

Yeats's concern for presenting the life and character of the Irish peasantry was basically the same intention which had motivated the majority of nineteenth-century Irish novelists. Numerous introductions and prefaces to Irish novels had declared the same goal : to represent Ireland 'as it really is' for the first time. Richard Lovell Edgeworth's comments as 'editor' of *Castle Rackrent*, which Yeats included in *Representative Irish Tales*, explained the need (which was to exist throughout the century) for novels based on Irish life : such works were 'a specimen of manners and character which are perhaps unknown in England'. What little the English reader did know of Ireland was usually unpleasant—insurrections, conspiracies, duels. But the Act of Union in 1800 had made Ireland a matter of direct concern to the English public. Numerous novels about life in Ireland were produced during the century in answer to this desire for information about Ireland.[7]

Although Yeats's selections in *Representative Irish Tales* represent most of the major Irish fiction writers of the century, he sought to counter three of the major ingredients of nineteenth-century Anglo-Irish fiction : political and religious propaganda; sentiment; and stage-Irish humour. Yeats's critical judgments of Anglo-Irish literature prior to his compilation of these two anthologies of Anglo-Irish fiction had demonstrated his deep bias against propaganda, sentiment and humorous caricature. Yeats had deplored Patrick Kennedy's use of Irish folklore to preach moral maxims, and the political propaganda of the Young Ireland movement. Nor had sentiment fared any better than propaganda in Yeats's early articles. Yeats had denounced David Rice McAnally because 'the Ireland he loves is not the real Ireland : it is the false Ireland of sentiment', and had criticised a collection of tales by a contemporary Irish writer because, 'Her whole book is simply a huge, iridescent tear. . . .'[8] In place of the pathetic Irishman depicted in the more lugubrious Irish fiction, Yeats extolled the 'serious, reserved' Irish peasant who was capable of deep passion.[9] In his articles Yeats continually referred to Irish character in terms of 'joy' rather than humour, and he had excluded materials from *Fairy and Folk Tales of the Irish Peasantry* which portrayed the foolish antics of the stage-Irishman.

The stories which Yeats selected for *Stories from Carleton* and *Representative Irish Tales* illustrate his attempt to replace political and religious propaganda with social history; lugubrious sentimentality with deep passion; and stage-Irish humour with joy and tragedy. Irish fiction was filled with propaganda about the heated political and religious controversies which character-ised Ireland's relations with England during the century. In 'The Trembling of the Veil' (1922) Yeats described the situation thus: 'All the past had been turned into a melodrama with Ireland for blameless hero and poet; novelist and historian had but one object, that we should hiss the villain, and only a minority doubted that the greater the talent the greater the hiss. It was all the harder to substitute for that melodrama a nobler form of art, because there really had been, however different in their form, villain and victim. . . .'[10] In selecting materials for his anthologies, Yeats tried to hold a middle course between the extreme characterisations of the Irish and the English as 'victim' and 'villain'. His selections do not belabour Irish suffering under English rule, nor do they depict the Irish peasantry as a group of barbarians about to overrun English outposts of civilisation in Ireland.

Yeats minimised Carleton's reputation as a propagandist and did not use the more propagandistic of Carleton's works, most notably Carleton's famous and most notoriously anti-Catholic tale, 'The Lough Derg Pilgrim'. Yeats used Rosa Mulholland's tale, 'The Hungry Death', which contained none of the intense Catholic and nationalistic propaganda so prevalent in most of her fiction. Yeats described *Representative Irish Tales* as 'a kind of social history' and praised Carleton as a 'historian', redefining history so as to exclude the divisive political and religious issues of Anglo-Irish relations and the 'hopelessly dry-as-dust' traditions of Irish historical scholarship: 'William Carleton was a great Irish historian. The history of a nation is not in parliaments and battlefields, but in what the people say to each other on fair-days and high days, and in how they farm, and quarrel, and go on pilgrimage. These things has Carleton recorded.'[11] Yeats here sounds very much like folklorists today who extol folklore for the invaluable insight it provides into the daily life of ordinary people in the past and present. Although Yeats is dealing with fiction his concerns are still those of a folklorist. His focus is on what folklorists today refer to as 'non-verbal' or 'customary' folklore such as weddings, wakes and other social customs and events in the life of the peasantry. When Yeats compared Anglo-Irish fiction with the poetry of Edward Walsh, J. J. Callanan, James Clarence Mangan, Samuel Ferguson and William Allingham in 1895 he declared: 'The tradition expressed by these poets was that of the bards and the Gaelic ballad-writers, but there was still another tradition, another expression of the same dominant moods, that which was embodied in the customs of the poor, their wakes, their hedge-schools, their factions, their weddings, their habits of thought and feeling, and this could best be described in prose.'[12] Both of Yeats's anthologies present a panorama of the social life of the Irish peasantry rather than the political and religious controversies of the century.

However, as much as Yeats deplored political propaganda, *Stories from Carleton* and *Representative Irish Tales* are a form of pro-Irish propaganda. Yeats did include some implicitly anti-British materials. In *Stories from Carleton* Yeats allowed Carleton's disgressions about the unfair rental practices of the Anglo-Irish landlords to remain in 'Tubber Derg', although they could have been removed without affecting the plot as he had deleted descriptive passages from selections in his folklore anthologies. Whenever the Anglo-Irish gentry appear in *Representative Irish Tales*, it is in an unfavourable light. The antics of the Rackrent family are well-known. In Yeats's selection from Gerald Griffin's novel *The Collegians*, 'The Death of the Huntsman', a drunken master requests a dying peasant to sound the fox-hunting call for the entertainment of his drunken friends; the noble peasant, whose peace had already been shattered by their boisterous, drunken revels complied with the request and died as a result. Yeats's selection by Charles Lever entitled 'Trinity College', describes the 'life of rackety and careless dissipation' of the 'young gentlemen' of Trinity College, and satirises a ped-

antic, ineffectual scholar. Yeats's other selections are an obvious
attempt to shape the reader's view of Irish life and character.
Yeats omitted all the virulent anti-Irish materials available to
him and concentrated instead on redefining the caricature of
sentiment and humour which had represented the Irish char-
acter throughout the century.

From the beginning of his involvement with an Irish subject
matter, Yeats had identified a depth and steadfastness in Irish
character quite different from the humorous, sentimental stereo-
types of Anglo-Irish fiction and the descriptions of James A.
Froude and of Matthew Arnold. In 1886 Yeats had praised
Samuel Ferguson as 'the greatest Irish poet' because his works
embodied 'more completely than in any other man's writings,
the Irish character. Its unflinching devotion to some single aim.
Its passion. . . . [and] faithfulness to things tragic and bitter. . . .'[13]
Yeats's early articles are filled with references to the implacability
of Irish 'passion', and the word 'sentimental' occurs only in a
derogatory sense. He inveighed against 'convivial Ireland with
the traditional tear and smile' throughout his life.

Yeats's search for examples of deep passion rather than
lighthearted sentiment in the Irish peasant character is apparent
in his selections for both anthologies of Anglo-Irish fiction. He
declared in his Introduction to *Representative Irish Tales* that
Carleton, in whom 'the true peasant was at last speaking',
brought 'a passion, a violence, new to [the] polite existence'
of anglicised Dublin literary circles; Carleton's fiction surpassed
that of Lover, Croker and Lever because Carleton combined
humour and passion and because of 'the sheer force of his
powerful nature . . . full of violent emotions and brooding
melancholy'. Carleton's 'Wildgoose Lodge', the only story to
appear in both *Stories from Carleton* and *Representative Irish
Tales*, is a horrifying example of the deep passions Yeats
believed characterised the Irish peasant. In the story, one
faction of Irish peasants set fire to the household of a rival
faction. Women and children were pushed back into the flames
when they tried to escape. Yeats included Carleton's note that
this 'scene of hellish murder' had indeed happened. In *Represen-
tative Irish Tales*, Carleton's 'The Battle of the Factions' des-
cribes how a young peasant killed a member of a rival faction
with his scythe. The killer's sister was in love with the murdered

man and, unaware that the murderer was her own brother, she killed the murderer with a blow from behind and then went insane. The line between 'passion' and sentimental melodrama in such tales is indeed thin, but Carleton's descriptions of violence, especially in 'Wildgoose Lodge', are generally unemotional and evoke a nightmarish world of undeniable energy and passion.

However, a number of Yeats's selections, even some by Carleton, inevitably verge on melodrama because there was so much more sentimentality than vehement, cold-blooded passion in nineteenth-century Anglo-Irish fiction. In *Stories from Carleton*, 'Tubber Derg', Carleton's tale of a peasant family's eviction, is filled with tearful partings and reunions sentimentalising the death of a young child and the family's visits to her grave. In 'The Poor Scholar' Carleton describes the departure of a young Irish peasant to seek a clerical education : 'This to him was the greatest trial he had yet felt; long and heart-rending was their embrace. Jemmy soothed and comforted his beloved brother, but in vain. The lad threw himself on the spot at which they parted, and remained there until Jemmy turned an angle of the road which brought him out of his sight, when the poor boy kissed the marks of his brother's feet repeatedly, and then returned home, hoarse and broken down with the violence of his grief.'[14] But both 'Tubber Derg' and 'The Poor Scholar' also contained nightmarish descriptions of famine which, if they did not actually convey passion, at least presented something far more serious in tone than 'convivial Ireland of the tear and smile'. In 'The Poor Scholar' Carleton matter-of-factly described starving and diseased peasants who, having been turned off their land and reduced to beggars, survived on weeds and furtively bled cows for food in prosperous landlords' fields while cartloads of Irish farm produce destined for English markets and under armed guard passed by the ditches in which the peasants lived and died.

Yeats's letters indicate that he consciously sought tragic material for his anthologies. Father Russell sent Yeats two humorous stories by Rosa Mulholland, but Yeats used neither, preferring instead 'The Hungry Death', her story about a young woman's heroically unselfishness deeds during a devastating famine on an island off the West coast of Ireland. In selecting materials from Carleton's *Traits and Stories*, the source of all but one of the stories by Carleton in Yeats's two anthologies, Yeats invariably chose the more sombre and least melodramatic. For example, the bloody death of the girl's lover and her brother and her own subsequent insanity in 'The Battle of the Factions' do indeed verge on melodrama. But Yeats could have used a similar story by Carleton, 'The Donagh or, The Horsestealers', in which a thief kills his daughter while aiming at his brother and is blinded by her spouting blood.

The nature of the peasant characters in 'The Donagh' is another indication why Yeats did not use it—the father is a thief and the daughter is about to betray him for a reward. Yeats used the stories from Carleton's *Traits and Stories* which contained the nobler and least humorous characters. The father in 'Tubber Derg' is reduced to pauperism but refuses to beg; the narrator of 'Wildgoose Lodge' has reservations about the violent action in which he participates. The peasants in the stories from *Traits and Stories* which Yeats did not use are generally foolish, lazy and mercenary. For example, 'The Poor Scholar' is a much more serious portrayal of a young Irish peasant seeking a clerical education than 'Denis O'Shaughnessy going to Maynooth', a story in *Traits and Stories* which Yeats did not use. James McEvoy in 'The Poor Scholar' wanted to become a priest for noble, unselfish reasons, but Denis O'Shaughnessy looked upon the priesthood as a call to the dinner tables and monetary endowments available to Irish priests. O'Shaughnessy, who really wanted to marry and eventually does, is a petty despot to silly peasants who mistake his unintelligible Latin gibberish for learning.

The serious and often noble characterisation of the Irish peasant was a criterion apparent in Yeats's selections from other authors as well. In Banim's 'The Stolen Sheep', under threat of imprisonment a father refuses to give evidence against his own son as a point of honour. The contrast between the nobility of the dying peasant and the shallow, drunken gentry is the focus of Griffin's 'The Death of the Huntsman'. The heroine of Rosa Mulholland's 'The Hungry Death' gives away her food to starving peasants and dies of starvation herself after having given food to the wife of the man she loves. In another obvious attempt to show that Irish subject matter was capable of seriousness and tragedy, Yeats used Griffin's 'The Knight of the Sheep' in which the Lear theme forms the basis of the plot.

Yeats did not completely ignore the humour which was an inevitable ingredient in most nineteenth-century Irish fiction; instead he attempted to transform it. Just as Yeats had admired Douglas Hyde as the best Irish folklorist because 'his work is neither humorous nor mournful; it is simply life,' Yeats's anthologies of Irish fiction contain humour as well as the seriousness and passion which Yeats intended to show were also part of the Irish character. Yeats admired Carleton because his work combined 'humour and passion'. In 1889 he wrote to Father Russell that Carleton and the Banims were the best Irish novelists of the century because 'they saw the whole of everything they looked at, the brutal with the tender, the coarse with the refined'.[15] Yeats's anthologies contain a large portion of brutality, immorality and drunkenness. He does not idealise the Irish peasants but attempts to portray their energy and extravagance which were as much a part of their comedy and immorality as of their tragedy and virtue.

Humour posed the least threat to Yeats's purposes. Sentimentality contradicted the depths of emotion he was seeking in Irish fiction and propaganda injected abstraction rather than energy into the fiction, but humour did not have to demean the Irish character as Yeats's selections indicate. When an author such as Charles Kickham offered only scenes of sentiment, propaganda or humour, Yeats invariably chose the latter. The humorous scene from Kickham's novel, *For the Old Land*, entitled 'The Pig-Driving Peelers' in *Representative Irish Tales*, is quite different in tone from the sentimentalism and propaganda which pervade the rest of the novel. The humour of 'The Pig-Driving Peelers' does not demean the character of the Irish peasants involved as humour had belittled the Irish gentry in 'Trinity College' by Charles Lever. The humorous tales in *Representative Irish Tales* convey a sense of energy and extravagance rather than mocking laughter. The Irish peasants are never portrayed as the foolish butts of laughter they had been as comic stage-Irish caricatures. In 'The Pig-Driving Peelers', Carleton's 'Condy Cullen and the Gauger', Lover's 'Barny O'Reirdon', Maginn's 'Father Tom and the Pope', and the anonymous 'Darby Doyle's Visit to Quebec', the fantastic actions of the Irish peasants ultimately succeed and get the best of the non-peasant characters—the peelers, the tax collector, the learned navigators, the Pope, and the wealthy passengers. According to Yeats, the wild comedy of 'Shane Fadh's Wedding' in *Stories from Carleton* possessed 'almost Chaucerian breadth and power'.[16]

The dramatic contrast between such humorous stories and the scenes of nightmarish violence and famine in other selections is quite effective. Benedict Kiely's description of Carleton's fiction—that it seemed 'as if he were writing about a wake where noise and merriment were a mask for mourning'[17]—conveys the mingled sense of comedy and pathos which characterises Yeats's anthologies. Their ultimate effect is one of reckless energy and vitality rather than light-hearted sentimentality.

The conception of the Irish peasant as visionary, so prevalent in Yeats's *Fairy and Folk Tales of the Irish Peasantry* (1888), is also apparent in his two anthologies of Irish fiction. When Yeats included Croker's 'The Confessions of Tom Bourke' in *Representative Irish Tales*, the only selection which had also appeared in *Fairy and Folk Tales*, he appended a lengthy extract concerning the aesthetic, religious and mysterious character of fairy doctors, men whose contact with the fairies gave them magical powers, from Lady Wilde's *Ancient Legends*. In his selection 'The Mayor of Wind-Gap', an excerpt from Michael Banim's novel *The Mayor of Wind-Gap*, Yeats introduces an aura of mystery that was not in his source. In the novel Banim had given twenty-three pages of explanatory commentary between the arrivals of two people during the Midsummer bonfires. Yeats omits the twenty-three pages and so in his excerpt the second figure arrives immediately after the first and, because of Yeats's deletion, his bizarre appearance and actions seem much more mysterious than they actually were:

At the crisis of the mystical festivity, a fellow uncouthly swathed from his neck to his heels in twisted straw ropes, wearing a ridiculous mask, and wielding a stick with a puffed bladder tied to its extremity, flapped and banged his way through the motley crowd with as much agility as his cumbrous clothing would permit. . . . He was followed by another man of proportions as muscular as his own, fantastically dressed in female attire, also wearing a grotesquely terrific

mask, and armed in the same manner as his supposed pro-
tector. This absurd pair dashed through the shouting throng,
dealing indiscriminately their blows on every head. . . .

The sense of mystery thus achieved is similar to the other-wordly
dimension Yeats had sought to convey in *Fairy and Folk Tales.*

Because Yeats minimised the propaganda, sentimentality and
comedy which had characterised nineteenth-century Anglo-Irish
fiction, *Representative Irish Tales* is more 'representative' of
Yeats's conception of the peasant than of Irish fiction in general.
In addition to selecting materials from representative authors
which reinforced his own notion of the Irish peasant, Yeats
omitted some important nineteenth-century Irish fiction and
novelists from *Representative Irish Tales.* He included none of
the historical fiction which had made up a major portion of the
Irish fiction of the century. Instead, he redefined 'history' in a
folkloristic way as the common everyday life of the people. Not
surprisingly, Yeats included no selection from Mrs S. C. Hall's
numerous tales of Irish life because her intention had been to
point out the defects in the character of the Irish peasant. In
the 'Dedication' to her *Stories of the Irish Peasantry* (1840),
Mrs Hall explained, 'My design was to exhibit and illustrate
those peculiarities in the Irish character which appear to be the
root of evils in their condition. . . .'[18] Even more significantly,
Yeats included no selection by Sydney Owenson, Lady Morgan,
the first of whose 'National Tales', *The Wild Irish Girl* (1806),
was one of the most popular and influential Irish novels of the
nineteenth century. *The Wild Irish Girl* went through seven
editions in two years and with Tom Moore's *Irish Melodies*
established the sentimental stereotype of Ireland which was
no truer than that of the eighteenth-century stage Irishman. The
following summary of *The Wild Irish Girl* describes the senti-
mental patriotism typical of Lady Morgan's fiction : 'A love
story of almost gushing sentiment . . . the "Prince" of Inismore,
though fallen on evil days, still keeps up all the old customs of
the chieftains, his ancestors. He wears the old dress, uses the
old salutations, has his harper and his sanachie. . . . His daughter,
Glorvina, is the almost ethereal heroine. The personages of the
book frequently converse about ancient Irish history, legend,
music, ornaments, weapons, and costumes. There is much acute

political discussion and argument in the book. It is fervently on the side of Irish nationality.'[19] Yeats's omissions of Lady Morgan's fiction would have been considered unusual by the nineteenth-century reading public. In the symposium discussing the 'Best Hundred Irish Books' in the *Freeman's Journal* in 1885 to which noted Irishmen, 'whose judgment on literary questions is held in universal and deserved esteem' contributed letters, only John O'Leary, Yeats's mentor, objected to including Lady Morgan's fiction.[20] Earlier in the century William Carleton praised both Mrs Hall and Lady Morgan as among those Irish authors who had all depicted the Irish as 'capable of thinking clearly and feeling deeply'.[21]

In the Introduction to *Representative Irish Tales*, Yeats admitted that there were many imperfections in the fiction he anthologised. But, as he explained in 1885, although there were 'many imperfect books' in nineteenth-century Irish literary tradition, 'under a mound of melodrama or sheer futility' there was hid a 'fire which cannot be had elsewhere in the world. . . .'[22] By his own account, Yeats sought 'powerful emotion' and 'noble types and symbols' in the life and character of the Irish peasantry.[23] But ultimately the Irish peasant depicted in Irish fiction was unable to satisfy Yeats's search for a uniquely Irish subject matter through which to convey passion and heroism. As Yeats declared in retrospect in 1908, it was often impossible to distinguish essential Irish elements from foreign qualities in 'Irish novelists of the nineteenth century', because it was 'impossible to divide what is . . . Irish, from all that is foreign, from all that is an accident of imperfect culture, before we have had some revelation of Irish character, pure enough and varied enough to create a standard of comparison'.[24]

Nevertheless, Yeats's involvement with Anglo-Irish fiction was not merely an isolated phase of his development. Yeats originally formed the critical vocabulary of 'joy' and 'vehemence' and 'tumultuous passion', which he applied to his characterisations of ancient Irish heroes in his later poems and plays, during his study of the Irish peasantry. Yeats's editions of Irish fiction are convincing proof that the early Yeats strove against the very sentimentality he has been accused of by critics of his early work, and that even during his so-called 'Celtic

Twilight' period he admired what he described as 'the abounding vitality' of Carleton's 'vast multitude of grotesque, pathetic, humorous persons, misers, pig-drivers, drunkards, schoolmasters, labourers, priests, madmen. . . .'[25] In 1908 Yeats summed up his involvement with nineteenth-century Irish fiction: 'I do not speak carelessly of the Irish novelists, for when I was in London during the first years of my literary life, I read them continually, seeking in them an image of Ireland that I might not forget what I meant to be the foundations of my art, trying always to winnow as I read . . . it was from the novelists and poets that I learned in part my symbols of expression.'[26]

For a time the peasants around Sligo seemed to offer Yeats the same living folk traditions Irish novelists and folklorists had recorded throughout the century. Yeats had known and sought out peasants in and around Sligo from the time he was a small boy, yet this remains one of the least explored areas of Yeats's early life. As noted a Yeats scholar as John Unterecker has declared his own keen interest in knowing more about Yeats's earliest contacts with the peasantry:

> One of the things I shall hope to find when a 'definitive' biography of Yeats finally comes along is an accurate picture of what life was like in the kitchens, stableyards, and barns of Rosses Point and Sligo. For it is these places, Yeats hints, that much of his character was shaped. I look forward to finding out who the stableboy was who, Yeats says in his autobiography, was his closest companion, the boy with whom Yeats climbed Ben Bulben's side in search of trout pools, who helped Yeats dig for earthworms with which they baited their fish-hooks, who shared with Yeats in a hayloft a book of political poems, Yeats's first experience, he tells us, of 'the pleasure of rhyme' . . . I look forward also to learning more, much more, about the Middletons who . . . 'took the nearest for friends and were always in and out of the cottages of pilots and tenants.'[27]

According to Yeats, 'It was through the Middletons perhaps that I got my interest in county stories, and certainly the first faery stories that I heard were in the cottages about their

E

houses.' One of them 'had the second sight' and these same Middleton cousins shared in some of his earliest visionary experiences of the fairies according to his later reminiscences. Folklore and the occult had thus been inextricably linked for Yeats from his earliest years.

Yeats had continued to collect Irish folklore all the while he had studied previously published Irish folklore and Anglo-Irish fiction during the late 1880s and early 1890s. His knowledge of actual oral traditions in the West of Ireland enabled him to evaluate previously published folklore and fiction : 'I had heard in Sligo cottages or from pilots at Rosses Point endless stories of apparitions, whether of the recent dead or of the people of history and legend, of that Queen Maeve whose reputed cairn stands on the mountain over the bay. Then at the British Museum I read stories Irish writers of the 'forties and 'fifties had written of such apparitions, but they enraged me more than pleased because they turned the country visions into a joke.'[28] So Yeats recorded the visions and beliefs of the countryside for himself. Much of what he recorded appeared in *The Celtic Twilight* in 1893. According to Yeats's letters during the summer of 1891, T. Fisher Unwin was planning to reprint several of Yeats's essays on folklore as a collection. This proposed collection was a casualty of Yeats's struggle with Sir Charles Gavan Duffy for the editorship of the 'New Irish Library'. T. Fisher Unwin chose Duffy as the editor of the series and Yeats's collection of folklore essays was published by the firm of Lawrence and Bullen. The collection, however, did not merely reprint previously published essays. Out of the twenty-two essays in the collection, only nine essays and parts of three other essays had been published previously. Yeats's sense of the significance of his early attempts to collect Irish folklore and of the resulting collection, *The Celtic Twilight*, is apparent in a statement he made in 1903 : 'When I was a boy I used to wander about at Rosses Point and Ballisodare listening to old songs and stories. I wrote down what I heard and made poems out of the stories or put them into the little chapters of the first edition of "The Celtic Twilight," and that is how I began to write in an Irish way.'[29] The nature and significance of *The Celtic Twilight* and Yeats's developing use of Irish folklore can best be understood when the collection is analysed as folklore, when it is com-

pared to Yeats's anthologies of previously published Irish folk-
lore and Anglo-Irish fiction, and when the 1893 edition of *The
Celtic Twilight* is compared to the 1902 edition.

The Celtic Twilight is, in many ways, a continuation of
attitudes and editorial practices which Yeats had first developed
when he compiled *Fairy and Folk Tales of the Irish Peasantry*.
However, *The Celtic Twilight* also embodies many develop-
ments and changes in Yeats's concept and depiction of Irish
folklore. The first edition of *The Celtic Twilight* was largely
composed of stories and essays which Yeats had written and
published in magazines and newspapers between 1888 and 1893
so it is not surprising that such materials echo *Fairy and Folk
Tales of the Irish Peasantry*. Indeed, some things in *The Celtic
Twilight* first appeared in his earlier anthologies. Paddy Flynn,
whom Yeats had described in his Introduction to *Fairy and
Folk Tales*, is the subject of Yeats's first essay, 'A Teller of
Tales', in *The Celtic Twilight*. The male 'Sceptic' from the
same Introduction reappears as a female 'doubter' in the second
essay 'Belief and Unbelief', where Yeats repeats the same
anecdotes he had first used in 1888. The tale which had ap-
peared under the title 'A Fairy Enchantment' in *Irish Fairy
Tales*, where it had been presented as having been told by
'Michael Hart' and recorded by W. B. Yeats, reappears almost
verbatim in the *Celtic Twilight* essay entitled 'Drumcliff and
Rosses' as the story of one 'Michael H—'. The fact that
Kathleen Raine, in her Introduction to a recent edition of
Fairy and Folk Tales, repeatedly quotes *The Celtic Twilight*
to explain the occult implications of *Fairy and Folk Tales*
demonstrates another direct link between the two anthologies.[30]

Considering the preference for legends which Yeats had
shown in his first two anthologies, it is not surprising that he
included only legends and no folk tales or myths in the first
edition of *The Celtic Twilight*. Any preference that Yeats had
for legends over the other genres of oral narrative, folk tale
and myth, was also encouraged by the nature of materials
available to him in oral tradition in and around Sligo. Because
of their simpler and more anecdotal form, legends survived
among the peasantry after lengthier and more complex forms
of narrative like folktales and myths had died out. Legends
also crossed over into English much more easily than folktales

and ancient hero tales whose complex plots were ornamented with lengthy and obscure passages known as 'runs' which were difficult to translate into English. Because Yeats did not speak Irish, the English-speaking informants he used were much more likely to give him fairy legends and beliefs even if he had preferred folktales and tales from ancient Irish mythology.

Although his earlier anthologies had been composed chiefly of previously published folklore, *The Celtic Twilight* includes only those materials which Yeats had collected himself or that he had heard secondhand from an oral informant or a written report. Yeats's reliance on oral materials in *The Celtic Twilight* represents a deepening sense of the essentially oral nature of folklore. Moreover, he not only used oral materials, but recorded them as accurately as possible. In contrast to most of his predecessors in the publication of Irish folklore, Yeats was able to declare at the beginning of *The Celtic Twilight*, 'I have therefore written down accurately and candidly much that I have heard and seen, and, except by way of commentary, nothing that I have merely imagined.'[31] However, Yeats's qualifying phrase 'except by way of commentary' makes it clear that the unvarnished oral traditions which Yeats has so 'accurately' recorded are to be accompanied by his comments. Yet his commentary was not to be either arguments concerning the truth or falsehood of folk belief or philological data such as had appeared in the editorial comments with which his predecessors had prefaced and annotated their materials. Instead, Yeats's 'commentary' would involve the presentation of his own visions and beliefs. He declared in the sentence which succeeded the one just quoted: 'I have, however, been at no pains to separate my own beliefs from those of the peasantry, but have rather let my men and women, dhouls [sic] and faeries, go their way unoffended or defended by any argument of mine.' Yeats had scrupulously avoided including his own beliefs in *Fairy and Folk Tales,* of which he had written to Katharine Tynan in 1888: 'All will go well if I can keep my own unpopular thoughts out. . . . I must be careful in no way to suggest that fairies, or something like them, do veritably exist, some flux and flow of spirits between man and the unresolvable mystery.'[32] Yeats had indeed maintained a strict silence concerning his own beliefs in that anthology, but descriptions of his personal visionary experiences abound in *The Celtic Twilight*.

However, rather than criticise Yeats for thus 'embellishing' the authentic oral materials he had collected, the reader should realise that Yeats' was simply using himself as an informant. Although he had chosen to present only the visionary experiences of Irish peasants in *Fairy and Folk Tales*, his presentation of such materials had developed considerably by 1893 and now included descriptions of how he and his friends, and even how middle-class clerks, had had contact with the fairies. Such a presentation of folklore, no matter how accurately Yeats recorded legends and beliefs from his informants, has not found much favour with the scientific folklorists of today. Richard Dorson has described *The Celtic Twilight* as 'a musing, introspective diary playing with the shadowy folk beliefs of fairy powers'.[33] However, such a judgement applies recent collecting standards to *The Celtic Twilight* without giving adequate credit to Yeats's sincerity in presenting his personal visionary experiences as the equivalent of those he recorded from his peasant informants. Folklorists today obviously use much more objective standards in collecting. Yeats recorded his materials as accurately as he could but he believed, or tried very hard to believe, in what he recorded as a folklorist. As a result he could not and did not approach his own beliefs and visionary experiences any differently than those of his peasant informants: he thus collected from them and himself and his juxtaposition of the two kinds of materials is not without rhetorical effect. The personal visionary experiences which Yeats incorporates into his accounts of peasant visions and beliefs reinforce their reality and vice versa. Yeats's visionary perspective is also characteristically Irish. According to a recent essay by Dáithí Ó hÓgáin, 'The Visionary Voice: A Survey of Popular Attitudes to Poetry in Irish Tradition', the ancient Irish concept of the poet as having visionary powers and of his poetry as a verbal manifestation of occult knowledge survived in peasant traditions.[34]

The visionary experiences which Yeats records also represent an early attempt to record what folklorists today call 'memorats'—first or secondhand accounts of encounters with supernatural creatures. *The Celtic Twilight* is filled with such 'memorats'. Richard Dorson has praised Lady Gregory for her pioneering efforts in recording memorats in *Visions and Beliefs in the West of Ireland*, which was based on material that she and Yeats had collected together in the late 1890s, because she reproduced exactly the highly personal, shapeless, often fragmentary confidences told her conversationally, although Dorson admitted that identification of her informants 'either by name or occupation' was not complete because she did not name the living or the deceased with living relatives.[35] In the same essay Dorson had criticised *The Celtic Twilight* as having been a 'musing, introspective diary playing with shadowy folk beliefs of fairy powers'. Obviously because Yeats had not 'reproduced exactly' his materials, or at least like Lady Gregory given the impression of having done so, Dorson was not prepared to admit that *The Celtic Twilight* too represented a pioneering attempt in the collection of memorats rather than the comical, literary, third-person accounts of the fairies given by Yeats's predecessors. Several of the essays which Yeats added to the 1902 edition of *The Celtic Twilight* included materials about Biddy Early and about the 'fool of the forth' which Lady Gregory and Yeats had collected together and which later reappeared in *Visions and Beliefs in the West of Ireland*.

The vivid presence of Yeats's voice, of his own beliefs and experiences in *The Celtic Twilight*, is all the more surprising because one of his major editorial emendations in tales he had included in *Fairy and Folk Tales* had been to remove the narrative device of an interlocutor. He becomes an interlocutor in *The Celtic Twilight* where he is by turn collector, interlocutor, informant. Although the removal of an interlocutor from tales Yeats used in *Fairy and Folk Tales* had improved the sense of immediacy in those selections, the presence of Yeats's personal voice in *The Celtic Twilight* increases rather than decreases the immediacy of his materials. The difference is that the selections in *Fairy and Folk Tales* were tales, whereas the selections in *The Celtic Twilight* are personal essays. The interlocutor whom Yeats had deleted from Samuel Lover's stories had been members of the gentry whose scepticism and laughter distanced the peasant and his lore from the reader. Rather than transforming his materials into fiction and inventing an interlocutor as a fictional character as Lover had, Yeats's personal voice is an integral part of the immediacy of his essays. Moreover, any folklore collector inevitably becomes an interlocutor because his function is to question and engage his informant in conversation. Yeats is simply recording his own part of the interviews with informants or acting as his own informant.

In *The Celtic Twilight* Yeats thus displayed an awareness of the effectiveness of the personality of the narrator, whether the peasant or himself, in the transmission of folklore decades before contemporary folklorists did. Yeats's careful descriptions of Mary Battle's and Paddy Flynn's personalities indicate he appreciated the significance of the storyteller's personality. His own vivid personal voice in *The Celtic Twilight* actually makes the collection resemble what folkorists today call a 'tale-telling event' in which the personality of the narrator naturally intrudes on and becomes a part of his materials. Richard Dorson himself remarked in an essay 'Esthetic Form in British and American Folk Narrative' that 'Legends are usually told in conversational and reminiscent fashion'[36] only a few years after he had criticised *The Celtic Twilight* for being introspective and 'playful'. Yeats explained in the following passage from 'Samhain: 1906' what he had already practised in *The Celtic Twilight*: 'Our own Raftery will stop the tale to cry, "This is what I, Raftery, wrote down in the book of the people"; or, "I, myself, Raftery, went to bed without supper that night". . . . He knows how to keep himself interesting that his words may have weight—so many lines of narrative, and then a phrase about himself and his emotions.'[37] Yeats's remarks foreshadow Kevin Danaher's much more recent description of Irish oral tradition: 'this is especially true of the Irish tradition of story-telling—the tales were not learned by heart. Instead, the storyteller knew the frame of the plot in detail, and clothed it with words to suit his audience, thus giving it the stamp of his own style and personality.'[38] Although Yeats was not narrating complex plots in *The Celtic Twilight*, the commentary with which he accompanied the anecdotes he recounted resembles oral narrative techniques. Moreover, Danaher's comment credits the traditional oral narrator with the prerogative of reworking his materials somewhat, another prerogative and technique of the oral narrator which Yeats emulates. Yeats's presentation compares much more favourably to that of an oral narrator than that of a folklorist.

Other features of Yeats's presentation of his materials in *The Celtic Twilight* both contradict and foreshadow methods used today. Folklorists today are expected to include data identifying their informant and the context in which they collected their material. *The Celtic Twilight* has been criticised for lacking such data because Yeats named and described only some of his informants. However, what seems at first glance to be due to careless, incomplete recording methods is again traceable to Yeats's personal involvement with his own materials and is most likely a conscious effort to protect his informants. A basic tenet of Irish fairy belief was that one should never talk about or reveal one's experiences with the fairies because the fairies jealously guarded their privacy and would punish anyone who revealed things about them. Consequently, Yeats's informants were often reluctant to speak of their experiences of the fairies. For example, Yeats presented the following description of his informant 'Biddy Hart' in the Introduction to *Irish Fairy Tales*:

> How firmly she believed in them! how greatly she feared offending them! For a long time she would give me no answer but 'I always mind my own affairs and they always mind theirs.' A little talk about my great-grandfather who lived all his life in the valley below, and a few words to remind her how I myself was often under her roof when but seven or eight years old loosened her tongue, however. It would be less dangerous at any rate to talk to me of the fairies than it would be to tell some 'Towrow' of them, as she contemptuously called English tourists, for I had lived under the shadow of their own hillsides. She did not forget, however, to remind me to say after we had finished, 'God bless them, Thursday' (that being the day), and so ward off their displeasure, in case they were angry at our notice, for they love to live and dance unknown to men.[39]

Yeats presumably identified 'Biddy Hart' by her real name in the Introduction to *Fairy and Folk Tales* but one cannot be sure. Lady Gregory's similar 'naming' of her informants was actually illusory: her folklore notebooks indicate she changed the names of her informants when she 'quoted' them in her collections. It is very likely that Yeats too exercised similar precautions when quoting living informants. In any event, by the time he quotes Biddy Hart and her husband Michael Hart, both of whom he had quoted by 'name' in *Irish Fairy Tales,* in *The Celtic Twilight* they have become 'Mrs H——' and Michael H——'.

In *The Celtic Twilight* Yeats usually identifies by name only those informants who have died. Yeats had described an informant named 'Paddy Flynn', a very common Irish name, in the Introduction to *Fairy and Folk Tales* but said merely that he was 'living' in 'the village of B——'. Hence, Yeats's Paddy Flynn was indistinguishable from the numerous other peasants of that name who were living in the West of Ireland. By the time Yeats described Paddy Flynn in *The Celtic Twilight* he was presented as having 'lived' in 'the village of Ballisodare' for 'Paddy Flynn is dead.' Likewise, the informant Yeats referred to throughout *The Celtic Twilight* as 'my old Mayo woman' was not identified until years afterward, by which time she had presumably died, as Mary Battle, Yeats's Uncle George Pollexfen's second-sighted servant. In the first section of his *Autobiography,* 'Reveries over Childhood and Youth' (1914), Yeats revealed that Mary Battle had been his source and that 'Much of my *Celtic Twilight* is but her daily speech.'[40] Occasionally, other circumstances made it impossible for Yeats to reveal the identity of his informants. For example, in 'Drumcliff and Rosses' Yeats identifies one friend who has successfully gathered folklore for him merely as 'the sweet Harp-String', a translation of his Irish name, 'for fear of gaugers' because his friend was a noted poteen-maker.

When Yeats did identify his informants and subjects in *The Celtic Twilight* by name, he was deliberately vague as to the locale. The anecdotes in the essay about 'Village Ghosts' all concern people identified by name, but all these ghosts 'inhabit the village of H——, in Leinster'. Other informants are simply identified as 'an old Miller at Ballylee' or, 'a doubter in Donegal'. Such vagueness about informants, even if attributable to a desire on Yeats's part to 'protect' the identity of his informants, also represents a literary technique which, whether it is intentional or not, has significant repercussions on the pre-

E*

sentation of Yeats's materials. The accuracy of Yeats's materials could, of course, never be checked. By not tying his materials to a specific informant Yeats also enhanced their mystery which, because they could possibly be traced to innumerable people and places in the West of Ireland, seemed all the more general and universal. Yeats's sense that such beliefs and legends were ancient and ultimately anonymous, that they belonged to tradition and not to a single informant, also helps to explain why he did not wish to present them as the property of a specific Irish peasant or locale. Here again, although Yeats fails to present the data which folklorists expect today, his presentation anticipates later theories about the nature of folklore. Folklorists today define legend as the possession of a group, because by its very nature a complete legend, whether a belief or a narrative, transcends the knowledge of a single individual. Consequently, collectors today are urged to present oral legends as a body of related texts rather than as a single fluent narrative. Richard Dorson's essay 'Defining the American Folk Legend' summarises such contemporary theories.[41] *The Celtic Twilight* presents its materials in the way Dorson suggests but without what he would call adequate ethnographic data.

Although Yeats was deliberately vague about the specific identity or locale of his informants, he carefully created the impression that the experiences and beliefs he recorded had occurred to real people in real places. He wrote in John Quinn's copy of *The Celtic Twilight* in 1904: 'All real stories heard among the people or real incidents with but a little disguise in names and places.'[42] Yeats is quite masterful at conveying a sense of reality about his informants while refraining from actually revealing their identity, as when he describes his informant in the essay 'Kidnappers': 'I heard it from a little old woman in a white cap, who sings to herself in Gaelic, and moves from one foot to another as though she remembered the dancing of her youth.' Occasionally Yeats hints at the context in which an item was collected—a technique used frequently by modern folklorists: 'One night as I sat eating Mrs H——'s soda-bread, her husband told me a longish story. . . .' Yeats often 'quotes' common opinion rather than specific informants. In such cases, he usually associates the beliefs he narrates with actual places which he does describe in detail: 'At the northern corner of Rosses is a little promontory of sand and rocks and grass: a mournful, haunted place. No wise peasant would fall asleep under its low cliff, for he who sleeps here may wake "silly", the "good people" having carried off his soul.' In such passages objective description imperceptibly shades into personal impressions and beliefs. The word 'may' can be read either as 'sometimes' in the sense that it can actually sometimes be carried off by the fairies, or as 'perhaps' in the sense that 'maybe' such reports are true. Elsewhere in the same essay, 'Drumcliff and Rosses', Yeats isn't the least ambiguous: 'Drumcliff and Rosses are chokeful of ghosts. By bog, road, rath, hillside, sea-border they gather in all shapes: headless women, men in armour, shadow hares, fire-tongued hounds, whistling seals, and so on. A whistling seal sank a ship the other day.'

The question inevitably arises as to how generalised such beliefs and visionary experiences actually were in and around Sligo. To his credit, later collectors have generally found similar materials in the West of Ireland. W. Y. Evans-Wentz, who had been influenced no doubt by Yeats's materials but who possessed his own extensive and firsthand knowledge of Irish oral tradition, found in 1911 that 'the Ben Bulbin country in County Sligo', the locale of much of Yeats's material in *The Celtic Twilight*, was especially full of fairy lore and that the fairies were seen by his Sligo informants rather than merely heard and felt. In contrast, Evans-Wentz quoted Douglas Hyde as saying that the fairies in Hyde's nearby native County Roscommon were 'rarely seen' and that beliefs about them had become relatively extinct.[43] Nevertheless, as late as the 1950s, D. A. MacManus, who had been a friend of Yeats's, claimed to have found fairy lore abundant in Ireland. MacManus declared in *The Middle Kingdom: The faerie world of Ireland* (1959):

Do not let anyone imagine that I have had to travel far and wide painstakingly collecting stories here and there as if plucking rare and precious flowers. Not in the least; for these stories have come to me without strenuous searching on my part . . . many of these tales I have known and lived with for years; others which are more recent, I have come across without special effort and in the course of my daily life.[44]

Lady Gregory also found a great deal of fairy lore still extant in County Galway and County Clare in the late 1890s. Daniel Deeney opened *Peasant Lore from Gaelic Ireland* (1900), a collection of folklore gathered mainly in Connemara and in Donegal, with a statement which echoed Yeats's finding in *The Celtic Twilight*: 'The life of the Irish-speaking peasant is inseparably associated with mysticism.'[45] Both Lady Gregory and Daniel Deeney had found such lore plentiful among 'Gaelic-speaking' peasants. One wonders how hard Yeats had to search for such lore among English-speaking peasants. Thomas Flanagan has praised *The Celtic Twilight*, saying it is 'at once the most ambitious and the most successful of his early prose works . . . a triumph of allusive style', yet Flanagan posed the question, 'It is difficult to resist the suspicion that the narrator has gone from one Sligo village to the next seeking out in each its resident idiot and listening with a sympathetic but defective ear.'[46] However, as eminent and as respected an Irish folklorist as E. Estyn Evans has recently published an essay on nineteenth-century Irish peasant beliefs which suggests that traditional beliefs remained relatively strong well into the late nineteenth century in rural Ireland, despite the famine, increased anglicisation and other social upheavals. According to Evans, a keen sense of and a reliance on pagan supernatural beliefs was actually encouraged by the disappearance of external features of traditional folk life such as language and customs: 'I see the crisis in the middle of the nineteenth century as marking in many ways the end of prehistory. At the same time the tensions produced by the fundamental changes in rural society brought about by the Famine appear to have resulted in secret recourse to supernatural forces during the second half of the century and, in some parts of the country, well into the present century.'[47] However, Evans does comment that it was a 'secret recourse' to such pagan beliefs and many informants may not have been willing to yield their secret beliefs to Yeats. Indeed, he frequently remarks on how difficult it was to get informants to discuss the fairies. Theoretically he should have been able to find many potential English-speaking informants around Sligo. In 1891, a census year, only one-third of the population of the western seaboard counties spoke Irish.[48] Whether or not these English-speaking informants would speak of fairy lore was another matter.

The fact that Yeats did not know Irish undoubtedly restricted the number of his potential informants because folklore, especially narrative, does not always cross over into English. He ultimately employed the same informants—Biddy Hart and her husband, Paddy Flynn, Mary Battle—again and again which implies his actual sources were few. Yeats also used the same materials repeatedly. He had already used four of the legends which he recounts in *The Celtic Twilight* in an essay on 'Irish Fairies' which he had published in 1890 : the anecdote about how a girl in service near Grange was 'taken' by the fairies reappears in the essay 'Belief and Unbelief'; the legend of the three O'Byrnes is repeated in 'The Three O'Byrnes and the Evil Fairies'; the legend of Michael Hart and the corpse is retold in 'Drumcliff and Rosses'; and the anecdote about a woman having danced all her toes off in fairyland reappears in 'Kidnappers'. Yeats had also used the tale of Michael Hart in *Irish Fairy Tales.* He ultimately used the anecdote about the toeless woman five times : in the introduction to 'The Trooping Fairies' in *Fairy and Folk Tales*; in an essay 'Irish Fairies, Ghosts, Witches, etc.' published in 1889; in the 'Irish Fairies' essay in 1890; in the Introduction to *Irish Fairy Tales*; and finally in *The Celtic Twilight.* Yeats was either very fond of some of his materials or else his actual fund of such accounts was limited.

Most of Yeats's sources, even the nameless ones, are referred to as 'old' : In *Fairy and Folk Tales* we are told 'Paddy Flynn is very old'; Biddy Hart is referred to as 'old Biddy Hart' in *Irish Fairy Tales.* The majority of the other informants he quotes in *The Celtic Twilight* in 1893 and 1902 are also old : his oft-quoted 'old Mayo woman' (Mary Battle); 'an old peasant' in 'A Visionary'; 'an old miller', 'an old man', 'an old woman' near Ballylee, 'an old weaver', 'another old man', another 'old woman' at Derrybrien in 'Dust Hath Closed Helen's Eyes'. Yeats is obviously recording the remnants of a dying tradition. Even the 'strong farmer' Yeats had described as so 'passionate' in the essay 'A Knight of the Sheep' in 1893 is referred to as 'the old man' in the essay about him, 'An Enduring Heart', which Yeats added to the 1902 edition. The question of senility inevitably arises when such elderly informants are used. Yeats's description of Paddy Flynn 'asleep under a hedge, smiling in his sleep' can suggest simple-mindedness as easily as visionary powers.

Yeats admits that his informant in the second section of the essay 'Happy and Unhappy Theologians' is thought by other villagers to be 'a little crazed', and Yeats refers to 'half-mad and visionary peasants' in 'A Visionary'. Likewise, Yeats says of 'old Martin Roland' who was dead when Yeats wrote 'Friends of the People of Faery' in 1897 : 'His neighbours were not certain he really saw anything in his old age, but they were all certain that he saw things when he was a young man. His brother said, "Old he is, and it's all in his brain the things he sees. If he was a young man we might believe in him".' Roland's brother's use of the word 'might' in the last sentence suggests a scepticism which belies Yeats's statement that Roland's neighbours were 'certain' he saw things when young. In any event, Yeats found informants to be relatively scarce and many of the Sligo peasantry probably did not share his credulity about the visions and beliefs he collected.

The 1893 edition of *The Celtic Twilight* develops as well as continues approaches to Irish folklore which Yeats had used in *Fairy and Folk Tales*. In that anthology he had presented fairy lore as a uniquely Irish phenomenon, experienced solely by the peasantry who encountered fairies much more frequently than any other kind of spirit. Yeats's perspective in *The Celtic Twilight* is much less pointedly Irish, less concerned with only peasants and much less concerned with the fairies. One essay, 'The Last Gleeman', does not even mention the fairies, any visionary experiences or rural Ireland. Yeats obviously found it unnecessary to be as militantly nationalistic as he had been when he compiled *Fairy and Folk Tales*. After all, he was able to boast in the final essay in the 1893 edition of *The Celtic Twilight*, 'The Four Winds of Desire' which he had originally published as a book review of Douglas Hyde's *Beside the Fire* in 1891, 'There has been published in the three years as much Irish folk-lore as in the foregoing fifty. Its quality, too, is higher.'[49] 'Irish' folklore had indeed come into its own as a literary tradition during the late 1880s. Having successfully propagandised its nationalistic significance as a uniquely Irish cultural and literary tradition, Yeats could begin to expand its significance by revealing its more universal and philosophical implications. So in *The Celtic Twilight* the visions and beliefs of the peasantry are linked to those of Yeats and his friends.

Visions and beliefs are no longer concerned primarily with the fairies. Ghost lore had accounted for only seven selections in *Fairy and Folk Tales*, but visions and beliefs about ghosts outnumber those about fairies in *The Celtic Twilight*. Here again the nature of the materials available to Yeats helps to explain the change of emphasis. The fairies had always been closely connected with the dead, especially those who had died suddenly or prematurely, in Irish folk belief. W. B. Evans-Wentz demonstrated how fairy lore and ghost lore were inextricably mingled in his comprehensive study *The Fairy-Faith in Celtic Countries* (1911) which he fittingly dedicated to Yeats and AE. Yeats's *The Celtic Twilight* also mirrors the declining popularity of fairy lore in rural Ireland. Yeats himself had noted in 1891 : 'In the towns the fairy tradition is gone indeed, but even there the supernatural survives in visions and ghost-hauntings.'[50] *The Celtic Twilight* makes clear that visions and ghost lore had begun to replace fairy lore in rural Ireland as well. Conrad Arensberg identified the replacement of fairy lore with ghost lore as a major trend in Irish folk belief in his landmark anthropological study, *The Irish Countryman* (1937): 'the fairy gives way more and more to the ghost in rural Ireland today.'[51]

Yeats suggests the fairies whom he does describe in *The Celtic Twilight* are 'bodiless moods'. Both the 1893 and 1902 editions open with an untitled poem which was originally and later entitled 'The Moods', addressed to immortal 'fire-born moods'. In the course of both editions Yeats associated the fairies more and more with his doctrine of universal moods. The opening essay about Paddy Flynn described literature as 'the expression of moods by the vehicle of symbol and incident'; in the essay 'Regina, Regina Pigmeorum, Veni' Yeats asks the 'gleaming' fairy woman he encounters 'whether she and her people were not "dramatisations of our moods"?', but she does not understand the question; and in the essay entitled 'The Golden Age' he refers to the fairies as 'those beings or bodiless moods, or whatever they be, who inhabit the world of spirits'.

The nature of Yeats's materials had also changed in other ways. *Fairy and Folk Tales* had delineated a veritable pantheon of individual spiritual beings who were collectively known as the fairies. Oral traditions about the fairies had obviously dwindled by the time Yeats attempted to tap the traditions which his predecessors earlier in the century had found so rich. When Yeats had sought a fairy lore characterised by seriousness and depth in previously published Irish folklore, he discovered that rationalising, humour and literary embellishments had disfigured any serious oral traditions his predecessors had encountered. The folklore available to Yeats from the Sligo peasantry also proved to be neither as abundant nor as serious a subject as he had hoped. Throughout *The Celtic Twilight* Yeats repeatedly used adjectives such as 'capricious', 'whimsical', 'pretty' and 'humorous' to describe the materials he had collected. In 1893 he has given up, at least for the time being, the attempt to inject seriousness and awe into his materials which had characterised his treatment of the pooka in *Fairy and Folk Tales*. When children mistake a Protestant girl dressed in blue and white for the Blessed Virgin in 'Our Lady of the Hills' the reader is presented with a willingness to believe rather than an actual visionary experience. Some of the visionary experiences Yeats records are indeed humorous, as when the boots of a 'doubter' come alive and kick him out of a haunted house in Donegal in 'The Man and His Boots'. But Yeats never elaborates such humorous incidents with stage-Irish antics as his predecessors had done. Indeed, he was obviously using the same editorial criteria in *The Celtic Twilight* which he had used in his presentation of the Irish peasant in *Representative Irish Tales:* he ignores political and religious issues and he avoids moralising, sentimentality and stage-Irish humour.

Although the nature and presentation of Irish folklore is decidedly different in *The Celtic Twilight*, many of his editorial criteria were the same ones he had used in *Fairy and Folk Tales*. Yeats obviously still preferred the weirdest, most mysterious, most inexplicable materials available to him. The anecdotes recorded in *The Celtic Twilight* may be whimsical and capricious but they are also undeniably extraordinary. According to one of Yeats's informants, hell is 'merely an invention got up by the priest to keep people good' and the fairies 'stand to reason'. Yeats had quoted the same beliefs in his Introduction to *Fairy and Folk Tales*. The tales the peasants related to Yeats in both editions of *The Celtic Twilight* were usually as weird as their beliefs. Mary Battle told of two friends who had been made love to by the devil, who had appeared to one in the form of the *Irish Times*. Another old man 'who found the devil ringing a bell under his bed' simply 'went off and stole the chapel bell and rang him out'. Another told of 'a servant girl who hung herself for the love of God', another of how Aristotle was outwitted by bees, another of how she 'had no toes left' when she returned from seven years in fairyland because 'she had danced them off'. Not surprisingly, Yeats frequently uses the word 'extravagant' which he had often used in *Fairy and Folk Tales* to describe his materials in *The Celtic Twilight*.

The Irish peasant is still presented as a visionary, as he had been in *Fairy and Folk Tales*, although he now encounters ghosts and devils as frequently as he does fairies. Two character-istics—'joy' and 'passion'—which Yeats had originally presented as essential to the Irish peasant's character in *Fairy and Folk Tales* and in *Representative Irish Tales* are also used to charac-terise the peasantry in *The Celtic Twilight*. Yeats claims that the peasantry in the West of Ireland 'do not fear spirits too much to feel an artistic and humorous pleasure in their doings,' and most of his informants do indeed seem to enjoy their beliefs and visions. According to Yeats, 'mainly small clerks and the like' en-counter 'the dark powers' who were relatively unknown among the peasantry. In 'A Remonstrance with Scotsmen for Having Soured the Disposition of their Ghosts and Faeries', Yeats de-clares that 'for the gay and graceful doings' of ghosts and fairies 'you must go to Ireland' where 'we exchange civilities with the world beyond' and 'for their deeds of terror [go] to Scotland'. Paddy Flynn is described as 'always cheerful'. Mary Battle's 'mind continually dwells on what is pleasant and beautiful' and 'her thoughts and her sights of the people of faery are pleasant and beautiful too, and I have never heard her call them the Fallen Angels'. Yeats recalled in his *Autobiography* how her 'merriment' had 'answered' his Uncle George Pollexfen's 'gloom'.

Yeats praised his informants for such 'joy', but he also at-tempted to discover a potential for passion and tragedy within their characters. Hence, Yeats saw in Paddy Flynn's eyes 'a melancholy which was well-nigh a portion of their joy'. Yeats's depiction of the character of 'the strong farmer' in the essay 'A Knight of the Sheep' is his most obvious attempt to find the same 'energy' and 'passion' in his Sligo peasants which he had so consciously sought when he assembled materials for *Representative Irish Tales*. Even the title of the essay, 'A Knight of the Sheep', was taken from *Representative Irish Tales* in which Yeats had included a tale by Gerald Griffin entitled 'The Knight of the Sheep'. Yeats had claimed the tale was from Griffin's collection entitled *Holland-Tide* (1827) but it was actually from Griffin's *Tales of my Neighbourhood* (1835). In any event the opening paragraph of Griffin's tale suggests the kind of heroic stature Yeats sought to give his own character: 'In the days of our ancestors it was the custom, when a "strong farmer" had arrived at a certain degree of independence by his agricultural pursuits to confer upon him a title in the Irish language, which is literally translated, "The Knight of the Sheep". Though not commonly of noble origin, these persons often exercised a kind of patriarchal sway, scarce less extensive than that of many a feudal descendant of the Butlers or the Geraldines.'[52] Yeats devoted his essay 'A Knight of the Sheep' to describing his 'strong farmer's' energetic, forceful and passionate personality. Not surprisingly then, when Yeats expanded *The Celtic Twilight* in 1902, he added another essay, 'An Enduring Heart', about the 'knight of the sheep's' unhappy love affair.

Obviously, if fairy lore had diminished and peasant customs were rapidly disappearing, the personality of the peasant offered Yeats the most hope of a vital, passionate and potentially tragic subject matter. His attempt to use the beliefs and legends of the peasantry as a revelation of their 'character' is in the tradition of his many predecessors who had also interpreted folklore as representative of the peasantry's character. Yeats merely concluded that folklore revealed different things: spiritual experiences rather than superstition, joy rather than ridiculousness, passion rather than farce, visionaries rather than buffoons. Folklore studies, from the Grimms to Douglas Hyde, had frequently been published as nationalist propaganda. Even today folklorists view folklore as a revelation of national character, although they are usually more cautious and objective in their interpretation. For example, the eminent Irish folklorist Sean O'Sullivan declared in a recent collection of Irish legends that 'legends' are much more truly Irish than 'folktales' because legends are based on folk belief and custom and thus 'reflect the inner mind and behaviour of peoples more closely than do folktales, and they offer a fairly sure key to the ways of thought of our ancestors'.[53]

The nature of the peasant personality, which had been a criterion for *Fairy and Folk Tales* and which had become an even more important criterion in *Representative Irish Tales*, is a major theme in *The Celtic Twilight*. The full title of the 1893 edition, *The Celtic Twilight: Men and Women, Dhouls and Faeries*, foreshadows how human personalities will have precedence over any depiction of the fairies. Human personalities are described in much greater detail than any fairy, in contrast to *Fairy and Folk Tales* where fairy attributes had been discussed at great length. However, Yeats's fascination with personality extends beyond the peasantry in *The Celtic Twilight*. 'A Visionary' describes in detail a visionary poet, probably AE, whose job was being a clerk in a large shop, but whose 'pleasure' was 'to wander about upon the hills, talking to half-mad and visionary peasants'. But rather than collecting folklore, this visionary poet explored the peasantry's personality for he sought 'to persuade queer and conscience-stricken persons to deliver up the keeping of their troubles into his care'. This poet shared other traits with the peasantry : he was a visionary, he epitomised 'the vast and vague extravagance that lies at the bottom of the Celtic heart', and he possessed an oral tradition for he chose to remember many of his poems rather than to write them down. Yeats also included another essay, 'The Last Gleeman', about another 'urban artist' who also shared traits with the peasantry. Michael Moran, or 'Zozimus' as he had been more popularly known, had been a 'celebrated Dublin street rhymer and reciter' in the early nineteenth century according to the *Memoir of the Great Original Zozimus* (1871) upon which Yeats based his essay. Although the *Memoir* was a written source, it recorded oral memories. The *Memoir* had opened with the argument that 'the memories of humble men' such as Zozimus were as significant as the lives of statesmen which were recorded in written histories.[54] Such an argument anticipates those used by folklorists today to explain the significance of folklore. The energy and extravagance of Zozimus' personality and life paralleled what Yeats had hoped to discover in Irish peasant life. The title of the essay 'The Last Gleeman' emphasises that Zozimus represented an oral poetic tradition similar to that Yeats was seeking in rural Ireland.

It is significant that the 'knight of the sheep' was old when Yeats visited him and that Zozimus had died in 1846 and was even then 'the last gleeman'. Moreover, the 'knight of the sheep' was not an ordinary peasant, and the visionary poet and Zozimus were not peasants at all. The passion and energy of the 'knight of the sheep', the vision and extravagance of the poet, and the energy and extravagance of Zozimus all resembled qualities Yeats had sought among the peasantry when he compiled *Fairy and Folk Tales* and *Representative Irish Tales* and when he collected materials during the late 1880s and early 1890s for *The Celtic Twilight*. The fact that Yeats found it necessary to include the aristocratic 'knight of the sheep' and the city-dwelling poet and Zozimus indicates that he had not found enough peasant personalities in the countryside who fulfilled his expectations. His descriptions of some peasants in *The Celtic Twilight* imply he found simplicity more often than depth of personality. Paddy Flynn's visionary melancholy is described as being like that 'of purely instinctive natures and all animals'. Yeats refers to 'the knight of the sheep's' daughters as 'robust children of nature' in the essay 'A Coward'. When peasant personalities had enough complexity to fascinate him, as had Paddy Flynn and Mary Battle, they were generally too old to be considered as representative of a still vital tradition. In addition, although both Paddy Flynn and Mary Battle may both have been visionaries with extravagant beliefs, their lives lacked the passion and energy which so intrigued Yeats in the lives of the 'knight of the sheep' and Zozimus, and the fictional peasant characters he had anthologised in *Representative Irish Tales*.

The essays about the 'knight of the sheep' and Zozimus had both been published previously. However, the other previously published essays which had been about the fairies had all been published several years before 'The Last Gleeman' (6 May 1893) and 'The Knight of the Sheep' (21 October 1893). 'A Visionary', which was about an artist rather than a peasant, had been published in October 1891. The only other previously published essay which had also appeared in 1893 was 'Our Lady of the Hills'. This essay too had nothing to do with the fairies; it told how several children had mistaken a Protestant girl dressed in blue and white for the Blessed Mother. The very presence of such an essay in the collection suggests continued visionary powers among the peasantry but ones which have obviously dwindled in their ability to see spiritual beings, whether pagan or Christian. The chronology of the publication dates of the previously published essays which Yeats included in *The Celtic Twilight* thus reflect his declining interest in the fairies and the peasantry.

The anglicised peasants whom Yeats encountered around Sligo indicated how the elemental energy of Irish peasant life had waned in the course of the century. As a consequence of his study of nineteenth-century Anglo-Irish fiction and of his collecting folklore around Sligo, Yeats realised the possibility of using Irish peasants as literary subjects had also waned. As early as 1889, he admitted that 'in Griffin and Kickham the tide began to ebb. . . . It has quite gone out now—our little tide. The writers who make Irish stories sail the sea of common English fiction', whereas the earlier writers such as Carleton and the Banims 'saw the whole of everything they looked at, . . . the brutal with the tender, the coarse with the refined', and had thus made one 'see life plainly but all written down in a kind of fiery shorthand that it might never be forgotten'.[55] The peasant life Yeats witnessed around Sligo could not compare to what Carleton and the Banims experienced earlier in the century. In 1896 he admitted :

Carleton lived only just in time to describe [the] manners and customs . . . [of] this strange Gaelic race . . . as they had been left by centuries of purely Gaelic influence, for the great famine changed the face of Ireland, and from that day a hundred influences which are not Gaelic began to mould [sic] them anew. His autobiography describes the actual wakes and faction fights and conspiracies and hedge schools and pilgrimages out of which he fashioned the half imaginary adventures of the 'Traits and Stories', and describes them not as one who observes them with the philosophical indifference of the historian, but with the moving sympathy of one who has himself mourned and conspired and learnt and taught and gone on pilgrimage, and to whom all these things are natural and inevitable.[56]

In 1901 Yeats characterised the mid-nineteenth century as a time of 'the great famine, the sinking down of popular imagination, the dying out of traditional fantasy, the ebbing out of the energy of race'.[57] Even the rich oral traditions to which Lady Gregory had introduced him in Galway in the late 1890s were obviously not as rich as he would have liked. In his 1903 essay 'The Galway Plains', Yeats recalled 'a day two or three years ago when I stood on the side of Slieve Echtge, looking out over Galway' with an 'old countryman.' The countryman told Yeats many anecdotes concerning fairy beliefs and visions at Slieve Echtge, but when Yeats 'asked him if he had himself seen any of its enchantments' he merely replied 'Sometimes when I look over to the hill, I see a mist lying on top of it, that goes away after a while.'[58] In this case, even an old Galway informant had not the firsthand anecdotes about the fairies such as old Paddy Flynn and Mary Battle had provided Yeats with a decade before. Even if the recurrent famines of the 1840s and what Douglas Hyde referred to as the 'anglicising' of Ireland had not destroyed Irish peasant life as Carleton knew it, the peasant life which Carleton celebrated could never have been 'natural and inevitable' to someone like Yeats who had not grown up a part of it.

Nevertheless Yeats did not give up his study of the beliefs and character of the peasantry after publishing *The Celtic Twilight* in 1893. The folklore he collected with Lady Gregory in County Galway in the late 1890s obviously encouraged him to publish an expanded edition in 1902. Lady Gregory's knowledge and collection of Galway folklore were indeed as extensive as Yeats and others have claimed, and as helpful to his playwriting. But Lady Gregory herself had been inspired to collect folklore by reading the first edition of *The Celtic Twilight* and Douglas Hyde's *Love Songs of Connacht*. She introduced Yeats to a rich oral tradition in Galway but Yeats's own interest in and attitudes about Irish folklore had arisen and developed quite independently of her influence. The second edition of *The Celtic Twilight* represented a deepening of all the elements in the first edition which themselves had been developments in earlier attitudes about Irish folklore he had shown in *Fairy and Folktales*. The second edition of *The Celtic Twilight* was even less specifically Irish and even less concerned with the fairies than the first edition had been; it placed even more emphasis on human personalities and on Irish folklore's occult significance and its relationship to ancient Ireland.

Yeats was able to expand *The Celtic Twilight* considerably in

1902, largely because of the Galway traditions he collected with Lady Gregory. The first edition had contained twenty-two essays. For the second edition he removed one essay and added eighteen new essays, plus footnotes and new paragraphs to about a half dozen others. Yeats presented the new edition as a continuation of the original collection: 'In these new chapters, as in the old ones, I have invented nothing but my comments and one or two deceitful sentences that may keep some poor story-teller's commerce with the devil and his angels, or the like, from being known among his neighbours.'[59] Yeats's waning enthusiasm for his materials is apparent in the note he added at the beginning: 'I have added a few more chapters in the manner of the old ones, and would have added others, but one loses, as one grows older, something of the lightness of one's dreams.' His sense, however, that his materials could be considered seriously from an occult perspective is obvious in his promise at the end of the note: 'I shall publish in a little while a big book about the commonwealth of faery, and shall try to make it systematical and learned enough to buy pardon for this handful of dreams.' The book to which he refers was Lady Gregory's *Visions and Beliefs in the West of Ireland* which did not appear until 1920 and to which Yeats appended two essays and lengthy notes about the mystical and magical connotations of Irish folklore.

Yeats repeatedly associated Irish folklore with universal occult and magical beliefs in the second edition of *The Celtic Twilight*. Indeed, such references reduced the Irish identity of his materials. The note which Yeats added in 1902 to a sentence about the 'Celtic' nature of his materials in the essay 'A Visionary' demonstrates how his nationalistic perspective had broadened: 'I wrote this sentence long ago. This sadness now seems to me a part of all peoples who preserve the moods of the ancient peoples of the world. I am not so pre-occupied with the mystery of Race as I used to be, but leave this sentence and other sentences like it unchanged.' Yeats's own responses to his materials were less pointedly Irish in 1902. For example, here is how he describes a conversation he had with a Sligo woman in the essay entitled 'War': 'And presently our talk of war shifted, as it had a way of doing, to the battle of the Black Pig, which seems to her a battle between Ireland and England, but to me an

Armageddon which shall quench all things in the Ancestral Darkness again. . . .' Yeats's imaginative distance from his informant is also quite obvious here.

Yeats did not quote any fairy lore or visionary experiences he had collected from this woman, but instead recounted her anecdotes concerning her adventures with soldiers during the Fenian times. The materials which Yeats added to the collection are generally more concerned with human loves and adventures than with encounters with ghosts and fairies. 'The Enduring Heart' concerns a love affair of the 'knight of the sheep'. 'Dust Hath Closed Helen's Eyes' concerns the legendary beauty of Ballylee, Mary Hynes, and the equally legendary poet Raftery who celebrated her beauty in poems still sung in the countryside. The mention of Biddy Early, the famous Clare wise woman, further underscores the human dimensions of the essay and Yeats's growing preference for peasants of legendary, even heroic, stature. Such a preference explains why Yeats filled the the essays he added in 1902 with references to the legendary heroes and heroines of ancient Ireland. The ancient heroes had been mentioned in the first edition. In the essay 'Drumcliff and Rosses' Yeats had said 'a fisherman saw, far on the horizon, renowned Hy Brazel [sic], where he who touches shall find no more care, nor cynic laughter, but shall go walking under shadiest boscage, and enjoy the conversation of Cuchullin and his heroes'. The poem 'The Host' which Yeats placed at the beginning of the 1893 edition and which was entitled 'The Hosting of the Sidhe' in the 1902 edition, described the Fenian hero 'Caolte' as riding with the fairy host. In the essay 'A Visionary' Yeats had claimed that the peasant visionaries and Cuchulain and Oisin all had 'within them the vast and vague extravagance that lies at the bottom of the Celtic heart' and were all 'a portion of that great Celtic phantasmagoria'. The vagueness and fluctuation implied in those phrases have sharpened into a steady concern with heroic traits by 1902. Rather than looking forward to idyllic conversations with Cuchulain and other ancient heroes in the happy otherworld, living Irish peasants enjoy contact with a heroic ancient Ireland. In the 1902 essay 'And Fair, Fierce Woman' Yeats describes how an old woman near Sligo saw the ancient Irish Queen Maeve and thus 'came face to face with heroic beauty'. In the same essay Yeats tells of an old poet who had seen Maeve and had a love affair with her, and of an old woman in a Galway workhouse who spoke of Maeve but refused to tell a scandalous story she knew about her.

Yeats also attempted to link the peasant's imagination with ancient Ireland. He said of his informant in the second part of the essay 'Happy and Unhappy Theologians' : 'some of his talk reminds one of those old Irish visions of the Three Worlds, which are supposed to have given Dante the plan of the *Divine Comedy.*' Yeats too is presented as trying to achieve contact with ancient Ireland. In the essay 'A Voice' he describes how once in the woods at Coole, while thinking of Aengus and Edain, and Mannanan, son of the sea, he was overcome momentarily with 'an emotion which I said to myself was the root of a Christian mysticism'. Shortly thereafter he experienced visions of heroic beings obviously associated with ancient Ireland, just as his vision of the tall gleaming woman which he had described in the 1893 essay 'Regina, Regina Pigmeorum, Veni' had presented her as of the fairies. By 1902 the fairies and the heroes and gods of ancient Ireland are all presented as 'the divine people'. In the essay 'Enchanted Woods' Yeats manages to link contemporary peasant and ancient wisdom : 'I say to myself, when I am well out of that thicket of argument, that they are surely there, the divine people, for only we who have neither simplicity nor wisdom have denied them, and the simple of all times and the wise men of ancient times have seen them and even spoken to them.' Yeats thus gives the fairies and visionary ex-periences of the peasants, and the peasants themselves, a new stature. Even in 1893 he had lamented in the essay 'Kidnappers' that 'so greatly has the power of Faery dwindled, that there are none but peasants in these sad chronicles of mine.'

Yeats had quite ingeniously solved these problems, the dwin-dling power of the fairies and having only peasants to write about, by greatly expanding the focus of his materials in 1902 on the basis of the theory that the fairies had once been the gods of ancient Ireland. This was one of the three major theories about the origin of the fairies he had outlined in his discussion of 'trooping fairies' in *Fairy and Folk Tales.* He quite handily disposed of the theory that the fairies were fallen angels when he said in 'Happy and Unhappy Theologians', of one of his most authoritative sources, the old Mayo woman, 'I have never heard her call them the Fallen Angels.' He had, of course, already made use of the theory that the fairies were the occult gods of the earth when he had associated the fairies with such spirits in the 1893 essay 'The Golden Age'.

In 1902 he was ready to equate the fairies with the pagan gods of Ireland. The only fairy lore in the essay 'Dust Hath Closed Helen's Eyes' concerned the legend that Mary Hynes had not died but had been 'taken' by the fairies. Yeats lost no time in identifying the Sidhe—the Irish term for fairies—as the gods, and in associating the peasants with the ancient Greeks: 'She died young because the gods loved her, for the Sidhe are the gods, and it may be that the old saying, which we forget to understand literally meant her manner of death in old times. These poor countrymen and countrywomen in their beliefs, and in their emotions, are many years nearer to that old Greek world, that set beauty beside the fountain of things, than are our men of learning.' Such a characterisation of the peasantry and their fairies forestalls any attempt to dismiss Yeats's materials as 'merely the small gossip of faerydom'—a phrase Yeats himself had used in 'Drumcliff and Rosses' in 1893. So by 1902 Yeats refers to a fairy pig as 'The Swine of the Gods' in the essay of that name, and other fairy creatures sighted in the woods at Coole are characterised as 'of the race of the white stag that flits in and out of the tales of Arthur, and of the evil pig that slew Diarmuid where Ben Bulben mixes with the sea wind'.

The notes which Yeats added in 1902 also increased the ancient, mythological and heroic significance of his materials. In 1893 he had briefly recounted the legend of a fairy woman named Clooth-na-bare in the essay 'The Untiring Ones': 'Such a mortal too was Clooth-na-bare, who went all over the world seeking a lake deep enough to drown her faery life, of which she had grown weary, leaping from hill to lake and lake to hill, and setting up a cairn of stones wherever her feet lighted, until at last she found the deepest water in the world in little Lough Ia, on the top of the Birds' Mountain at Sligo.' In a note to this essay in 1902 in which Yeats tries to correct his bad Irish he also reveals that Clooth-na-bare could perhaps be the mother of the gods: 'Doubtless Clooth-na-bare should be Cailleac Bare, which would mean the old Woman Bare. Bare or Bere or Verah or Dera or Dhera was a very famous person, perhaps the mother of the Gods herself.'

John Kelleher has written a masterful analysis of the written and imaginative resources from which Yeats produced the 1893 legend, the 1902 note and a much lengthier note about Clooth-na-bare in *The Wind among the Reeds* (1899).[60] Kelleher's scholarly research among Yeats's written sources is dazzling, but his analysis and conclusions completely discount the possibility that some of Yeats's sources were oral. Kelleher says that Yeats's information is 'so jam-packed with error and innovation that for a long while I thought Yeats had simply made it up'. After searching through the innumerable books and articles on Irish folklore which Yeats read in the 1880s and 1890s, Kelleher identified two major written sources for Yeats's material about Clooth-na-bare, but found no source for the impossible Irish in the name. Kelleher concluded that the only possible written source for the legend Yeats recounted about Clooth-na-bare in 1893 was a somewhat similar legend in W. G. Wood-Martin's *History of Sligo*: 'On the mountain overlooking the scene of this catastrophe lived a giantess named Veragh. She was so tall that she could easily wade the rivers and lakes in Ireland. One day, however, when trying to cross *Loch-da-ghedh*, it proved to be beyond her depth, and she was drowned; but her house on the mountain still remains, and is styled Calliagh-a-Veragh. This lake has the reputation of being the deepest in the County Sligo.'[61] Kelleher comments that Wood-Martin's book is 'the sort of amateur pseudo-scholarship that Yeats *would* choose to forage from' and argues that the legend in *The Celtic Twilight* is so different from Wood-Martin's version because 'neither the name nor the story was at all graceful. Something had to be done; and something was. Clooth-na-bare, and her story as retold by Yeats, is little more than a tidying up of inconvenient fact.' Even if Yeats did 're-tell' Wood-Martin's version, it becomes more passionate and tragic rather than graceful. However, why not take Yeats's word that the story as he told it in *The Celtic Twilight* came from an oral source? In his notes to the *Wind among the Reeds* he says of his source for the legend, 'I forget, now, where I heard this story, but it may have been from a priest at Collooney.' Kelleher claims to 'have strong doubts about the priest' and the reality of Yeats's oral sources in general.

Yet Yeats had claimed in his Introduction to *The Celtic Twilight* that he had 'accurately and candidly' written down what he had heard. Even in his revisions in the materials he used in *Fairy and Folk Tales* he had altered only the form not the substance.

Kelleher is equally certain that Yeats's source for elevating Clooth-na-bare to being the mother of the gods was a written one: 'Yeats's fantastic memory reaching back, perhaps twenty years, to his reading of O'Kearney's article in which . . . the Carthagenian Anu is equated with Juno who is equated with Diana who is equated with the Irish Aine who is the sister of Milucradh who is the Cailleach Biorar, the mistress of the waters.' Yeats did read and mine Nicholas O'Kearney's notes to the Fenian tale 'Feis Tigh Chonain' for *Fairy and Folk Tales*, and he did have a prodigious memory and an equally prodigious imagination. But it is just as possible that his version of the Clooth-na-bare legend in 1893 and his note associating her with the gods came from oral tradition. Even his incredibly corrupt version of her Gaelic name could easily have been the result of his hearing but not understanding how to write down a Gaelic name. Irish oral tradition is full of lore about hags or 'cailleacha' whose traits often resemble those of a goddess. Even Kelleher admits that 'We find fragmentary recollections of "hag" stories. Hag stories are a widely-known type of rather low-level folk-lore, possibly degenerated from myth and generally pretty vague.' It is very likely that Yeats heard just such a scrap of oral tradition around Sligo. Sean O'Sullivan, in his *Handbook of Irish Folklore*, says that Cailleach Bhéara is one of the most well-known hags in Irish oral tradition. The questions which O'Sullivan suggests that collectors ask their informants about hags underscore their divine traits: Are the hags regarded as being very old and wise and possessed of supernatural powers? Were they looked upon as supernatural beings? Had they unusually great wisdom? Could they cause sudden storms and sickness?[62] Even Kelleher admits that Yeats's version of the legend and later notes about it resemble genuine oral tradition: 'Yet though the substance of Yeats's note is mainly a frustrating mish-mash of misremembered misquotation of bad nineteenth-century pseudo-learning, at the very bottom there is a stratum of genuine folk-belief.' We should not be too hasty in discounting Yeats's oral sources or in applying standards from written literature to his memory and use of quotations. Yeats's own memory and the oral lore he recorded as a folklorist were both oral memories which belie our literate notions that a tale must be a single, unchanging, printed entity.

Whatever the source of Clooth-na-bare's transformation from a fairy in 1893 to a goddess in 1902, her elevation to an ancient and heroic stature typifies the added significance Yeats has bestowed on his materials in 1902. Even in 1902 it was hard to find much passion or tragedy in the beliefs of an informant such as Mary Battle whose 'mind continually dwells on what is pleasant and beautiful'; likewise her sober counterpart in the second part of the essay 'Happy and Unhappy Theologians' was 'a little-crazed'. The imaginations of both informants were indeed lively and extravagant, but their age, possible senility and inactive lives left little room for passion, heroism or tragedy. At least the divine beings their imaginations dwelled on—whether fairies, ancient gods or ancient heroes—had supposedly led 'passionate' lives. Yeats had used his memory of the lively faction fighting among peasants near Sligo as an example of the peasantry's passion and violence in the 1893 essay 'The Thick Skull of the Fortunate'. In 1902 he appended the following paragraph to the essay : 'I wrote all this years ago, out of what were even then old memories. I was in Roughley the other day, and found it much like other desolate places. I may have been thinking of Moughorow, a much wilder place, for the memories of one's childhood are brittle things to lean upon.' He no longer had to rely on memories of a disappearing peasantry for such passion; their ancient heroes obviously had become more suitable vehicles for it by 1902.

The second edition of *The Celtic Twilight* demonstrated several other developments in Yeats's concept of Irish folklore. He had concluded the first edition with the essay 'The Four Winds of Desire', a review of Douglas Hyde's *Beside the Fire.* He omitted this essay in 1902. He obviously had more original folklore to include because of the materials he had gathered with Lady Gregory. The essay had reviewed the previous nineteenth-century collections of folklore as well as Hyde's book and thus had been literary criticism. The inclusion of the essay in 1893 had indicated that Yeats considered his first original collection of Irish folklore to be a part of the preceding tradition. By 1902 Yeats obviously had concluded that his collection with its record of his personal beliefs and visions had marked a radical departure from previous literary folklorists like Croker and from scientific folklorists like Hyde. In 1902 he had expanded the occult dimensions of the previous edition. The deletion of the review-essay, and of any reference to previous collections, presented Yeats's collection as the unique achievement it indeed was. He had succeeded in combining the two major forces in nineteenth-century folklore studies he had wrestled with when he compiled *Fairy and Folk Tales* and *Irish Fairy Tales*. He had blended the freedom of the creative artist and the accuracy of the folklorist. In the process he created a work which is unique among his works and in modern literature, and one for which Yeats, who was an extremely demanding critic of his early works, never lost his admiration.

One essay, 'Dreams that have No Moral', which Yeats added in 1902 demonstrates an interest in an entirely different genre of Irish oral narrative. Yeats's preference in *Fairy and Folk Tales*, in *Irish Fairy Tales* and *The Celtic Twilight* had been for legends. Whereas Douglas Hyde preferred folktales to legends, Yeats and Lady Gregory preferred legends to folktales. Nevertheless in 'Dreams that have No Moral' Yeats records what at first glance appears to be a folktale; in any event it is definitely not a legend. Yeats introduces the story with the following apologetic comment :

> The story, which I am going to tell just as it was told, was one of those old rambling moralless tales, which are the delight of the poor and the hard driven, wherever life is left in its natural simplicity. They tell of a time when nothing had consequences, when even if you were killed, if only you had a good heart, somebody would bring you to life again with a touch of a rod, and when if you were a prince and happened to look exactly like your brother, you might go to bed with his queen, and have only a little quarrel afterwards. We too, if we were so weak and poor that everything threatened us with misfortune, would remember, if foolish people left us, every old dream that has been strong enough to fling the weight of the world from its shoulders.

The story has a long involved plot typical of a folktale : A king who wishes a son is told by his adviser to have the queen eat a fish which is to be caught at a certain place. The cook inadvertently also eats a bit of it and both she and the queen give birth to sons before the year is out. Their sons are like twin brothers. The mare and greyhound who had eaten bits of the fish which were thrown into the yard likewise had two foals and two pups respectively. The queen sends the cook's son, Jack, away but before he leaves he tells his twin brother Bill, the queen's son, that the water at the top of the well will turn to blood if he, Jack, is ever in danger. Jack takes one of the pups and one of the horses along on his journey and soon becomes the cowherd for a king. While searching for better grass for the cows, Jack confronts and overcomes a giant from whom he gets a magical object, an invincible sword. The next day Jack defeats a two-headed giant and receives a suit that makes its wearer invisible. The third day Jack defeats a four-headed giant and gains shoes that enable him to run as fast as the wind. Jack has earned all three magical objects just in time to use each in turn to defend the princess against a great serpent while the bully who was supposed to defend the princess hides in a tree. On the third day Jack fights the serpent, kills him with the sword and then disappears, but not before the princess has secretly cut off some of his hair which she plans to use to identify her unknown hero. The bully, of course, claims to have saved her and is rewarded by the king with the hand of the princess in marriage. But the princess refuses to marry anyone whose foot will not fit into the magical shoes and whose hair does not match the hair she clipped from her real protector. The king gives a ball at which all the men in the kingdom try on the shoe. Jack, the lowliest cowherd, is revealed as the hero and marries the princess. Unfortunately, Jack then is accosted by the mother of the three giants he had killed. She enchants the dog and horse, who normally would have aided Jack, and turns Jack into stone. At this point the twin brother Bill sees the water in the well turn to blood and he sets out to find Jack. He is mistaken for Jack by Jack's wife, he sleeps with her one night then goes off and rescues Jack and countless others from the hag's enchantment.

This plot, commonly called 'The Twin or Blood Brothers' and identified by the Aarne-Thompson number A-T303, is one of the most well-known folktales in the world and in Ireland. Sean O'Sullivan, in *The Types of the Irish Folktale* lists hundreds of

manuscript versions of the tale in the archives of the Irish Folk-
lore Commission as well as numerous printed versions, including
Yeats's tale in *The Celtic Twilight.*[63] Yeats's version, as do many
of those cited by O'Sullivan, incorporates some details of the
equally famous folktale plot known as 'The Dragon Slayer'
(A-T300).

The tale Yeats recounts contains all the generic character-
istics of an international folktale. At first glance, nothing in
Yeats's tale seems uniquely Irish, other than the giant's saying
'I smell the blood of an Irishman.' When Lady Gregory included
the same tale with a few different details in her *Kiltartan Wonder
Book* under the title 'Shawneen' she gave the heroes Irish names:
the queen's son was named Shamus and the cook's son, Shaw-
neen. But both the giant's statement and Lady Gregory's use
of Irish names are really only surface details. However, this tale
can also be categorised as a uniquely Irish oral narrative genre
known as the 'hero tale'. Many such hero tales are purportedly
about the adventures of a legendary Irish hero from either the
Red Branch or the Fenian cycles. Many hero tales combine
international and uniquely national motifs within a freely
adapted but still recognisable international folktale plot; others
are based on uniquely Irish plots. For example, 'The Dragon
Slayer' plot (A-T300) is a folk version of the classical tale of
Perseus, while the successive slaying of three giants by Jack is
possibly a purely Irish motif according to Sean O'Sullivan.[64]

Although Bill and Jack are the stereotyped figures of the com-
mon folktale, their adventures resemble a 'hero tale' in several
ways. The description of Jack's fight with the giant echoes the
formulaic descriptions known as 'runs' which are characteristic
in hero tales: 'So then they began to fight. The ground that was
hard they made soft, and the ground that was soft they made
hard, and they made spring wells come up through the green
flags.' Compare that with the following passage describing a
fight between Céatach and the Magician from the hero tale
entitled 'Céatach' which is reprinted in Sean O'Sullivan's *Folk-
tales of Ireland*: 'They made the hard places soft and soft places
hard. They drew wells of spring water up through the centre
of the green stones.'[65] The giant had asked Jack before they
began to fight: 'Would you sooner be driving red-hot knives into
one another's hearts or would you sooner be fighting one another

on red-hot flags?' The Magician had asked Céatach a similar
question before their fight began: 'Which do you prefer: to
wrestle on red flagstones or to stab with grey knives against each
other's bulging ribs?' The giant had greeted Jack with the
words: 'Fee-faw-fum I smell the blood of an Irishman . . . you
are too big for one mouthful, and too small for two mouth-
fuls, and I don't know what I'll do with you . . .' The Magician
had spoken a similar greeting to Céatach: 'Fú fá féasóg I can
smell a lying, thieving Irishman. To eat you in one bite would be
too little for me, and to eat you in two bites would be too much.
I don't know what I'll do with you . . .' The Magician, after
he had been defeated by Céatach gave him a magic sword and
a horse as fast as the wind. Earlier in the tale when Céatach
had fought a giant named Steel Skull he had cut off the giant's
head: 'The head went up into the air whistling and came down
humming in hope of joining the body again.' But Céatach
kicked the head seven acres away and the severed head tells him
'Lucky for you that you did that, had I joined the body again
it would have taken more than half of the Fianna to prise me
loose.' Likewise Jack 'cut off the giant's head that it went into
the air, and he caught it on the sword as it was coming down,
and made two halves of it. "It is well for you I did not join the
body again", said the head, "or you would have never been able
to strike it off again." ' When Bill sets off to rescue his twin-
brother Jack he puts himself under an oath or what is known
as a 'geasa' in the hero tales: 'I will never eat a second meal
at the same table, or sleep a second night in the same bed, till
I know what is happening to Jack.' Oscar, in another hero tale
in O'Sullivan's *Folktales of Ireland* entitled 'The Coming of
Oscar', had put himself under a similar 'geasa' when he set
off to find his father Oisin and the Fianna: 'I won't eat three
meals at the same table or sleep three nights in the same bed,
until I see him.'[66] Such descriptive 'runs', and such motifs as magic
swords, talking severed heads, and 'geasas' are characteristic of
innumerable Irish hero tales. Moreover, although Bill and Jack
retain the generic names of typical folktale heroes, they rely
much less on magical objects than ordinary folktale heroes
generally do. Bill and Jack both possess more innate courage
and strength than is usual to folktale heroes, and thus they share
the heroic stature, if not the legendary names, of the figures in

F

many Irish hero tales. So, although Yeats had offered the story apologetically to his readers as 'one of those old rambling moralless tales', it was much more than an ordinary folktale. Yeats had actually recounted a rare narrative because relatively few such hero tales ever passed into English. All of the hero tales included in Sean O'Sullivan's *Folktales in Ireland* had been collected in Irish and then translated into English.

Yeats does not say whether the friend, Lady Gregory, who collected the tale heard it in Irish or in English. Nor does Lady Gregory indicate whether she originally collected it in Irish or in English when she included it in her *Kiltartan Wonder Book*. In any event, the fact that Yeats's version follows hers almost word for word attests to the truth of his claim to have presented his materials as accurately and as candidly as possible. The details of plot in which Yeats's version differs from Lady Gregory's is accounted for by her note concerning 'Shawneen' at the end of the *Kiltartan Wonder Book*. She explained her version was a combination of a tale she heard at a workhouse and of a similar tale related 'at my own door by a piper from County Kerry'.[67] Yeats presented his version as having been collected by a friend at a workhouse and his is obviously the original version Lady Gregory had collected. The conclusions of both their versions are identical except for one interesting difference. Yeats's version glosses over but at least implies the sexual connotations of Bill having spent the night with Jack's wife—a somewhat euphemistic handling compared with other European versions of the tale which deal with the episode in detail. However, Lady Gregory, who is known to have bowdlerised her materials, completely ignores even mentioning the episode and Jack's consequent jealousy. She must have consciously omitted the episode because Yeats's tale demonstrates it had been included in one of her sources.

The inclusion of what was actually an Irish hero tale in the second edition of *The Celtic Twilight* typifies Yeats's growing concern with heroic personality and other kinds of traditional narrative. However, the ancient heroes, though frequently alluded to in these new essays, remain somewhat shadowy presences. They are the subject of the peasantry's visions and imagination but the major focus of the second edition remains the peasantry—only it has become a peasantry much more closely associated with ancient Ireland.

When Yeats had begun collecting the folklore which eventually appeared in *The Celtic Twilight* he was mainly interested in gathering lore about fairies and other supernatural creatures. So he gathered beliefs and legends rather than folktales. As he declared in 'The Four Winds of Desire', the concluding essay to the first edition, he believed that although oral traditions were rapidly disappearing 'Much, no doubt, will perish—perhaps the whole tribe of folk-tales proper; but the fairy and ghost kingdom is more stubborn than men dream of.'[68] However, although he remained fascinated with the occult significance of the fairies, he became disenchanted with their literary possibilities and more and more intrigued with the character of the Irish peasantry. By the time he compiled the second edition, his conception of both the fairies and the peasantry had become increasingly associated with the gods and heroes of ancient Ireland.

Lady Gregory had introduced him to oral traditions which offered uniquely Irish narrative possibilities rather than the narrative traditions of English fiction which he had found superimposed on Irish folklore and on fiction about Irish peasant life which had been published earlier in the century. The heroic legends which Lady Gregory and others were publishing at the turn of the century were of far better literary quality than the translations which had been available to him in the 1880s. The essay 'Dreams which have No Moral', in which he recorded the folktale which resembled a hero tale in so many ways, was the penultimate essay in the second edition. His final essay 'By the Roadside' further illustrates his deepening interest in more complex forms of traditional narrative than simple, anecdotal belief legends. He describes how 'Last night I went to a wide place on the Kiltartan road to listen to some Irish songs.' The focus in the entire essay is on narrative songs and tales, on their ancient significance, rather than on contemporary beliefs and visionary experiences. Yeats recalls how hearing the songs and stories the peasants narrated 'carried my memory to older verses, or even to forgotten mythologies'. When he refers to the collectors of folklore he does so in terms of song and story—'we, who would re-awaken imaginative tradition by making old songs live again, or by gathering old stories into books'. The fairies will still be of occult significance but his literary hopes for Irish folklore obviously have come to focus on the human personalities and the narratives it offers him, on the peasants and ancient heroes who people legend, folktale, hero tale and myth :

> There is no song or story handed down among the cottages that has not words and thoughts to carry one as far, for though one can know but a little of their ascent, one knows that they ascend like medieval genealogies through unbroken dignities to the beginning of the world. Folk art is, indeed, the oldest of the aristocracies of thought, and because it refuses what is passing and trivial, the merely clever and pretty, as certainly as the vulgar and insincere, and because it has gathered into itself the simplest and the most unforgettable thoughts of the generations, it is the soil where all great art is rooted.

Yeats's emphasis at the conclusion of the 1902 edition of *The Celtic Twilight* is on folklore as a matter of art rather than as a matter of belief. He had kept his occult beliefs out of *Fairy and Folk Tales*. He presents a unique combination of the literary and the occult sides of Irish folklore in *The Celtic Twilight* where visions of the peasantry are openly presented as a matter of occult significance. But it was the lives of the peasantry and of their legendary heroes that offered the most poetic promise, hence the literary emphasis of the concluding essay in *The Celtic Twilight*. Yeats spoke for himself as well as for many in his generation when he recalled in 1931 that 'forty years ago intellectual young men, dissatisfied with the political poetry of Young Ireland, once the foundation of Irish politics, substituted an interest in old stories and modern peasants.'[69] 'Old stories and modern peasants' became his concern more and more during the 1890s. It was his study of the 'modern peasant', of his energetic life in *Representative Irish Tales* and of his visionary extravagance in *The Celtic Twilight*, that led Yeats to the 'old stories' of Ireland's legendary past.

Yeats's major focus, then, in both *Representative Irish Tales* and *The Celtic Twilight* is the character of the Irish peasant. Consequently, one might expect these works to corroborate the charges of having idealised the peasantry which have so frequently been levelled at Yeats and other members of the Irish Literary Revival by literary critics, historians and folklorists. Maurice Harmon's recent comment—'the Literary Revival was generally weak in dealing with rural Ireland, tending to transform peasants into angels in red petticoats'—typifies the judgement of many literary critics.[70] Lawrence T. McCaffrey's characterisation of Anglo-Irish writers represents the view of many historians : 'Their view of Ireland, the inheritor of a colourful paganism illustrated in epic poems and tales, a rural, spiritual bastion in an industrial, materialistic world, had little relationship to an economically and culturally underdeveloped island on the fringes of Western Europe. Their spiritualized peasants, descendants of folk heroes, had little resemblance to men and women grubbing out an existence on an inhospitable soil'.[71]

An Irish folklorist, Kevin Danaher, has been equally critical, especially of Yeats : 'W. B. Yeats, it is to be feared, often blunders. He himself dabbled in folk lore, but all too often brings into his poems, and even into his prose, an air of mystical moonshine which is very far from the clear black and white of folk tradition, in which magic is only one more of the hard facts of life.'[72]

Both *Representative Irish Tales*, which has been virtually ignored even by Yeats's scholars, and *The Celtic Twilight* actually qualify such conclusions. Yeats had selected materials for *Representative Irish Tales* which reflected ignoble as well as noble aspects of peasant life. His major concern had been with the 'abounding vitality' of a peasant life which included brutal and earthy as well as pleasant and visionary dimensions. The detailed panorama of everyday peasant life which Yeats presents in *Representative Irish Tales* prevents one from concluding on the basis of *The Celtic Twilight* that Yeats sought only a 'visionary' peasantry. Even in *The Celtic Twilight* Yeats elevates only the peasant's imagination, and later collectors have also found a similar mystical streak to be characteristic of the peasantry. Walter Starkie's recollection of his initial response to the 'earthiness' of *The Celtic Twilight* suggests that Kevin Danaher's charge of 'mystical moonshine' should not be applied too readily :

> *The Celtic Twilight*, which was published in 1893, is in every way a contrast to all the other works of Yeats, and its general note is one of complete sincerity and simplicity. The title would lead us to expect the prevailing misty melancholy

of the poems of these years, whereas it is full of freshness and early-morning sunshine, and might have been written in the open air. Occasionally, we catch a glimpse of the rarefied world of the Sacred Rose, but all around us we see the familiar scenes of the countryside near Sligo.[73]

Magic is indeed a 'fact of life' to Yeats's informants. The few details which he presents about them are matter-of-fact and down-to-earth. Although the other 'hard facts of life' to which Danaher alludes are not dwelt upon, they are alluded to: Yeats says of Paddy Flynn, 'And yet there was much in his life to depress him, for in the triple solitude of age, eccentricity, and deafness, he went about much pestered by children.' Nor does Yeats shrink from describing the ignoble manner in which Paddy Flynn died: 'a friend of mine gave him a large bottle of whiskey and though a sober man at most times, the sight of so much liquor filled him with a great enthusiasm, and he lived upon it for some days and then died. His body, worn out with old age and hard times, could not bear the drink as in his young days.' The 'hard times' the peasantry endured are likewise referred to in 'Dreams that have no Moral,' when Yeats generalises that the peasants 'were so weak and poor that everything threatened [them] with misfortune'. Although Yeats has been criticised by folklorists such as Richard Dorson and Kevin Danaher, Yeats's presentation of his materials in *The Celtic Twilight* resembles that of an oral narrator if not that of a scientific folklorist, and in many ways Yeats actually anticipates later theories about the nature of folklore which both Dorson and Danaher have promulgated.

5

Rakes and Rapparees: *Irish Adventurers*

Yeats's growing interest in personality during the 1890s, as reflected in *Representative Irish Tales* and in the two editions of *The Celtic Twilight*, was largely influenced by and expressed in terms of the folklore materials he was using. He selected materials for *Representative Irish Tales* which highlighted the energy, the passion and the heroism of the peasant characters. The first edition of *The Celtic Twilight* presented many visionary peasant personalities and even more dynamic peasant and non-peasant characters such as the knight of the sheep and Zozimus. Yeats added the heroic personalities of several ancient heroes to the second edition in 1902. This change of emphasis from peasant personality to ancient heroic personality represented several major developments in Yeats's conception of Irish folklore during the 1890s.

During the late 1880s Yeats had admired Samuel Ferguson's poetry for both its ancient heroic and more recent peasant subjects. Yeats's first essay on Ferguson distinguished two kinds of poetry : poems based on ancient Irish heroes which presented 'instants of heroic passion' and poems based on more recent events in the life of the peasantry, such as 'The Welshmen of Tirawley' and 'The Fairy Thorn', in which 'character is subordinated to some dominant idea or event.'[1] Yeats admired both kinds of poems but his own needs as a poet demanded that he choose the peasant tradition for his inspiration. The old myths were either inaccessible in Irish manuscripts or available in unsatisfactory translations and popularisations. Peasant traditions, which Yeats believed would help to simplify his poetry and bring it back down to earth, were readily available to him in both written and oral form.

Yeats's early distrust of emotion and personality in life and

in literature also explained why he chose the peasantry's folklore
rather than the ancient heroic tradition. His father taught him
to both distrust and admire passion and personality. Yeats
describes in the first section of his *Autobiography* how much his
father admired intensity in life and passion in literature, and
how his father had taught him to admire reserve and laugh at
displays of emotion in life. As a poet he originally sought to
avoid the 'sad soliloquies of a nineteenth-century egoism' which
to him characterised too much English Romantic poetry.[2] Yeats
declared in 1889 that the 'Saxon' was too 'full of self-brooding.
Like his own Wordsworth, most English of poets, he finds his
image in every lake and puddle. He has to burthen the skylark
with his cares before he can celebrate it. He is always a lense
coloured by self.'[3] Yeats concluded that Shelley's poetry had
lacked a living folk tradition which gave 'the greatest poets of
every nation . . . symbols and events to express the most lyrical,
the most subjective moods'.[4] Even the Victorians, as Yeats re-
called in his essay on 'Modern Poetry' in 1936, had seemed to
him during the 1880s to have been overly concerned with
'psychology' in their poetry. Emotion was to be filtered through
folklore : 'Emotion, on the other hand, grows intoxicating and
delightful after it has been enriched with the memory of old
emotions, with all the uncounted flavours of old experience; and
it is necessarily some antiquity of thought, emotions that have
been deepened by the experiences of many men of genius, that
distinguishes the cultivated man. The subject-matter of his
meditation and invention is old, and he will disdain a too
conscious originality in the arts.'[5] Emotion could thus be ex-
pressed through the symbols and events preserved by oral
tradition.

Yeats initially preferred the beliefs and the events rather than
the personalities recorded in folklore for his own literary sub-
ject matter. Richard Ellmann has analysed the early Yeats's
distrust of personality in literature. Yeats's father insisted upon
the value of personality and emotion in literature and in life : 'It
seems to me that the intellect of man *as man*, and therefore of
an artist, the most human of all, should obey no voice except
that of emotion. . . . Art has to do with the sustaining and in-
vigorating of the Personality.'[6] The elder Yeats, who read only
the most passionate parts of plays and poems to his son, taught

him that the highest form of literature was dramatic poetry be-cause it was the form most crammed with life and passion, and least tainted by beliefs. Ellmann claims, however, that the young Yeats shared his generation's distrust of passionate personality: the Romantic hero had too often been preyed upon and even-tually destroyed by the intensity of his passions, but by the end of the century such a hero had been brought under control by aesthetes to whom all passion was repugnant.[7]

Not surprisingly then, in October 1886, Yeats praised Ferguson for presenting the 'passion' of the ancient heroes, especially the passion and lyricism of Ferguson's Deirdre in her 'Lament for the Sons of Usnach', which he quoted at length in November 1886.[8] But less than a month later, in an essay on the poetry of Robert Dwyer Joyce, Yeats praised Joyce's handling of the same Deirdre legend for having 'all the essentials for a popular poem—a fine story, swiftness of narration, richness of colouring, typical character, a hero for its centre'. Individual passion and personality are notably absent. Yeats describes Joyce's Deirdre as having been 'as simple as children who had never been to school' and in an earlier essay on Joyce's ballads remarked that 'the aim of a ballad writer is not character or passion—the story is everything with him'. Yeats praised Joyce, as reteller of ancient legends and as a creator of ballads, for having been 'the poet of all the external things that apertain to the barbaric earth . . . he was in no way a singer, also, of man's inner nature of the vague *desires,* though it takes from his stature as a poet, makes him so much the dearer to many worn with modern unrest.'[9] Three months later Yeats published an essay on James Clarence Mangan which depicted Mangan as a man over-whelmed and defeated by the intensity of his passions and as a poet whose poems expressed 'passionate self-abandonment' rather than 'the thoughts of normal mankind'.[10] When Yeats wanted to write 'popular poetry' in the late 1880s, the events recorded in folklore and the impersonality of what he then be-lieved to be true, folk ballads seemed to offer the means. The early poems which Yeats did write about ancient Irish heroes lamented the disappearance of heroic personality. Oisin, King Goll and Cuchulain in Yeats's early poems were not especially energetic or heroic; Oisin and Cuchulain's became more and more dynamic only in later revisions which Yeats made under the

F*

influence of his new conceptions about ancient Irish heroes and about the place of personality in literature.

Yeats later recalled in his essay 'What is "Popular Poetry"?' that for a time the ballads by Allingham and Ferguson based on the beliefs and the events recorded in oral tradition had seemed an alternative to the political opinions of Young Ireland poetry.[11] Clearly, in 1886 and 1887, he had not yet experienced the intensely personal and passionate peasant songs which Douglas Hyde published in 1893 in *Love Songs of Connacht*. In the meantime he wrote impersonal ballads such as 'The Ballad of Father O'Hart' and 'The Ballad of Father Gilligan' in imitation of Ferguson and Allingham in which he subordinated character to event. Even in his earliest poetry, written before he sought an Irish subject matter based on folklore, Yeats had conceived of poetry as providing a refuge from the unrest of the world of passion and action. Richard Ellmann has described one of the unpublished poems Yeats wrote in the early 1880s: 'He began an epic on Sir Roland in Spenserian stanzas and set forth his theories in rhyme. The poet should deal commonly, harmoniously, and sadly with love, not passionately with war and suffering. He should load his rhymes with metaphor so that they would move slowly with their precious freight.'[12] Yeats later described his 'first thought of what a long poem should be' in a letter to Katharine Tynan as follows: 'I thought of it as a region into which one should wander from the cares of life. The characters were to be no more real than the shadows that people the Howth thicket.'[13]

Yeats's involvement with Irish folklore becomes all the more significant when it is considered in light of Yeats's early theories about personality and passion in literature. Although he was undeniably attracted to the passionate personalities of Ferguson's ancient heroic characters, Yeats turned to the beliefs and legends of the peasantry for his first Irish subjects. His first anthology of Irish folklore, *Fairy and Folk Tales of the Irish Peasantry*, had been composed chiefly of peasant beliefs and legends about the fairies. But even in that 1888 anthology the nature of the peasant characters had been an important criterion in his selection of materials. His growing interest in personality is even more apparent in the passionate, often heroic personalities of the peasants in *Representative Irish Tales*. The visionary peasantry of *Fairy and Folk Tales* return in 1893 in *The Celtic Twilight* where their visionary powers and beliefs are characterised by the same energy and extravagance that had marked the lives and character of the peasants who peopled *Representative Irish Tales.* But the personalities of Yeats's peasant informants and other characters in *The Celtic Twilight* were as much his focus as were their visions and beliefs. Yeats's study of previously collected Irish folklore, nineteenth-century Anglo-Irish fiction and oral traditions around Sligo obviously encouraged and provided materials for his fascination with personality. However, the anglicisation of the Irish peasantry which became more and more apparent to him as he compiled materials for *Representative Irish Tales* and *The Celtic Twilight* encouraged him to look elsewhere for the quintessential Irish personality.

The ancient Irish heroes eventually replaced the peasantry as a personification of energy and extravagance, passion and heroism, as is evident in the materials concerning ancient Irish heroes which Yeats added to *The Celtic Twilight* in 1902. However, Yeats's involvement with another lesser known area of Irish folklore—an early interest which has been virtually ignored by Yeats scholars—provided a vital link between his interest in the peasants and his interest in ancient heroes. Between 1890 and 1893 he was actively involved in the preparation of an anthology of traditional lore about duellists, rogues and outlaws for T. Fisher Unwin's 'Adventure Series' which was to be entitled *Irish Adventurers.* Yeats wrote to Katharine Tynan on 5 July 1890, 'I have been in the Museum much lately reading up the duellists and outlaws for this Unwin book—going through contemporary and chap-book records. Whether the book comes off or no, they will serve me for articles at any rate.' In September 1890 he again wrote of the project to her : 'I am also editing, or trying to edit, a book of Irish Adventures for Unwin. If my introduction pleases him I am to get twenty pounds; if not five pounds. Whether it will please him I do not know. I am to give in it "A vivid view of Irish Life in the eighteenth century" and am quite new to historical writing.'[14] Yeats solved both his ignorance and dislike of 'historical writing' by gathering materials which were more legendary than historical as his reference to going through chapbooks indicates.

Yeats obviously expended a great deal of time and effort on

the introduction. In June 1891 he wrote to John O'Leary: 'I want to get to Dublin not merely to see you and other good friends but to have some talk with knowledgeable folk about my essay on Ireland in the eighteenth century for Unwin's Adventure Series.' He wrote to Katharine Tynan in July 1891 : 'I have likewise the Introduction to those wretched "Irish Adventures" waiting writing.'[15] In September 1891 he published an essay entitled 'A Reckless Century: Irish Rakes and Duellists' based on the materials he was assembling for *Irish Adventurers*.[16] This essay was not the introduction to the projected anthology because on 16 October 1892 he wrote to John O'Leary from Sligo where, according to Allan Wade, he had continued to work on the anthology throughout the summer of 1892 : 'I have almost finished my introduction to the volume of "Irish Adventures".' Later that month he wrote to his friend Edward Garnett, who was Unwin's reader : 'I shall finish my introduction to the "Irish Adventurers" tomorrow and post it to you. I hope the thing will do. It is I think fresh and has a little novel information in it.'[17]

Yeats's doubts about his introduction pleasing Garnett and his comment that it contained 'novel information' were evidently justified. Garnett's reader's report, now in the Berg Collection of the New York Public Library, preserves Garnett's reaction and provides a clue to the nature of Yeats's introduction : 'Yeats's Introduction is very original, very poetic and quite in his best vein. It is dreamy and impressionistic, but it has very little to do with the subject matter we count on. What to do with it?'[18] Yeats obviously had discarded any earlier intention to attempt 'historical writing'. Garnett, at the end of his reader's report, answered his own rhetorical question about what to do with Yeats's introduction : 'Yeats's Preface can be preserved as a sort of flying Foreword. . . . And he might or he might not, write a biographical introduction.' Unfortunately, Fisher Unwin never published Yeats's *Irish Adventurers* and all traces of Yeats's work, except for his 1891 essay on rakes and duellists, Garnett's reader's report and references to the project in Yeats's letters, have disappeared. In a letter to Garnett, which Wade tentatively dates November 1892, Yeats wrote 'Thank you for good offices in the matter of Adventure volume.' Evidently the project was still underway in early 1893 because Yeats, in a letter which Wade dates simply '1893' but places with letters written early that year, referred to having sent Garnett 'part of the contents of "The Adventurer volume" ' and went on to list the contents.[19] After that there is no further mention of the project in Yeats's letters. *Irish Adventurers* was probably a casualty of Yeats's unsuccessful battle with Sir Charles Gavan Duffy for control of 'The New Irish Library' series which Fisher Unwin was to publish.

Although *Irish Adventurers* was never actually published, Yeats's compilation of it reveals his developing attitudes about Irish folklore and the nature of the heroic personality. *Irish Adventurers,* although an anthology of written sources, was indeed another collection of what can legitimately be called folklore. Oral and written accounts of the legendary exploits of Irish adventurers—be they duellists, rakes or outlaws—were frequent in nineteenth-century folklore. Folklorists today recognise that oral traditions remain folklore even when transmitted in printed form. As Kevin Danaher has argued in a recent essay entitled 'Oral Tradition and the Printed Word', Irish oral tradition during the past century and a half was 'deeply influenced by the written word' and such an 'intimate connection' existed between oral tradition and the printed word 'that we can no longer discount its relevance in the study of any aspect of folk life and tradition'.

> Half the population in the early nineteenth century could read English. That they did is shown by the volume of traffic in printed books. A work published in 1818 estimates the number of books sold annually in Ireland at 300,000; these were for the most part small cheap books, 'chapbooks' which were carried throughout the country by pedlars as well as being sold in the towns . . . Since the reading aloud of material in English was at least as popular as the reading of material in Irish, the written word was also available to the illiterate.[20]

Yeats's own letters acknowledge that he was using chapbooks as a source for materials, and the 'contemporary records' which he also referred to using were just as likely to have recorded oral traditions as historical fact. Patrick Dowling in *The Hedge Schools of Ireland* discusses the great popularity among the peasantry of the cheap reprints issued at Dublin, Limerick and Cork known as the 'Burton Books' or 'sixpenny books'. Dowling quotes a list of typical books which Hely Dutton in *A Statistical*

Survey of the County of Clare (1808) observed in use in County Clare: With the exception of 'a few universal spelling books', the 'general cottage classics' were:

> *History of Seven Champions of Christendom*
> *Irish Rogues and Rapparees*
> *Freney, a notorious robber*
> *The Most Celebrated Pirates*
> *Jack the Bachelor, a noted smuggler*
> *Fair Rosamund and Jane Shore, two prostitutes*
> *History of Witches and Apparitions*[21]

Yeats's book on Irish Adventurers, as outlined in his letter to Edward Garnett in 1893, was to have contained six sections—one of which was entitled 'Freney the Robber', another 'Rogues and Rapparees'. Thackeray, in Chapter Fifteen of his *Irish Sketch-Book*, recalled purchasing a copy of the popular Freney autobiography for threepence in Ireland.

Many of the sources Yeats drew upon when compiling *Fairy and Folk Tales of the Irish Peasantry* alluded to the popularity of such chapbooks among the peasantry. According to an article on 'Irish Literature' in the *Dublin and London Magazine* of August 1825, 'The number of "sixpenny" or "Burton" books annually sold, was formerly immense. Four booksellers in Dublin used to deal exclusively in them, and one had four presses constantly employed, and published on an average fifty thousand annually; besides these there were presses in Cork and Limerick employed on no other work. It was supposed that in this way three hundred thousand were every year printed and circulated.'[22] Patrick Kennedy mentioned in *Legendary Fictions of the Irish Celts* that the chapbook *The Adventures of Irish Rogues and Rapparees* was exceedingly popular among the peasantry. Sir William Wilde in *Irish Popular Superstitions* described a peasant named Paddy Welsh at great length and remarked of him: 'His readings were confined to "Raymond the Fox", "The Irish Rogues and Rapparees", "Moll Flanders", "The History of Freney the Robber", and "The Battle of Aughrim".'[23]

William Carleton's fiction frequently referred to the popularity of chapbooks about rogues and outlaws among the peasantry. Carleton even wrote a short melodramatic and sentimental novel loosely based on the life of a famous seventeenth-century Armagh outlaw, *Redmond Count O'Hanlon, The Irish Rapparee* (1862). Yeats himself in the early versions of his stories about Red Hanrahan referred several times to Hanrahan owning a copy of a reading-book used by him in his hedge-school, and called *The Lives of Celebrated Rogues and Rapparees'*. John Edward Walsh in *Ireland Sixty Years Ago* (1847), Yeats's source for much of his material in his essay on Irish rakes and duellists, described how Freney's autobiography was a 'cottage classic' with which children were taught to read towards the end of the eighteenth century.[24]

Such written traditions were inseparable from oral tales and ballads about Freney and other rogue heroes. Crofton Croker remarked in *Researches in the South of Ireland* that it was common 'to hear the adventures and escapes of highwaymen and outlaws recited by the lower orders with the greatest minuteness, and dwelt on with surprising fondness'.[25] Georges-Denis Zimmermann, in his comprehensive study of *Songs of Irish Rebellion: Political Street Ballads and Rebel Songs 1780–1900,* has described the popularity and significance of the outlaw-hero in Irish oral tradition:

> One of the typical characters was the gallant outlaw who scorns the police and sympathises with the poor, the highwayman whose daring deeds, hairbreadth escapes and high spirits at the moment of death fascinated the popular audience. The 'noble bandits' were dear to the people mainly for romantic reasons, as in other countries, but in Ireland they were more than just heroes of adventure stories or charming bad men. The social background of their exploits should not be underestimated. These outlaws who 'robbed the rich and helped the poor' and defiantly refused to surrender and to 'work for the government' were *also* heroic symbols of freedom, of resistance to a law which was called injustice by many.[26]

Such outlaws were frequently referred to as 'tories' or 'rapparees'. 'Tories' had been a generic term for Irish outlaws since the time of the Desmond rebellion during the reign of Queen Elizabeth, and the term had acquired even more patriotic overtones when it was applied to the seventeenth-century Irish, of aristocratic as well as peasant origin, who took shelter in the woods and mountains and waged a kind of guerilla war on the English who had taken their lands. Likewise, the term 'rapparee' had originally been applied to the Irish who had become outlaws after their defeat in the Jacobite and Williamite wars. In his study, *Irish Tories, Rapparees and Robbers*, John G. Marshall concluded that after the first quarter of the eighteenth century most so-called tories and rapparees were little more than common outlaws.[27] Nevertheless, they still enjoyed the same admiration from the peasantry which their more patriotic and chivalric predecessors had earned. The exploits of Irish outlaws, whether based on patriotic or selfish motivations, became a nationalistic symbol. For example, in 1833 a reader wrote a letter to the editor of the *Dublin Penny Journal* about how reading 'Irish Rogues and Rapparees' had given him 'my early fostered and long-matured hatred of tyranny'.[28] Charles Gavan Duffy reprinted a peasant ballad of 1691 entitled 'The Rapparees' in *Ballad Poetry of Ireland* (1886). The ballad's references to 'the Master's son' having become 'an outlawed man . . . riding on the hills' and its last stanza typify the peasantry's conception of a 'rapparee':

> Now Sassanach and Cromweller, take heed of what I say—
> Keep down your black and angry looks that scorn us night
>   and day;
> For there's a just and wrathful Judge that every action sees,
> And He'll make strong to right our wrong the faithful
>   Rapparees!
> The men who rode by Sarsfield's side, the roving Rap-
>   parees![29]

Yeats's inclusion of Freney and other rogues and rapparees in *Irish Adventurers* thus represented a major element in the written and oral literature of the nineteenth-century peasantry. However, Yeats did not only intend to include outlaw heroes. His book was also to include sections about various eighteenth-century duellists and rakes. Yeats's letter to Edward Garnett describing the contents read as follows:

> My dear Garnett, I sent you from Dublin part of the contents of 'The Adventurer volume'. You have somewhere a list of the total contents. It was somewhat as follows

Introduction
1 Fighting Fitzgerald
2 Tiger Roche
3 ———Maguire (British Museum)
4 Freeney the Robber
5 Rogues and Rapparees
6 Michael Dwyer

I have sent you no 1, no 2, no 4, no 5—3 and 6 will have to be got at Unwin's expense—at least 3 will. 6 I could get probably.[30]

Garnett's reader's report reflects a slightly different list of contents: two chapters about Col. Blood, a chapter about Tiger Roche, another about G. R. Fitzgerald and a final section about Freney and other Irish highwaymen. Yeats's letter had said the content was 'somewhat as follows' so he had probably merely forgotten to list Col. Blood. Three chapters indicated in Yeats's letter—Maguire, Rogues and Rapparees, and Michael Dwyer —are not specifically mentioned in Garnett's reader's report. However, the chapter about 'Irish highwaymen' to which Garnett refers is probably the same one Yeats referred to as 'Rogues and Rapparees'. Yeats had indicated in his letter that Unwin would have to procure the materials about Maguire and Michael Dwyer at his own expense and, according to Garnett's report, Unwin had obviously not done so.

On the basis of information provided by Yeats's letter and Garnett's report, the contents of *Irish Adventurers* can be summarised as follows: Col. Blood; Tiger Roche; G. R. 'Fighting' Fitzgerald; Bryan Maguire; Freney and other Irish highwaymen, rogues and rapparees; Michael Dwyer.

Thomas Blood (1618?-1680), according to the *Dictionary of National Biography* (1908), was an adventurer better known as 'Col. Blood'. He was the son of a blacksmith and was probably born in Ireland. When the lands in Ireland he had acquired during Cromwellian times were threatened by the Restoration he joined with insurrectionists who plotted to seize Dublin Castle. In 1663 his plot to kidnap the Lord-Lieutenant, James Butler, Duke of Ormonde, failed because of an informer. Most of his cohorts were captured but Blood escaped to the mountains where he was assisted in his attempts to rescue them by native

Irish and old Cromwellians. Blood assumed various disguises and spent time in England and Holland before returning to Ireland. Around 1670 he was wounded in an attempt to rescue his friend Capt. Mason from a guard of eight troopers. Angry at the Duke of Ormonde's punishments of his fellow conspirators, Blood captured Ormonde with the intention of hanging him but did not. Blood's attempt to steal the Crown Jewels in 1671 ultimately led to his regaining his Irish estates. When Blood and his cohorts were captured after stealing the jewels his audacity saved him. He refused to confess to anyone except King Charles, who, it turned out, was desirous to see so bold a ruffian and granted him an audience. Blood confessed his part in the capture of Ormonde and obtained his forfeited Irish estates. Shortly thereafter, Blood fell out with his protector, the Duke of Buckingham. Blood was charged with slander and fined £10,000 in damages for having falsely accused Buckingham of sodomy. He died two weeks later but reportedly was 'still strong in spirit'. When it was rumoured he had not really died, his body was exhumed. His notorious exploits were celebrated legends both during and after his life.

According to Garnett's report, Yeats devoted two separate chapters to Blood. The first, which Garnett referred to as 'Eminent Passages in the Life of Col. Blood', was probably concerned with several of Blood's adventures. Garnett said of it, 'a splendid narrative and may be printed verbatim'. The 'contemporary record' upon which Yeats based this first chapter about Blood was very likely an account, supposedly written by Blood himself and published in 1680, entitled *Remarks on the life and death of the fam'd Mr. Blood; giving an account of his plot in Ireland, to surprize Dublin Castle, Rescue of Capt. Mason, Attempt on Duke of Ormond.* However, Garnett recommended that the second chapter about Blood, 'The Narrative of Col. Blood', be omitted: 'This is simply a confused account of a very unpleasant affair Blood was mixed up in, and it is really unfit to print.' Yeats's title for this section indicates he based it on *The Narrative of Col. Thomas Blood*, the subtitle of which reads: 'concerning the design reported to be lately laid against the life and honour of his Grace George Duke of Buckingham. Wherein Col Blood is charged to have conspired with Maurice Hickey, Philip le Mar, and several others, to suborm the testimony of

Samuel Ryther and Philemon Coddan to swear Buggery against the said Duke.' This book, published in London in 1680, claimed to give 'an extremely detailed, cloak-and-dagger account of an attempt to pin a charge of heterosexual sodomy on the Duke' and declared that 'Col. Blood is more usually associated with an attempt to steal the Crown Jewels.' The book, and presumably Yeats's chapter, described how Blood 'with several others conspired to rob the Duke of his honour and his reputation and his life, upon a presumption of committing Sodomy with one Sarah Harwood'.[31] Supposedly Blood bribed the Duke's servants to swear they heard Sarah Harwood declare such things against the Duke. Little wonder, considering the nature of the slander which Blood supposedly instigated, that Garnett found it 'unpleasant' and 'unfit to print'.

Yeats had been charged by Unwin to give a 'vivid view of life in the eighteenth century'. Blood's exploits were certainly vivid, although they had occurred in the seventeenth rather than the eighteenth century. Yeats obviously conceived the subject 'Irish Adventurers' to transcend the eighteenth century. He was also obviously recording history in terms of legend and anecdote rather than the personalities and events of national significance recorded in history books. His account in the first section of his *Autobiography* of the numerous local legends he heard while growing up in Sligo demonstrates he learned early that it was the extravagant deed, even when inconsequential or sordid, and the eccentric personality which survived in folk legend that often outlasted what history books chose to record. Even the oral traditions within his own family attested to that fact:

There had been among our ancestors a King's County soldier, one of Marlborough's generals, and when his nephew came to dine he gave him boiled pork, and when the nephew said he disliked boiled pork he had asked him to dine again and promised him something he would like better. However, he gave him boiled pork again and the nephew took the hint in silence. The other day as I was coming home from America, I met one of his descendants whose family has not another discoverable link with ours, and he too knew the boiled pork story and nothing else. We have the General's portrait, and he looks very fine in his armour and his long curly wig, and underneath it, after his name are many honours that have left no tradition among us.[32]

Yeats's second adventurer, 'Tiger Roche', as he was called, was the younger son of an old aristocratic Norman family and had been born in Dublin in 1729. John Edward Walsh had devoted an entire chapter in *Ireland Sixty Years Ago*, Yeats's source for some materials in his essay on Irish rakes and duellists, to Roche whom he said was especially celebrated 'for unbridled indulgence and fierce passions'. Edward Garnett's report indicated that Yeats's piece on Roche was an article of three thousand words from the *Dublin University Magazine*; however, no such article ever appeared in the *Dublin University Magazine*. Yeats's probable source was thus Walsh's chapter on Tiger Roche which was approximately three thousand words in length.[33] Walsh's account of Roche can be summarised as follows : Roche received the finest education Dublin could offer and was so highly skilled in gentlemanly accomplishments that Lord Chesterfield, then Lord Lieutenant of Ireland, offered him gratuitously a commission in the army. Roche declined because his friends convinced him he could do better. Unfortunately he idled the next several years away by indulging in 'all the outrages and excesses which then disgraced Dublin'. One night, after he and his associates attacked and killed a watchman who had attempted to quell a riot they had excited, he escaped to America where he joined one of the provincial regiments. He soon distinguished himself for the same fierce and cruel qualities which supposedly characterised the Indians. At the height of his reputation for fearlessness and spirit, he was accused and convicted of a false charge of robbery. According to Walsh, Roche was so angered by his disgrace that :

> Roche immediately challenged the officer who had prosecuted him. He refused, however, to meet him, on the pretext that he was a degraded man, and no longer entitled to the rank and consideration of a gentleman. Stung to madness, and no longer master of himself, he . . . insulted the officer in the grossest terms, and . . . attacked the corporal with his naked sword, declaring his intention to kill him on the spot. The man with difficulty defended his life, till his companions sprung upon Roche and disarmed him. Though deprived of

his weapon, he did not desist from his intention; crouching down like an Indian foe, he suddenly sprung, like Rhoderick Dhu, at his antagonist, and fastened on his throat with his teeth, and before he could be disengaged nearly strangled him, dragging away a mouthful of flesh, which, in the true Indian spirit, he afterwards said, was 'the sweetest morsel he had ever tasted'. From the fierce and savage character he displayed on this occasion, he obtained the appellation of 'Tiger', an affix which was ever after joined to his name.

A few days later when the English army advanced to Ticonderoga, Roche was left behind in the wilderness but soon joined up with a party of friendly Indians and 'by extraordinary exertions and forced marches' he reached the fortress. Once there he distinguished himself by his courage and military abilities and received four serious wounds. But, according to Walsh, 'the stain of robbery was upon him, and no services, however brilliant, could obliterate it.' Roche suffered 'incredible afflictions from pain, poverty, and sickness' in New York but his indomitable spirit persevered and he eventually reached England in 1785 where he continued to avenge his honour with incredible diligence and ferocity.

After several duels and wounds, his name was cleared unexpectedly when the real robber confessed on his death bed. He was lionised and soon returned in triumph to Dublin where he delighted in recounting his now legendary adventures and hairbreadth escapes. Soon after his return he heroically rescued a gentleman and his two children as they were being attacked by some of the so-called 'pinkindindies' who roamed the streets of Dublin in those days. Roche subsequently formed a group of fellow officers and patrolled the dangerous streets of Dublin at night. His extravagant habits soon brought him to an English debtor's prison where 'his mind appears to be completely broken down, and the intrepid and daring courage, which had sustained him in so remarkable a manner through all the vicissitudes of his former life, seemed to be totally exhausted.' He submitted to the indignities and insults he underwent while in prison with either patience or tears. An unexpected inheritance suddenly released him from prison : 'With his change of fortune a change of disposition came over him; and in proportion as he had shown an abject spirit in confinement, he now exhibited even a still more arrogant and irritable temper than he had ever before displayed.' The contradictions within his character continued to display themselves : he humanely interceded on behalf of two ruffians who were apprehended when attacking him, but remorselessly dissipated the entire fortune of a young heiress he married. When a 'sudden and unaccountable fit of terror' seized him in a confrontation with another officer on board a ship bound for India, he was expelled from the officer's table. When the officer was mysteriously and ferociously murdered, Roche was accused. He was acquitted by Dutch authorities at the Cape and at a later trial in England. Disgraced again, he retired from England to India and disappeared from public view.

Edward Garnett declared the Roche material 'unfit to be printed' and judged it 'rather hearsay'. The fundamentally oral and legendary nature of Yeats's chapter on Roche was obviously too much 'hearsay' and not enough historical fact for Garnett who shared Yeats's passion for spiritualism but not his enthusiasm for folklore. Nor did Garnett evidently care for the qualities for which legend had commemorated Roche. Roche was indeed a personality whose passions at times overwhelmed him. Yet the passion and intensity of his life and personality obviously appealed to Yeats who, of course, became increasingly fascinated with dual personalities such as Roche's. Walsh concluded his chapter on Roche with a comment on Irish character and on Roche which echoed many similar nineteenth-century statements on Irish character :

A writer of the last century, in speaking of the Irish character, concludes with this remark :—'In short, if they are good, you will scarcely meet a better : if bad, you will seldom find a worse.' These extremes were frequently mixed in the same person. Roche, at different periods, displayed them. At one time, an admirable spirit, great humanity, and unbounded generosity; at another, abject cowardice, ferocity, treachery, and brutal selfishness. The vicissitudes of his fortune were as variable as his character : at times he was exposed to the foulest charges, and narrowly escaped ignominious punishment; at others he was the object of universal esteem and admiration.

Yeats's third Irish adventurer, George Robert Fitzgerald, 'Fighting Fitzgerald', possessed an inherently contradictory personality such as Roche's. According to Walsh, Fitzgerald's career and personality represented 'a characteristic sample of the spirit of the times . . . in the strange and almost incompatible traits of character; his alternate gentleness and ferocity, love of justice, and violation of all law; his lenity and cruelty, patient endurance of wrong, yet perpetration of foul and atrocious murders'. Walsh claimed Fitzgerald's wild Irish character was less an anomaly because he was from Connacht—'on the remote shores of the Atlantic, seldom visited by strangers, having little intercourse with England, and either generally ignorant of its laws, or, from longer impunity, setting them altogether at defiance'.[34] Walsh refers his readers who wished more information about Fitzgerald to another volume, 'Fighting Fitzgerald', in the series of which his book was a part. He is evidently referring to a reprint of an anonymous book entitled *The Life and Times of G. R. Fitzgerald, commonly called Fighting Fitzgerald* which was originally published in 1787. This was evidently Yeats's source because Garnett refers to Yeats's materials on G. R. Fitzgerald as 'a reprint' of 'G. R. Fitzgerald. Life and Times. Dublin '42'. The *Dublin University Magazine* had reprinted this account of Fitzgerald from July to October 1840 as part of a series entitled 'Connaught Legends'. The editors claimed that the purpose of the reprint was 'to exhibit the diseased state of society, in the province of Ireland, previous to the Union'.[35] Walsh had written *Ireland Sixty Years Ago* with a similar purpose in mind : to show how things were before the Irish began to learn from the English about 'propriety and decency, peace and good order'. Yeats, of course, admired Col. Blood, Tiger Roche and Fighting Fitzgerald because their adventures represented a passionate Irish character which English gentility and culture had never quite succeeded in civilising. Blood, the son of a blacksmith; Roche, the scion of an old Norman family; and Fitzgerald, a descendant of a branch of an old Desmond family which had been transplanted to Connaught in 1641, all represented an old Irish stock who could never assimilate the ways of the English gentry.

George Robert Fitzgerald (1748-1786) was born in County Mayo and, according to *The Life and Times of G. R. Fitzgerald,*

'This insolent oppressor—this lawless rioter—this reckless duellist
—this bold, calculating murderer—could not have lived and
moved and had his horrid being in any other place, or under
any other circumstances than in Ireland before the close of the
eighteenth century.'[36] Fitzgerald was noted for his both noble
and ignoble traits. In appearance he was the epitome of an ele-
gant gentleman. He supported the legislative independence of
Ireland and instituted useful agricultural improvements on his
Mayo estates where he lived most of his life and where he was
a favourite with his tenantry in a time when cruel absentee
landlords were all too frequently the rule elsewhere in Ireland.[37]
But neither his family's Protestantism nor his Eton education
succeeded in controlling his wild Irish nature. Even his some-
what gallant deeds often demonstrated a certain barbarism. Once
he rode over to Westport House, where he took a pot-shot at
Denis Browne, and then killed the Brownes' giant wolfhound
and left a note with the servants which declared that until Lord
Altamont showed more charity to the poor, who up until now
had only come to his doorway to be barked at and bitten by
the overfed monster he had just shot (which ate all the meat due
to them), he could not allow any such beast to be kept at West-
port.

Most of Fitzgerald's bizarre behaviour was completely devoid
of noble motive and displayed only his incredible arrogance and
ferocity. When someone once dared to insult him for a wager
and approached him muttering, 'I smell an Irishman!', Fitz-
gerald reportedly replied, 'You shall never smell another!' and
took up a knife and cut off his challenger's nose. He fought his
first duel at sixteen and hundreds thereafter. He continually
fought with his fellow Mayo gentry whom he detested.
In Dublin when the mood took him to fight, he would
strike out at people or snatch at their rings and watches. Once
he shot off a man's wig. When challenges to duels were not
frequent enough to suit him, he would resort to standing in the
middle of a narrow street crossing and wait for someone of
promising fighting material to jog him so that he could demand
immediate satisfaction. While visiting the court of Louise XV
at Versailles, Fitzgerald was discovered using loaded dice and
during a royal hunt confounded court etiquette by riding in
front of the royal party and bringing the stag to bay, a privilege

exclusively reserved for the king. He courted and married the rich and beautiful Jane Conolly, a sister of Thomas Conolly of Castletown House. But she soon refused to live with him because of his debts and wild ways. He reportedly had many personal 'eccentricities', including 'a passion for strange pets; and he kept, for his own amusement, and no doubt to terrify others, bears, foxes, and foreign ferocious dogs.'[38]

If Fitzgerald's treatment of his father is taken as typical of his treatment of his family, his wife was wise to leave him. He continually quarrelled with his father about money and once when his father refused to change his will, Fitzgerald knocked out three of his teeth. On another celebrated occasion he manacled his father to a pet bear for an entire day and then locked him up in a cave on the grounds of his estate. Fitzgerald was fined and sentenced to two years' imprisonment after his brother had him charged with 'extreme cruelty'. But Fitzgerald was released when the local militia, which he had organised because of the threatened French invasion and which under his leadership had become the terror of the neighbourhood, rioted in front of the jail. Furious with his father, he abducted him to an isolated island and threatened to remain there until they both starved unless his father dropped all charges. His father agreed, only to change his mind after they returned to the mainland. Fitzgerald, who appeared in court dressed as a beggar except for the diamond band worth fifteen hundred pounds stuck in his ragged hat, was convicted but was able to obtain a quick release from prison through influential relatives.

When Fitzgerald returned to Mayo he found a new enemy in a Patrick McDonnell who had been elected as Colonel of the Mayo Legion of Volunteers, a position that Fitzgerald coveted for himself. He reportedly arranged to have McDonnell arrested and shot while trying to escape. Fitzgerald, only thirty-eight years old, was convicted and hanged in June 1786. But even his execution was bizarre. On the day of his execution he drank a bottle of port and appeared perfectly composed when he approached the gallows. He hurled himself from the gallows but the rope broke in two and he fell to the ground. By the time a new rope was prepared some hours later, Fitzgerald had sobered up and lost his nerve. According to local legend, the sheriff had a reprieve in his pocket when he executed Fitzgerald.

Fitzgerald's character and exploits were legendary in Mayo both before and after his death where he was locally referred to as 'mad Fitzgerald'. His passionate, solitary nature obviously fascinated Yeats. Garnett found the chapter on Fitzgerald acceptable, but suggested the *Dictionary of National Biography* be consulted concerning some new facts which had come to light concerning Fitzgerald since the narrative of his *Life and Times* had been published the year after his death. Here again Garnett preferred historical facts to any purely legendary accounts. The *Dictionary of National Biography* presented the bare facts of Fitzgerald's life and few of the bizarre anecdotes which abounded in *The Life and Times of G. R. Fitzgerald* whose author had obviously recorded all the oral legends and anecdotes about Fitzgerald with little concern for their factual accuracy. That anonymous author concluded his account of Fitzgerald with an assessment quite similar to Walsh's summary of Tiger Roche's personality. In his opinion, Fitzgerald's 'courage was of a very uncertain character, for though he was often known to show great bravery and subsequent generosity in duels and rencontres, yet on some occasions he acted a sly, scheming, and over-reaching part, would take a dirty advantage, and, as the phrase is, show the white feather.'[39]

While a child Yeats experienced firsthand a 'brawling squireen' near Sligo who represented a degenerate echo of the tradition of Fighting Fitzgerald. In his *Autobiography* he recalled:

Sometimes I would ride to Castle Dargan, where lived a brawling squireen, married to one of my Middleton cousins . . . It was, I daresay, the last household where I could have found the reckless Ireland of a hundred years ago in final degradation. . . . He himself, with a reeling imagination, knew not where to find a spur for the heavy hours. The first day I came there he gave my cousin a revolver . . . and to show it off, or his own shooting, he shot a passing chicken; and half an hour later . . . he fired at or over an old countryman. . . . Once he had asked a timid aunt of mine if she would like to see his last new pet, and thereupon had marched a racehorse in through the hall door and round the dining room table. And once she came down to a bare table because he had thought it a good joke to open the window and let his harriers eat the breakfast. There was a current story, too, of his shooting, in the pride of his marksmanship, at his own door with a Martini-Henry rifle till he had shot the knocker off.[40]

The Adventurer listed in Yeats's letter of 1893 as '———— Maguire' was undoubtedly Brian Maguire. Yeats had described Brian Maguire in his essay on Irish rakes and duellists in 1891 :

> The bragadocio [sic] of Brian Maguire—huge, whiskered bully that he was—standing at a narrow crossing and daring the passerby to jostle him, is not so pleasant an object even though his skill was so great that he always rang his bell with a bullet and could snuff a candle held in his wife's hand with a pistol shot; nor does the statement of a certain contemporary pamphleteer that his ancestors were once kings in Ireland, but that 'the infamous invader had been impoverishing Mr Maguire's for centuries', make us any the more anxious to see his like again.[41]

The contemporary pamphlet to which Yeats alludes in this article was probably the source about Maguire which he said Unwin was to procure at his own expense at the British Museum. As mentioned earlier, Yeats had written to Katharine Tynan in 1890 that he was assembling materials for the Irish adventurers book from chapbooks and 'contemporary records' at the museum. The same contemporary pamphlet was probably Walsh's source for his account of Maguire in *Ireland Sixty Years Ago*. In addition to eccentricities Yeats summarised in the sentence about Maguire quoted above, Walsh described the following :

> He assumed on all occasions a truculent and menacing aspect. He had been in the army serving abroad, and, it was said, dismissed the service. He availed himself of his military character, and appeared occasionally in the streets in a gaudy glittering uniform, armed with a sword, saying it was the uniform of his corps. When thus accoutred he strolled through the streets, looking round on all that passed with a haughty contempt. His ancestors were among the reguli of Ireland, and one of them was a distinguished Irish leader in 1640. He therefore assumed the port and bearing which he thought became the son of an Irish king. The streets were formerly more encumbered with dirt than they are now, and the only

mode of passing from one side to the other was by a narrow crossing through mud heaped up at each side. It was Bryan's glory to take sole possession of one of these, and to be seen with his arms folded across his ample chest, stalking along in solitary magnificence. Any unfortunate wayfarer who met him on the path was sure to be hurled into the heap of mud at one side of it.

This proud solitary descendant of Irish kings was as much at odds with anglicised and dirty Dublin, as Col. Blood, Tiger Roche and Fighting Fitzgerald had been with English gentility and social order. But in Maguire, whom Walsh says was of a 'more recent period' than other rakes and duellists, the titanic Irish personality has degenerated into a mere urban bully and rather pathetic eccentric. According to Walsh, he was reduced to the following activity to vent his passions :

> Another of his royal habits was the mode of passing his time. He was seen for whole days leaning out his window, and amusing himself with annoying the passengers. When one went by whom he thought a fit subject, he threw down on him some rubbish or dirt, to attract his notice, and when the man looked up, he spat in his face. If he made any expostulation Bryan crossed his arms, and presenting a pistol in each hand, invited him up to his room, declaring he would give him satisfaction there, and his choice of the pistols.[42]

Maguire's ancient Irish blood and passions obviously found no suitable outlet in eighteenth-century Dublin.

Although Maguire's actions lacked the heroic dimensions of those of Blood, Roche and Fitzgerald, his eccentric behaviour too was the very stuff of which folk legends have always been made. Indeed, Sir William Wilde mentioned both Maguire's duelling and Fitzgerald's wild deeds in *Irish Popular Superstitions*.[43] All of Yeats's adventurers, whether rakes or rapparees, represented a combination of heroic and anti-heroic traits. Such personalities were common to many folk heroes among the nineteenth-century peasantry. James MacKillop, in his essay on 'Finn Mac Cool : The Hero and the Anti-Hero in Irish Folk Tradition' demonstrates that 'an unheroic or anti-heroic Finn existed side by side with the hero' in oral tradition among a peasantry who enjoyed seeing Finn as simultaneously crafty as well as brave, vindictive as well as generous.[44] Yeats, of course, had included such a legend about a simultaneously and anti-heroic Finn in *Fairy and Folk Tales.* Standish O'Grady and William Carleton, two of Yeats's major influences on the use and significance of Irish folklore, also offered comments which illuminate the inherently antithetical personalities of Yeats's rogue heroes in *Irish Adventurers.* O'Grady remarked in his *History of Ireland* that 'Heroes expand into giants, and dwindle into goblins, or fling aside the heroic form and gambol as buffoons. . . .'[45] The rakes in Yeats's collection of Irish adventurers illustrate comments which William Carleton made about their character in an essay entitled 'The Irish Rake'. According to Carleton, 'the Irish rake has never been properly described because of the difficulty of blending so many antithetical traits of temper and modes of life into one harmonious picture'; he was 'composed of many traits which singly would make up the personality of an ordinary man . . . a kind of proteus'.[46] In Carleton's estimation, the Irish rake was at once an elegant ladies' man and a buffoon, all the while as mysterious as the Wandering Jew whose background was unknown. Carleton also mentioned that the rake seemingly never died because no one ever hears of his death. Indeed, it had been rumoured that Col. Blood had never really died, Roche had simply disappeared from view in India, and Walsh remarked of Maguire that 'after a time Bryan disappeared from Dublin.'

The fifth subject in Yeats's *Irish Adventurers* was to be James Freney and other highwaymen or 'rogues and rapparees' as they were more commonly known. Many such highwaymen were indeed 'gentlemen' rapparees either by birth or the chivalric nature of their actions. According to the most popular peasant chapbook, usually referred to in contemporary accounts as *The History of Irish Rogues and Rapparees,* the seventeenth-century Ulster rapparee Redmond O'Hanlon was 'more remarkable and notorious' than any other Irish robber. The full title of this chapbook was *A Genuine History of the Lives and Actions of the Most Notorious Irish Highwaymen, Tories and Rapparees* by J. Cosgrave. 'The History of Irish Rogues and Rapparees' is printed across the top of each page in the copy of the ninth edition, printed in Belfast in 1776, of this chapbook in the National Library of Ireland. It opens with a thirty-three page chapter entitled 'The Surprizing History of Redmond O'Hanlon, Protector of the Rights and Properties of his Benefactors, and Captain General of the Irish Robbers; a most notorious though a Gentleman-like Robber'. According to Cosgrave's account, O'Hanlon's family had been displaced from their lands in Armagh by English settlers and O'Hanlon became an outlaw when he returned to Ireland after having fled abroad rather than face trial on an accusation of almost killing a gentleman in a quarrel.

William Carleton wove a sentimental novel, entitled *Redmond Count O'Hanlon, The Irish Rapparee*, about O'Hanlon's supposed rescue of a lovely young peasant girl who had been abducted by a profligate Anglo-Irish rake. Carleton's descriptions of O'Hanlon's outlaw band and of O'Hanlon himself reflect a combination of lawlessness and nobility :

> At this period, too, the country was overrun and ravaged by lawless bands of Rapparees, and the still more atrocious body of Tories, the latter of whom spared neither life nor property in their merciless depredations. With them [the Tories] religion, of which they were as ignorant as the brutes about them, was no safeguard whatever. The Catholic was robbed and slaughtered with as little remorse as the Protestant, whilst among the Rapparees, on the other hand, there was moderation and forbearance—the great and established principle on which they acted being never to shed blood unless in defense of life, and under no circumstances to injure or maltreat any of the female sex.

Carleton mused about the inherent contradictions represented by the rapparees :

> It is singular to reflect upon the strange perversion and involution of moral feeling by which this desperate and terrible confraternity was regulated. The three great principles of their lawless existence [sobriety, avoidance of bloodshed, and the protection of women] were such as would reflect honour upon the most refined associations and the most intellectual institutions of modern civilization. . . . Yet, upon the basis of principles involving so much that was noble and lofty in morality, was erected such a superstructure of theft and

robbery as Ireland never saw, either before the period we wrote of or since.

Although the rapparee system itself was antithetical in Carleton's view, the picture he painted of O'Hanlon was one of pure nobility :

The individual who commanded this formidable gang of Rapparees was, considering his position in the world, probably the most extraordinary man of his age, or of any age before or since. Carte, in his life of Ormond, after giving an authentic account of his death, states, that for a series of many years he kept the whole province of Leinster, in such a state of terror and alarm as was almost incredible. He asserts, that the whole military force of the kingdom was not able to apprehend him, nor to preserve the peace of the country, or to establish the security of life and property so long as he lived. It is true he was often made prisoner, but he never failed by the exercise of his wit, ingenuity, or courage, to escape from the hands of his captors. His personal and mental accomplishments were amazing. That, however, is not extraordinary; for, as we said, the man was not only a gentleman by birth, but Count of the French Empire—a title which was conferred upon him during his residence in that country. He is said to have been the most perfect specimen of a man in the kingdom. He was well educated, and could speak the English, Irish, and French languages to perfection. His athletic powers, strength, and activity, were unrivalled, but if there was anything more extraordinary about him than another, it was his wonderful Protean power of assuming all characters with such ease and effect, that when he chose to discard his own, and assume another, his most intimate friend could not recognise him. He could pass himself, whenever he wished, for an Englishman, Scotchman, or Frenchman, without the slightest risk of detection, and such was the flexibility of the muscles of his face, that he could transform himself into an old man of seventy with scarcely an effort. He is said to have been the handsomest man of his day, and of the most perfect symmetry. We may judge of what his popularity among the people must have been, when, notwithstanding the enormus rewards that were offered by the government of his day for his head, living or dead, he was never betrayed during a period of about twenty-five years, either by any of the people or his own gang. . . . This, in a great measure, was owing to his generosity to the poor and struggling people, whom he frequently assisted, and to his liberality in sharing his plunder with his own men.[47]

Carleton seems to have followed oral tradition in Ulster and Cosgrave's *History of Irish Rogues and Rapparees* in his account of O'Hanlon. Other sources corroborate that O'Hanlon was indeed kind and generous to the poor and needy and that the peasantry, in their turn, protected him; but they also point out that he blackmailed or extorted what was known as 'black rent' from the peasantry in return for his protection.[48] Some of his incredible physical endowments were probably more legendary than real. Even Cosgrave admits at the end of his account of O'Hanlon that legends about him often involved folklore as well as fact : 'But stories concerning him differ greatly; nevertheless, had all his exploits and actions been recorded, they would have made as remarkable a history as most of the Irish giants.'[49] A twentieth-century commentator on O'Hanlon agrees that legends about O'Hanlon frequently represented more folklore than fact : 'Folklore has gathered about him and he is liable to be credited with the deeds of more obscure individuals.'[50]

Accounts of O'Hanlon's death in 1681 vary greatly in detail and thus demonstrate the stability-plus-variation which characterises folklore. According to Cosgrave, O'Hanlon died through the combined forces of a traitorous relative and a treacherous woman—a common motif in the death of a legendary hero in folklore. Cosgrave and twentieth-century accounts agree that O'Hanlon's severed head—a common motif in Irish hero tales—was carried on a staff by his murderer to Armagh, but later accounts omit the treacherous woman motif. Carleton's claim that O'Hanlon was Count of the French Empire is likewise denied by twentieth-century accounts which claim O'Hanlon never actually received such a title when in France.[51]

Yeats probably included O'Hanlon in his general discussion of rogues and rapparees, but it is significant that Yeats singled out James Freney rather than Redmond O'Hanlon for emphasis in *Irish Adventurers*. Carleton's idealisation of O'Hanlon and the innumerable legends about noble rapparees available to Yeats makes his selection of Freney all the more noteworthy. Freney was not treated in Cosgrave's *History of Irish Rogues and Rapparees* but Freney's supposed autobiography was a chapbook whose popularity rivalled Cosgrave's. Walsh discussed Freney's exploits at length in his chapter on 'Rapparees and Robbers' in *Ireland Sixty Years Ago*, but dismissed O'Hanlon in one sentence in the same chapter. The noble O'Hanlon obviously did not suit Walsh's purpose of presenting the negative aspects of the wild Irish character. Freney—of whom Walsh could remark 'He was a coarse, vulgar, treacherous villain, much of the highwayman, and nothing of the hero'—did suit his purposes.[52] Yet Yeats, who so often has been accused of sentimentalising the Irish peasant character during the 1890s, preferred Freney to O'Hanlon.

Freney was born in the early eighteenth century to servants in the house of a gentleman named Robbins in County Kilkenny.[53] Freney's first person account of his life in his autobiography, *The Life and Adventures of James Freney*, inevitably presents a more sympathetic account of his life than that in Walsh. According to Freney's account he was an idle youth but forces beyond his control drove him into becoming an outlaw : after he married and set up business in Waterford he was opposed by several gentlemen of the city who said he 'had no right, as not being free of the city'. After they summoned him to court and drove him out of the city, he became a highwayman when his money ran out. His autobiography describes his daring robberies—how he once robbed ten different men in a day—and hairbreadth escapes in detail. He summarily describes his surrender and subsequent pardon through the intercession of Lord Carrick, and claims to be writing his autobiography to raise money in order to leave Ireland because 'gentlemen of the country refused to subscribe' to Lord Carrick's proposed subscription to help Freney and his family emigrate. In any event he never did leave Ireland because his patron, Lord Carrick, secured him a good post as tide-waiter at New Ross and Freney lived to a ripe old age.

Walsh's account credits Freney's own idle and degenerate nature as the reason for his career as an outlaw because neither his friends nor the 'efforts of his kind patron [his father's employer] could turn him from low dissipation'.[54] Walsh describes how

G

Freney 'collected round him all the idle and worthless fellows of his neighbourhood, whom he formed into a gang of robbers' and how by 'daring deeds and hair-breadth escapes' Freney 'astonished the country, and kept it in alarm, and, to a certain degree, in subjection, for five years'. According to Walsh, Freney's own treachery and that of other gang members in the form of informing brought out their demise : 'They turned informers against each other, and were hanged in succession, till but one, named Bulger, remained with him.' During an ambush Freney carried his wounded comrade Bulger off on his back, only to purchase his own safety shortly thereafter by turning Bulger in. This 'treachery' and the intercessions of Lord Carrick earned him a pardon. Walsh remarks that 'Freney is still well remembered in the south-east of Ireland . . . [where] his character has been much over-rated . . . He had nothing of dignified appearance or gentlemanly manners. Those who saw and conversed with him described him as a mean-looking fellow, pitted with the small-pox, and blind of an eye.' Freney was indeed a far cry from Redmond O'Hanlon. Walsh, however, too easily discounts the legend-making power of Freney's 'Robin-Hood' actions among the poor and the selective powers of oral tradition. The peasantry remembered what they chose to about Freney—the sly trickery of his bold confrontation with a Quaker in the ballad 'Bold Captain Freney' and the daring deeds and hairbreadth escapes recounted in his autobiography and in oral tradition.

Both Lord Carrick's patronage of Freney and Freney's inform-ing on his comrades would not have seemed an anomaly either to Freney or to the peasantry who sang of his deeds. *The Journal of the Kilkenny and South-East of Ireland Archeological Society* (1856-57) referred to many oral legends about Freney in existence among the peasantry and quoted 'a letter from the middle of the last century' concerning Freney which declared that a 'system of secretly countenancing and protecting highwaymen was pretty general amongst the better classes throughout all parts of Great Britain and Ireland, but seems to have prevailed to a much larger extent in the county of Kilkenny as to cast a particular stain upon the character of the district.'[55] The letter describes how gentlemen would 'set a thief to catch a thief' and how informing was a common practice. Freney himself dedicated his

autobiography to Lord Carrick and praised him for abolishing
the scheme of protection whereby members of the gentry sup-
ported outlaws who levied 'black-rent' on loyal subjects of the
crown. Freney claimed such a system had been the source of
his own crimes.

The other rogues and rapparees whom Yeats included in
Irish Adventurers would very likely have been less tainted in
their nobility than Freney because the vast majority of such
highwaymen conformed to 'noble bandit' stereotype best repre-
sented by O'Hanlon. Many were even artists as well as outlaws.
Cosgrave's *History* claimed a rapparee named William Peters
'composed several songs and put tunes to them' and that when
John MacPherson 'a notorious Robber' was brought to the gal-
lows 'he play'd a fine tune of his own composing on the bag-
pipes, which retains the name of MacPherson's tune unto this
day.'[56] Most rapparees were celebrated in song as well as in
story. 'Crotty's Lament' was supposed to have been composed
by the wife of the eighteenth-century outlaw William Crotty at
his execution. Crotty, whom Walsh claimed was even 'more
eminent' than even Freney or O'Hanlon, probably would have
been included in Yeats's section about 'rogues and rapparees'.
According to Walsh, 'Crotty was a man of desperate courage and
unequalled personal agility; often baffling pursuers even when
mounted on fleet horses. . . . Like many other highwaymen he
was in the habit of sharing with the poor what he plundered
from the rich.'[57] As in many of Yeats's other adventurers and,
according to Walsh, 'as in many of his countrymen, the ex-
tremes of ferocity and kindly feeling were combined in Crotty.'
Crotty was even more ferocious than Tiger Roche for 'Crotty was
reputed to be a cannibal, and he was believed to fill these
recesses [of his cave] with stores of human flesh, on which he
fed.' After his execution his severed head was put on display
and for a long time was an object of grisly horror.

Walsh's description of how Crotty eluded his pursuers could
also describe Yeats's final adventurer figure, Michael Dwyer,
except his depredations had a clearly nationalistic motive which
Crotty's robberies lacked: 'Men from the woods and moun-
tains infested the neighbourhood of populous towns, having holes
and dens from which they issued to commit their depredations,
and to which they retired, like wild beasts to their lair; when

pursued, they thus suddenly sank into the earth and disappeared, and were passed over by their pursuers.' Indeed, Yeats's inclusion of Dwyer, a hero of noble patriotic motives, would have retro-actively strengthened the nationalistic implications of the accounts of the other outlaws who preceded him. Dwyer's exploits were closer in spirit to those of the original seventeenth-century rap-parees than those of Freney or any other eighteenth-century out-laws had been.

Michael Dwyer (1771–1826) was a native of County Wicklow where in 1798 he joined the United Irishmen, bringing with him a band of twenty or thirty insurgents from the Wicklow Mountains.[58] After the rebellion was defeated Dwyer led a band of fellow-insurgents who held out for five years, until 1803, in the Wicklow Mountains. In 1803 Dwyer was concerned in Emmet's insurrection and brought five hundred men with him to Rathfarnham, but he refused to concur in Emmet's attempt upon Dublin. Dwyer's niece, Anne Devlin, sheltered Emmet for a time after the failure of his plans. Dwyer himself surrendered on 17 December 1803. He was sentenced only to be transported to Australia on the grounds of the humanity he had displayed. He became high constable of Sydney in 1815 and died there in 1826. His exploits were commemorated in numerous songs and legends. The broadside ballad 'Dunlavin Green', the place where a Captain Saunders in the Yeomanry corps shot thirty-six of his men who were suspected of being United Irishmen, sings of Dwyer:

> Some of our boys to the hills they are going away,
> There are some of them shot, and the rest of them going to
> sea;
> Michael Dwyer in the mountains to Saunders he owes a
> spleen,
> For his loyal United who were shot on Dunlavin Green.[59]

A collector for the Irish Folklore Commission still found vivid oral memories of Michael Dwyer as late as 1934 in County Wicklow. The recollections of a Mrs O'Tool of Ballinglen, whose grandfather had hidden out with Dwyer in the Wicklow Mountains, contained many anecdotes about Dwyer and his adventures.[60] After a bird warned Dwyer, her grandfather and two others who were hiding in a cave that a large group of

British soldiers with bloodhounds were approaching, their trickery and bravado made the soldiers flee in terror and report 'that the hills were full of rebels'. She told of numerous hairbreadth escapes Dwyer engineered and of 'all his bravery and the good acts he had done'. Once at Glendalough when Dwyer was hiding in the recessed ledge known as St Kevin's Bed, 'he jumped into the lake which was never done since nor before by any man.' When an English lord attempted to bribe Dwyer's wife into informing on him, Dwyer disguised himself as a woman and went to the meeting the officer had arranged with his wife and there 'he started to have a loving conversation with the old officer.' Soon 'Dwyer jumped to his feet and whipped hold of him by the throat, and threw him into the Slaney, and hammered him against the stones there till he had him boneless and senseless and lifeless.' When Dwyer finally surrendered, according to Mrs O'Tool, he did so on his own terms. Dwyer insisted the English Capt. Hume come to him and he did. As Mrs O'Tool described their encounter it sounded as if Hume surrendered to Dwyer rather than vice versa : 'Hume, delighted to hear of a chance of getting shut of him at all, to get him out of Ireland, threw up his arms and he said : "All right, Dwyer, all right. Go where you please. We'll send you anywhere." So Dwyer said he'd go to Sydney in Australia, and if they did not send him there he'd go nowhere at all but would stay at home and give them more of it. So they sent him to Sydney in Australia, and he brought his pike along with him.' Sean O'Sullivan's *Handbook of Irish Folklore* lists Michael Dwyer as a person about whom collectors could still expect to find oral traditions.

Yeats's list of the contents of *Irish Adventurers* in his letter to Garnett indicated that Unwin should get the Dwyer material but that otherwise he probably could. Shortly after Dwyer's surrender, the *Belfast News-Letter* on 23 December 1803 and 17 January 1804 published detailed accounts of his appearance and manners. Perhaps those were to be the 'contemporary records' upon which Yeats intended to draw. In any event, he could easily have heard oral accounts of Dwyer during his numerous visits to Katharine Tynan's at her father's thatched farmhouse in Clondalkin at the foot of the Wicklow Mountains during the 1880s and early 1890s. Katharine Tynan herself had written a poem entitled 'The Grave of Michael Dwyer' which was included in the anthology *Poems and Ballads of Young Ireland* (1888). Yeats's poem 'A Fairy Song', first published in *The National Observer* on 12 September 1891, included the following note after its title in its first several printings: 'Sung by "the Good People" over the outlaw Michael Dwyer and his bride, who had escaped into the mountains'.[61]

Garnett's reader's report does not allude to Michael Dwyer so evidently the material about him which Yeats desired to include had never been procured by Unwin. Garnett, however, did object to Yeats's material about Freney and other Irish highwaymen and remarked, 'We cannot help thinking that better material than this might be got.' Indeed, Garnett did not seem very taken with any of Yeats's materials except for the first section about Col. Blood. Garnett concluded his report with the following comments: 'We want better *original* material than the present' and 'What we would suggest is that Mr Seccour be consulted as to whether he will advise or supply him with other material to supplement the Blood narrative.' Perhaps the failure of Unwin to ever publish Yeats's *Irish Adventurers* was due to the reservations which Garnett voiced in his reader's report as much as to Yeats's battle with Duffy over the 'New Irish Library' series.

The fact that Yeats's *Irish Adventurers* was never published is ultimately irrelevant. What matters is that in compiling it he changed and developed his attitudes to folklore and about personality in literature. Although all trace of his introduction to the volume has disappeared, the essay he published in September 1891 entitled 'A Reckless Century: Irish Rakes and Duellists' suggests what Yeats probably said in the introduction which he finally finished writing thirteen months later. The rakes and duellists essay is a collection of anecdotes, most of which Yeats admitted garnering from Walsh's *Ireland Sixty Years Ago* (1847) and from Sir Jonah Barrington's *Personal Sketches of His Own Times* (1869). Yeats also refers to materials from 'old magazines' and 'popular tradition'. Indeed he is careful to present his anecdotes, whatever their source, as legendary lore and oral tradition. He introduces his anecdotes with phrases such as: 'the neighbourhood still mutters', 'the story is', 'the peasants will have it', 'the tale goes'. Yet 'for all this copious tradition not much is known for certainty of this Hellfire Club.'[62] Clearly this is legendary lore not historical fact. Yet this lore obviously expresses the violent and reckless character of the century more fully than any textbook could.

Yeats interwove these legendary anecdotes with personal musings supposedly generated when he stood on top of Mount Pelier and looked on the ruins of the Hellfire Club which had been the scene of the notorious meetings of eighteenth-century rakes known as 'Bucks' : 'Such were the thoughts and stories brought to my mind the other day by that grinning skull at Mount Pelier.' Walsh had summed up these Bucks as follows : 'Among the gentry of the period was a class called "Bucks," whose whole enjoyment and the business of whose life seemed to consist in eccentricity and violence.'[63] Yeats declared the Bucks and their Hellfire Club to have been a 'hideous symbol of an age without ideals, without order, without peace', yet Yeats admires their times as 'an age in whose unbridled life there was something essential'.

Yeats found the duellists to be 'somewhat more worthy of sympathy' than the Bucks and gives a nationalistic explanation for the origin of the century's wild passion for duelling : 'The destruction of the national forces at the battle of the Boyne had filled the land with Catholic gentlemen who had no defence against insult but their own unaided swords, and from their contests with their supplanters spread through the country a habit of fighting for anything and everything.' Whereas Walsh ignored such historical origins and preferred to present duellists and rapparees as examples of the wild Irish character so badly in need of England's civilising influence, Yeats extols the passion of the rakes and duellists and presents it as of both nationalistic and literary significance. Yeats says of duellists like Fitzgerald and Maguire, 'A little conviction would have made them good rebels.'

Yeats was careful to ascribe a similar energy to the leaderless peasantry—'This reckless and turbulent spirit was by no means confined to the upper classes.' As an example he alludes to the reckless gaiety embodied in the popular folk ballad 'The Night Before Larry was Stretched' although he does not actually name it : 'Poor men, when condemned to death, would spend the night before their hanging gambling upon the lids of their own coffins, making amends for a life without dignity by a death without fear.' He argues that, to the credit of the peasantry, more of a sense of 'national duty' and 'patriotic hope' motivated their 'excesses'. *Irish Adventurers*, of course, also contained a similar dual focus on the Irish gentry and peasantry.

Yeats concludes his essay with the observation that the vast energy embodied in these 'tales of forgotten violence and dead recklessness' were 'fortunate prophesies' of nationalistic and cultural success : 'I see there the Celtic intensity, the Celtic fire, the Celtic daring wasting themselves, it is true in all kinds of evil, but needing only the responsibility of self-government. . . . The vast energy that filled Ireland with bullies and swash-bucklers will some day give us great poets and thinkers. . . . Their swords were strong, at any rate, though they were not turned often enough, or persistently enough, towards the enemies of their country.' John Frayne remarked of Yeats's rakes and duel-lists essay, 'The Hellfire Club, Power of Dargle, and Brian Maguire were all, whether they knew it or not, preparing the way for the Celtic Revival.'[64] Likewise, the presence in *Irish Adventurers* of Michael Dwyer, whose heroic defiance of the English from 1798–1803 spanned the two centuries, was ob-viously a prototype of what was to come. *Irish Adventurers* prophesied the political possibilities of Irish energy and passion just as the stories about the eighteenth-century poet Red Hanrahan, which Yeats began writing during the early 1890s, foreshadowed the poetic genius of the Literary Renaissance.

Yeats's rakes and duellists essay represented a development in his earlier attitudes. Less than two years previously he had displayed little interest in or admiration for Irish adventurers. In an article entitled 'Chevalier Burke and Shule Aroon', pub-lished on 28 December 1889, Yeats criticised Robert Louis Stevenson's sketch of 'the blackguard adventurer, Chevalier Burke' who was a true enough type 'but Mr Stevenson is certainly wrong in displaying him for a typical Irishman' :

He is really a broken-down Norman gentleman, a type found only among the gentry who make up what is called 'the English garrison.' He is from the same source as the Hell Fire Club and all the reckless braggadocia of the eighteenth century in Ireland; of that class who, feeling the uncertainty of their tenures, as Froude explained it, lived the most devil-may-care existence. One sometimes meets even at this day vulgar, plausible, swaggering 'Irishmen' who are its much decayed survivals, and who give Mr Stevenson his justification. They are bad, but none of our making; English settlers bore them, English laws moulded them. No one who knows the serious, reserved and suspicious Irish peasant ever held them in any way representative of the national type.[65]

Clearly in late 1889, shortly after compiling *Fairy and Folk Tales of the Irish Peasantry* and before he had discovered the passion and energy of the peasantry he anthologised in *Representative Irish Tales* (1891), Yeats's conception of the peasantry was the antithesis of the reckless energy of the Irish adventurers.

By the following spring, when he sent off his manuscript of *Representative Irish Tales* and began reading about duellists and outlaws for the Irish adventurer book, his conception of the peasantry and the adventurers had developed significantly. The adventurers' exploits, whether rake or rapparee, were clearly as extravagant and weird as any legend he had included in *Fairy and Folk Tales*. The adventurers obviously shared the same reckless energy he had admired in the lives of the peasantry portrayed in *Representative Irish Tales*. He had been forced to supplement the visionary powers of Mary Battle and Paddy Flynn in *The Celtic Twilight* with accounts of the aristocratic knight of the sheep and the eighteenth-century Dubliner Zozimus because Mary Battle and Paddy Flynn's lives did not equal the extravagance and energy of their imaginative powers. If the quintessential Irish energy and passion had waned among the peasantry in the course of the nineteenth-century, it was still available in legends about Irish rakes and rapparees of the preceding century. The closest Yeats came to finding violent passions among the peasantry he depicted in *The Celtic Twilight* was in the essay 'The Thick Skull of the Fortunate' in which he described the skull-breaking which went on at faction fights at the village of Roughley. In 1902 he added a note to the essay which declared that even in 1893 such events had been no more than 'old memories'. By contrast, fighting was anything but rare during the eighteenth century when, according to Walsh, it had been the pre-eminent Irish pastime: 'There was, however, one most singular pursuit in which the highest and lowest seemed

G*

alike to participate with an astonishing relish, viz., fighting, which all classes in Ireland appear to have enjoyed with a keenness now hardly credible even to a native of Kentucky.'[66]

Yeats's account in his *Autobiography* of his own woeful inadequacies in the fights he had experienced so frequently as a schoolboy suggests he would have vicariously enjoyed the fighting abilities of his Irish adventurers. As a child he dreamed of being an adventurous sea rover someday and both he and his brother Jack delighted in playing pirates when they were boys. Jack eventually wrote plays about pirates, but the pirates in chapbooks were usually English rather than Irish. The wild Irish nature of Yeats's duellists and rapparees was much more suitable to his literary nationalism. The cunning and trickery displayed by many of his Irish adventurers would also have been especially appealing to Yeats. He recalled his youthful enthusiasm for the tricks of cunning, devil-may-care rogue heroes when he explained the genesis of his tale 'Michael Clancy, the Great Dhoul, and Death': 'When I was about eighteen I came upon a Connaught folk tale of a tinker and Death and the Devil. . . . I began what was to be a long poem . . . meaning to make the tinker a type of that kind of jeering, cheating Irishman called "a melodious lying Irishman" in another folk tale; and to bring him through many typical places and adventures.'[67] However, the scope of such a lengthy project soon dampened his enthusiasm and 'I gave up my epic and wrote this little tale instead.'

Michael Clancy in the resulting tale is still as cunning a rogue as had first attracted Yeats's attention. Indeed Yeats's hero is even more roguish and more heroic than the protagonist in the standard version of that folktale. Yeats's plot is an interesting variation of the popular folktale plot of 'the smith outwits the devil' (A-T330). Four of Yeats's sources for *Fairy and Folk Tales*—Kennedy's *Legendary Fictions*, Lover's *Legends and Stories*, the chapbook *The Royal Hibernian Tales*, and William Carleton's *Tales and Sketches*—contained versions of A-T330. Carleton's version, which was entitled 'The Three Wishes' and which Yeats included in *Fairy and Folk Tales*, typifies most versions of the tale: a blacksmith, 'the completest swindler' in the whole parish but who also possessed the entirely antithetical character trait of pity towards strangers, one day is kind to an old beggar who actually is the devil. When the devil rewards the smith with three wishes, the smith chooses three seemingly ridiculous powers which he cunningly uses to outwit the devil himself. The incorrigible smith is refused entrance to heaven when he dies, and after the torment he had put the devil through, the devil declares: 'Don't admit that rascal, bar the gate . . . I won't be safe—and I won't stay here, nor none of us need stay here, if he gets in—my bones are sore yet after him.' So the smith is doomed to roam the world as the will-of-the-wisp. A character such as the smith is what folklorists call a 'trickster' figure and is one of the most ancient and most popular kinds of heroes in world folklore.

Yeats's Michael Clancy is not a blacksmith but is a wandering tinker and folk doctor and is far superior to the blacksmith in Yeats's version who is so terrified when he meets the devil that he faints and is never the same. Michael Clancy, on the other hand, outwits not only the devil but Death as well. After out-witting Death for years, he becomes bored, chooses to die and sends the fairies, whom he seems to respect enough not to treat as horribly as he does the devil and Death but whom he is evi-dently superior to if he can use them as his messengers, to sum-mon Death. When he is denied entrance at heaven and hell, the fairies turn him into a salmon in the river at Ballisodare. Wizards and ancient heroes frequently lived as enchanted, mirac-ulous salmons during one of their many lives. While 'the smith outwits the devil' plot is generally told as a folktale and while Carleton's version has just enough real life details to make it a legend, Yeats's version is so filled with details of Sligo geography and daily peasant life that it is unmistakably a legend. Yeats's amplification of the roguish and heroic traits in his hero's char-acter suggests he had a natural sympathy for his Irish adven-turers.

In any event, by the time Yeats wrote his rakes and duellists essay and compiled *Irish Adventurers*, the adventurer had be-come the peasant's kindred spirit rather than his antithesis. Yeats himself summed up the pivotal importance of the eighteenth-century adventurer to his developing conception of the heroic personality and of the quintessential Irish character in a statement he made in his essay 'A Visionary' in the first edition of *The Celtic Twilight*: 'The peasant visionaries that are, the landlord duellists that were, and the whole hurly-burly of

legends—Cuchulain . . . Caolte . . . Oisin . . . —all are a portion
of that great Celtic phantasmagoria whose meaning no man
has discovered, nor any angel revealed.' Irish adventurers did
indeed represent a transitional interest between Yeats's early
preoccupation with the peasant and his eventual fascination
with the ancient heroes. Peasant visions, eighteenth-century
duels and heroic legends were all folklore, but they represented
three distinct phases in his developing conception of Irish folk-
lore and of the quintessential Irish character.

6

Poets and Heroes: *The Secret Rose*

The stories which Yeats published in collected form as *The Secret Rose* (1897) were in many ways the culmination of his activities as an anthologist and collector of Irish folklore. Most of the plots, situations and details in the stories in *The Secret Rose* were based on legends and other folklore which Yeats knew either from oral tradition or from printed versions. The quintessential Irish personality, as Yeats portrays it in *The Secret Rose*, is a combination of the visionary powers which he had associated with the Irish peasantry in *The Celtic Twilight* and of the passionate energy and extravagance he had found among the peasants in *Representative Irish Tales* and the duellists and outlaws in *Irish Adventurers*. Red Hanrahan, the hero of many of the stories in *The Secret Rose*, is at once peasant visionary and passionate poet. *The Secret Rose* stories, in which the fairies are continually associated with the gods of ancient Ireland and in which the nobility of a character is in direct proportion to his visionary or legendary knowledge of ancient Ireland, also represent a pivotal stage in the development of Yeats's attitudes about heroic personality and about ancient Ireland. *The Secret Rose* anticipates and explains how his focus shifted from fairies and peasants in *The Celtic Twilight* (1893) to ancient gods and heroes in the materials he added to *The Celtic Twilight* in 1902.

The publishing history of the stories which Yeats wrote during the 1890s and eventually anthologised in *The Secret Rose* reveals several major kinds of revisions—all of which reveal his growing preoccupation with ancient Ireland, especially with its mythology and its heroic legends. The stories which Yeats collected in *The Secret Rose* in 1897 had all been published previously. The following summary of their publishing history, based on information in Allan Wade's *Bibliography*, will provide a framework in which to discuss the significance of the revisions the stories underwent.[1] *The Secret Rose* (1897) contained the following stories—the original title, if any, and the date of publication of the earlier version is given in parentheses:

'The Binding of the Hair' (September 1896).
'The Wisdom of the King' ('Wisdom'—September 1895).
'Where there is Nothing, there is God' (October 1896).
'The Crucifixion of the Outcast' ('A Crucifixion'—March 1894).
'Out of the Rose' (May 1893).
'The Curse of the Fires and of the Shadows' (August 1893).
'The Heart of the Spring' (April 1893).
'Of Costello the Proud, of Oona the Daughter of Dermott and of the Bitter Tongue' ('Costello the Proud, Oona Mac-Dermott and the Bitter Tongue'—1896).
'The Book of the Great Dhoul and Hanrahan the Red' ('The Devil's Book'—November 1892).
'The Twisting of the Rope and Hanrahan the Red' ('The Twisting of the Rope'—December 1892).
'Kathleen the Daughter of Hoolihan and Hanrahan the Red' ('Kathleen-ny-Houlihan'—August 1894).
'The Curse of Hanrahan the Red' ('The Curse of O'Sullivan the Red upon Old Age'—September 1894).
'The Vision of Hanrahan the Red' ('The Vision of O'Sullivan the Red'—April 1896).
'The Death of Hanrahan the Red' ('The Death of O'Sullivan the Red'—December 1896).
'The Rose of Shadow' ('Those Who Live in the Storm'—July 1894).
'The Old Men of the Twilight' ('St Patrick and the Pedants'—December 1895).
'Rosa Alchemica' (April 1896).

During 1903–1904 Yeats rewrote the stories about Red Hanrahan with Lady Gregory's help 'in very simple words like those the country people tell their stories in'.[2] The collaboration between Yeats and Lady Gregory resulted in the separate edition of *Stories of Red Hanrahan* (1905). Yeats twice revised the texts of the other stories included in *The Secret Rose*, once he was preparing his *Collected Works* (1908) and again when he was preparing *Early Poems and Stories* (1925).[3] In the section of *Collected Works* called *The Secret Rose,* Yeats dropped two stories entirely, 'The Binding of the Hair' and 'The Rose of Shadow' and he revised the texts of the other stories and arranged them in different order: 'The Crucifixion of the Outcast', 'Out of the Rose', 'The Wisdom of the King', 'The Heart of the Spring', 'The Curse of the Fires and of the Shadows', 'The Old Men of the Twilight', 'Where There is Nothing, There is God', 'Of Costello the Proud, of Oona the Daughter of Dermott and of the Bitter Tongue'.

The stories about Red Hanrahan had recounted a sequence of events revolving around a separate hero even in the 1897 edition of *The Secret Rose,* and because Yeats later published them as a separate collection, they should be explored separately. Hanrahan is also the logical point at which to begin an analysis of the prose fiction in *The Secret Rose* because the first two Hanrahan stories were written and published in 1892 before any of the other stories in *The Secret Rose.*

Douglas Hyde's translations of Irish love songs, especially *The Love Songs of Connacht* which Yeats would have known even before its publication in 1893, had been a crucial influence on Yeats's conception of Irish folklore and of the peasant personality. He had originally been attracted to Irish folklore because of his interest in the impersonal Irish ballads which narrated peasant legends. *The Love Songs of Connacht* justified the preoccupation with the character of the Irish peasantry which Yeats had shown in *Representative Irish Tales*. Hyde's *Love Songs* revealed a lyrical power and a passion which Yeats later recalled had been to him the coming of a new power into literature. The peasant personality was no longer capable only of fairy visions or energetic, extravagant acts; Hyde's songs showed the peasantry had also created great lyrical poetry. Yeats had argued in his essay 'The Message of the Folk-lorist' in August 1893 that the greatest poets had found 'symbols and events to express the most lyrical, the most subjective moods' in folk narratives. Less than two months later when he reviewed Hyde's *Love Songs* Yeats could argue that the peasantry themselves had created great lyrics out of their boundless emotions: 'sheer hope and fear, joy and sorrow, made the poems, and not any mortal man or woman' and 'every powerful emotion found at once noble types and symbols for its expression'.[4] Yeats had associated the peasantry with his doctrine of the moods by placing the poem he later titled 'Moods' at the beginning of the first edition of *The Celtic Twilight*, published in December of 1893. But the peasants in that collection are visionaries not poets. It was in the early versions of the Hanrahan stories that Yeats began to describe the poetic powers inherent in the emotions of the peasantry.

It is generally agreed among Yeats scholars that he modelled Red Hanrahan on two eighteenth-century Munster peasant poets, Owen Rua O'Sullivan (1748–1784) and William Dall O'Heffernan (1720–1760). Richard Finneran has pointed out that Yeats would have learned about both poets in John O'Daly and Edward Walsh's *Reliques of Irish Jacobite Poetry* (1844) and about O'Sullivan from Edward Walsh's *Irish Popular Songs* (1847) and from conversations with Douglas Hyde.[5] In the earliest versions of the Hanrahan stories the title character is named O'Sullivan the Red and lives in Munster. The real O'Sullivan and O'Heffernan were not only poets but also popular figures in Munster folklore, so here again, although his knowledge was drawn largely from printed sources, Yeats is drawing upon what was ultimately oral tradition or folklore for his materials. According to *Reliques of Irish Jacobite Poetry*, in 1844 legends of O'Sullivan survived throughout Counties 'Cork, Kerry and Limerick, where his memory survives, his poems are recited, and the brilliant effusions of his happy wit, shine familiar as household words'; likewise, the subjects of O'Heffernan's songs had all disappeared but his 'fame, the smallest traits of his character, the most trivial incidents of his life, and those rich and exuberant strains of Celtic eloquence, which came with the force and copiousness of a torrent upon his enemies, are remembered and recited by the people as if they were the productions of yesterday.'[6] More than half a century later Lady Gregory remarked that the old Jacobite songs of O'Sullivan and O'Heffernan and others were 'still sung . . . not for the sake of the kings, but for the sake of the poets who made them'.[7] Daniel Corkery in *The Hidden Ireland* (1924) claimed O'Sullivan was still a living legend among the Munster peasantry.[8]

O'Sullivan's life was the major source for Yeats's Hanrahan. Yeats credited his O'Sullivan, whom he later renamed Hanrahan,

with two of the blind O'Heffernan's most famous songs, 'Caitilin
ni Uallacain' and 'Shaun Bui', both of which had been published
in Mangan's *Poets and Poetry of Munster* (1849), a source
Yeats knew well. But Hanrahan's personality was most clearly
based on O'Sullivan who had been described in *Reliques of
Irish Jacobite Poetry* as 'wild and irregular' and as noted for
his 'uncontrolled passion'.[9] Yeats ignored the more virulent
aspects of O'Sullivan's anti-English sentiments and the more
prosaic of his activities as an itinerant potato-digger and mower
and as a soldier. Yeats concentrated instead on O'Sullivan's
reckless, wild nature and his poetic powers, and gave him
visionary powers which he had not possessed either in real life
or in oral tradition. The reckless energy Yeats had so admired
in duellists and outlaws thus acquired the serious poetic and
visionary powers it had not had among Irish adventurers. Daniel
Corkery describes the O'Sullivan of legend as 'a wastral with
a loud laugh'[10]; the visionary powers of Yeats's Hanrahan make
him much more than that. Yeats's Hanrahan is not only different
from the legendary O'Sullivan; his conception of Hanrahan
underwent significant developments in each new version of
the stories about him. All of the original versions of the Hanrahan
stories had been written about O'Sullivan the Red and had been
published separately between 1892 and 1896 in the same order
they follow in *The Secret Rose* and in *Stories of Red Hanrahan*.
The changes which Yeats made in each new version of the six
Hanrahan stories reveal significant developments in his attitudes
about the fairies, the peasants and ancient Ireland. The follow-
ing analysis is based on Michael Sidnell's invaluable reprinting
of the periodical versions of the stories, which also indicates
changes made in 1897, in *Yeats Studies* I.[11]

'The Devil's Book', published in November 1892, was Yeats's
first fictional portrait of the legendary O'Sullivan. In the story
O'Sullivan buys a supposed 'devil's book' full of curses, love
charms, and invocations and charms with which to contact
the spirits. O'Sullivan invokes 'Cleona of Ton Cleona, the Queen
of the Munster Sheogues' by writing the necessary names in
bat's blood on the back of his copy of *The Lives of Celebrated
Rogues and Rapparees*. When she appears to him, he asks a
question about the legendary salmon of knowledge, but 'finding
it useless to try and talk with this beautiful phantom, he sank

into a very rapturous silence.' The next day he invokes Cleona again by placing a pan of milk and a griddle-cake under a haunted thorn-tree but this encounter proves as fruitless as the first. When O'Sullivan invokes Cleona the third time, she appears in human form but he rejects her because she is no longer 'the Woman o' the Shee'. She, however, loves O'Sullivan for his human qualities: 'the fire in yer heart would not let ye rest. I love ye, for ye are fierce and passionate, now good and now bad, and not free and dim and wave-like as are the Sheogues.' Nevertheless O'Sullivan sends her away, his cabin is destroyed by a fairy whirlwind, he sells the devil's book to a local fairy doctor, spends the money on poteen, and is driven from the parish after the priest preaches that the wrath of God rather than the fairies had destroyed O'Sullivan's cabin.

Yeats's 'Note' after the 1892 version presented his materials as a legend: 'O'Sullivan the Red was really a noted peasant-poet of the last century. His character was much as I have described it. The Gaelic poets were often thought to have a Lianaan Shee or Fairy-mistress. Cleona of Ton Cleona is the Queen of the Munster Fairies.' Yeats's O'Sullivan does reflect many details of the life and character of the real O'Sullivan: he lives in Munster, he is notorious for his drinking and his escapades with women which frequently cost him his job as hedge-school master, and he maintains a running battle with the rural clergy. Yeats's O'Sullivan refers to his 'trouble about Molly Casey, her I made the song to'. The reference to the Molly Casey episode is clearly based on the account in *Reliques of Irish Jacobite Poetry* of how O'Sullivan's love for the village beauty, Mary Casey, caused such a scandal 'the school was given up' and O'Sullivan's 'licentiousness denounced from the altar'.[12] On this occasion O'Sullivan supposedly composed the song 'Molly Casey's Charms'. Yeats invented O'Sullivan's relationship with Cleona but Yeats's note makes clear that he considered this 'invention' to be an elaboration of a popular folk belief about poets. His seeming 'innovation' was indeed traditional.

Yeats remarked that Cleona was 'Queen of the Munster Fairies' and referred to her as 'Cleona of Ton Cleona'. 'Tonn-Cliodna' means Cliodna's Wave and refers to the wave which supposedly washes against Cliodna's Rock in Glandore Bay in County Cork. In *Gods and Fighting Men* (1904) Lady Gregory would recount the legend behind 'Cliodna's Wave' in a short chapter of that name which was based on Standish Hayes O'Grady's *Silva Gaedelica* (1892). According to the O'Grady-Gregory account, Cliodna was the daughter of Gebann, the chief druid of Manannan. Cliodna drowned in Glandore Bay while running away from Tir-na-nog with Ciabhan, the handsome son of the King of Ulster. Although O'Grady's account of Cliodna, in which she is clearly one of the Tuatha De Danaan, was available to Yeats in 1892, he presents Cleona as a fairy queen rather than as an ancient goddess. Cleona's fairy palace was supposedly at Carrig-Cleena near Mallow in County Cork, but Yeats, perhaps influenced by a Roscommon oral legend from Douglas Hyde, transposed O'Sullivan's first encounter with her to 'Cruchan' (Cruachan) in County Roscommon, the legendary capital of ancient Connacht. That change anticipated Yeats's transposition in the 1905 edition of all the events in the Hanrahan stories to Connacht. The legendary importance of Cruachan in ancient Ireland reinforced Yeats's identification of both O'Sullivan and Cleona with ancient Ireland. In this story O'Sullivan recounts an anecdote about the 'Finians' (Fenians) and Cleona appears 'dressed in saffron like the women of ancient Ireland'. Both O'Sullivan and the fairies would be associated with ancient Ireland more and more each time Yeats revised the stories.

This story was revised and retitled 'The Book of the Great Dhoul and Hanrahan the Red' in *The Secret Rose.* Yeats's explanation to John Quinn in 1905 of the change in the title character's name from O'Sullivan to Hanrahan reflects the fact that Hanrahan was a composite portrait of the eighteenth-century peasant poets: 'Red Hanrahan is an imaginary name— I saw it over a shop, or rather part of it over a shop in a Galway village—but there were many poets like him in the eighteenth century in Ireland.'[13] In the 1897 version Molly Casey was transformed into the fictional Maive Lavell. The artificial dialect which O'Sullivan and Cleona spoke in the 1892 version was removed. The specific place names of the early version became vaguer and less specifically Irish: Cork becomes 'the Town of the Grey Lough', the villages of Tailteen, Conroy and Shronehill become 'the Great Spring', the Rath of Cruchan

becomes 'the Grey Rath'. As the events become less identified
with specific contemporary Irish place names, they also become
more definitely associated with ancient Ireland. O'Sullivan's
anecdote about how God's admiration for the Fenians' great
strength and their stories merited them special treatment in hell
is expanded with a list of the gods and goddesses they wor-
shipped : 'Dana and Angus and the Dagda and Lir and Man-
nanan'. The fairies become 'the Shee' or 'the People of Dana'
and are thus given mythological origins. Cleona, now Cleena,
is summoned by charms of occult as well as of folk detail, and
she is clearly an incarnation of the Rose for she refers to herself
as such and her robe is embroidered with roses. Hanrahan asks
her about the ancient god 'Angus' rather than about the legen-
dary salmon of knowledge and thus a figure from Irish myth-
ology no longer spoken of in contemporary oral tradition replaced
one that was.

Hanrahan is a less dynamic figure than O'Sullivan had been
in the 1892 version. O'Sullivan had bought the book of his
own volition in order to demonstrate that he had the same
spirit that God had so admired in the Fenians :

> Well, their way is my way, for whatever men do agin me,
> and wherever I am I get the best out of things, whether they
> be most like Hell or Heaven; and now that Father Gillen
> is turnin' the neighbours on me, I am goin' to meet them fair
> and square. They say, ye know, that I got me songs on the
> Rath of Cruchan. Well, now I am goin' to make them say
> I get them straight from the Ould Boy himsel', and when
> they say it I will laugh, and laughter will be like smooth green
> grass before me and behind.

In the 1897 version such a declaration becomes an after-the-fact
rationalisation by Hanrahan of why he bought the book. When
he bought it he obviously did so under the influence of the
fairies in the form of winds such as 'are held to be the passing of
a troop of the Shee. At the same moment his eyes fell upon
a little shop-window . . . and a book whose pages were open
and full of singular diagrams. He at once remembered having
heard the owner of the shop talking of this book . . . and he won-
dered he had never thought of looking at it, and perhaps of
buying it and taking it home.' Hanrahan's will is clearly under

a fairy enchantment and Cleena says to Hanrahan later in the story: 'It was I who put a thought of the Devil's Book into your head.' O'Sullivan in the earlier version had displayed much more dynamic initiative. These changes typify how the fairies would gain in stature, being more and more associated with ancient Irish gods and goddesses, while any stature or nobility which the peasant Hanrahan would possess would be in direct proportion to his relationship to ancient Ireland.

Any initiative O'Sullivan or Hanrahan had displayed in the first two versions disappeared in 1905 because Yeats replaced the Faust-like story about the Devil's Book with an entirely new story entitled 'Red Hanrahan' in which Hanrahan's acts are completely under enchantment. Yeats later said that this new Hanrahan story was based on 'a Sligo tale about "a wild old man in flannel" who could change a pack of cards into the likeness of a pack of hounds'.[14] In the new opening story, Hanrahan is bewitched by 'an old mountainy man' on Samhain Eve. Samhain had originally marked the beginning of the ancient Irish winter and among the peasantry the festival was celebrated as a night when fairies were especially active and when humans were especially susceptible to fairy enchantment. The 'strange old man', who is obviously a fairy creature, enchants Hanrahan away, not to a fairy queen such as Cleena, but to Echtge, a personage much more closely associated with Irish mythology. Echtge was the daughter of Nuada of the Silver Hand who was the king and leader of the Tuatha De Danann against the Firbolgs at the First Battle of Moytura where he lost his hand and consequently the kingship. According to John Rhys' *Lectures on the Origin and Growth of Celtic Heathendom*, a source Yeats knew well, Nuada was 'a divinity of the sun and of light'.[15] Wood-Martin's *History of Sligo* had also told of Nuada. But Yeats is clearly modelling Echtge on local legends about Slieve Echtge, now Slieve Aughty, an area in Galway where he and Lady Gregory had collected a great deal of folklore.[16] In Yeats's new story Hanrahan is spirited away inside Slieve Echtge in Galway where the De Danann Echtge is in an enchanted sleep from which Hanrahan is not hero enough to wake her. He is consequently cursed never to find happiness in earthly love and this curse functions to explain the subsequent stories just as Cleena's curse had generated his adventures in the earlier stories about him. Echtge and the four old women who guard her obviously represent Irish mythology much more than fairy lore. The four old women are each associated with one of the four treasures of the Tuatha De Danann, the gods of ancient Ireland: the Cauldron of the Dagda, the Stone of Destiny, the Spear of Lug and the Sword of Nuada.[17] Yeats thus carefully links contemporary fairy legends with ancient Irish mythology.

Yeats based his second story about O'Sullivan, 'The Twisting of the Rope', on a song of the same title by O'Sullivan which Edward Walsh had included in *Irish Popular Songs*. Lady Gregory quotes some stanzas from a Connacht version of O'Sullivan's song 'The Twisting of the Rope' in *Poets and Dreamers* which justify Yeats's transposition of the O'Sullivan legends to Connacht:

> What was the dead cat that put me in this place,
> And all the pretty young girls I left after me?
> I came into the house where was the bright love of my heart,
> And the old hag put me out by the Twisting of the Rope.
>
> It is down in Sligo I got knowledge of my love;
> It is up in Galway I drank my fill with her.
> By the strength of my hands, if they do not leave me as I am,
> I will do a trick will set these women walking.[18]

Yeats opened his 1892 version of 'The Twisting of the Rope' with a description of O'Sullivan walking from Munster to Connacht: 'And as the imperfect English of the Munster peasants gave place to the perfect Gaelic of them of Connaught, he became a new man for was he not the last of that mighty line of poets which came down from Sancan Torpeist . . . and mightier Oisin . . . and day by day as he wandered slowly and aimlessly he passed deeper and deeper into that great Celtic twilight, that shadowy sunset of the Gaelic world.' Sancan, of course, is Seanchan the bard, the subject of one of Lady Wilde's tales Yeats had included in *Fairy and Folk Tales* and the hero of Yeats's play, *The King's Threshold* (1904). Yeats, in order to find the last of this ancient line of Gaelic poets, had to go back in time to eighteenth-century Ireland. O'Sullivan's wanderings themselves are a kind of trip backwards in time—he bathes under the shadow of the hill where the ancient God

Balor sleeps and he sleeps in the cave where the legendary Grania had once slept.

Once O'Sullivan arrives at the farm house which is to be the scene of his next adventure, he broadcasts himself as the author of 'Shawn Bui', which was actually a song composed by O'Heffernan. Yet O'Sullivan goes on to sing an untitled lyric about his wanderings which was actually composed by Yeats and titled 'Maid Quiet' when later published in 1897. Yeats never has O'Sullivan or Hanrahan sing any of O'Sullivan's own songs, probably because the majority of O'Sullivan's poems which were available to Yeats during the 1890s were political and Yeats scrupulously avoids depicting O'Sullivan's notoriously anti-English sentiments. Moreover, the non-political songs by O'Sullivan had not been translated into the spare Kiltartan idiom Lady Gregory was to use in her translation of 'The Twisting of the Rope'. For example, the translation of the one stanza of O'Sullivan's Molly Casey's Charms' which had been printed in *Reliques of Irish Jacobite Poetry* began as follows :

> One evening late it was my fate
> To meet a charming creature,
> Whose airy gait and nice portrait
> Excels both art and nature . . .[19]

The translation faithfully reproduces the internal rhyme characteristic of the traditional Irish amhrán or song-poetry. Although its content is obviously in the visionary tradition of the Irish aisling, Yeats preferred his O'Sullivan to have visions of occult or mythological rather than nationalistic significance. Indeed, Yeats described O'Sullivan as having had a quasi-mystical experience of ancient Ireland when he slept in the same cave Grania had : 'and upon him there fell the fascination of ancient white-haired Fion; and, as he lay there, the immense shadows seemed to be taking him to themselves, unhumanising him away into the dim life of the Powers that have never lived in mortal bodies.'

O'Sullivan's association with ancient Ireland is deepened by the fact that his attempted seduction of the young girl, to whom he tells tales of the legendary Deirdre and Adene (Edain), takes place on May Eve, the ancient Irish festival of Beltaine which marked the beginning of summer. Yeats also filled the story with detailed descriptions of peasant customs such as dances, the May bush and protective charms. In *The Secret Rose* story, 'The Twisting of the Rope and Hanrahan the Red', Yeats changed the name of the hero to Hanrahan but otherwise the story remains essentially the same. The only significant difference in the 1897 version concerns Cleena. In the 1892 version she passed O'Sullivan on the shore surrounded by 'grey forms' referred to as 'spirits'. In 1897 they are referred to as 'the daughters of Dana' and thus are much more closely identified with the mythological Tuatha De Danann. In the 1905 version of the story Cleena has, of course, become Echtge.

Yeats removed most of the details about peasant life and about ancient Ireland in the 1905 version of 'The Twisting of the Rope'. Hanrahan's mention of Deirdre is the only allusion to ancient Ireland left in the story. The long introductory passage which connects both Hanrahan's poetic powers and the Irish speaking peasantry to ancient Ireland is removed. Hanrahan's vigour has also diminished because certain details are no longer included. O'Sullivan in 1892 and Hanrahan in 1897 had each delivered a vivid curse as parting words to those who had tricked them out of the house by having them 'twist the rope' : 'May the ravens and the crows and the hawks get your body, and the demons get your soul, and may your bed be made for all eternity upon the red hearth-stone of hell!' In 1905 the actual curse is not included. In 1892 and 1897 'his anger gave way to a profound melancholy' and he has something of a visionary experience as Cleena and the other spirits pass him; in the later version both anger and courage simply leave him and give place to nothing.

The third story in the O'Sullivan-Hanrahan series also takes its title from an Irish folksong, 'Caitlin ni Uallacain', but one by O'Heffernan rather than O'Sullivan. Nevertheless, in 'Kathleen-ny-Houlihan' (1894) in *The Secret Rose* version and in 1905, Yeats credits its composition to O'Sullivan or Hanrahan. The song, which was greatly revised in each successive version of the story, is actually Yeats's creation although it is derived from O'Heffernan's song and from oral traditions about female images of Ireland. This song is the closest Yeats's O'Sullivan or Hanrahan ever come to overt nationalism or what Yeats alludes to in the 1894 and 1897 version as 'passionate patriotism'. The only major revision in the story, besides those to the song itself, are the anglicisation or the deletion of the many specific place names of the 1894 version—something Yeats did to all of the O'Sullivan stories when he revised them for publication in *The Secret Rose*. In the 1894 version O'Sullivan journeyed 'in the direction of Sligo, through Drumahair and Drumease' and met Margaret Rooney 'on the road between Drumease and Sligo and close to Colgagh Lough'. In the 1897 version Hanrahan journeyed 'in the direction of the Town of the Shelly River, through the Ridge of the Two Demons of the Air' and met Margaret Rooney 'between the Ridge of the Two Demons of the Air and the Lough of Swords'. Such names seem needlessly artificial and elaborate today, as they did in retrospect to Yeats himself when Lady Gregory helped him simplify the elaborate prose of the 1897 stories in 1903-4. Perhaps, Yeats's intention in substituting English equivalents for Irish names in 1897 had been to make them more prosaic and literal. The Irish for Sligo is Sligeach and means 'shelly river'. Names referring to 'Demons of the Air' also served to underscore the occult implications of his materials. Yeats had after all claimed in a letter to John O'Leary in 1897 that *The Secret Rose* was an attempt to write an 'aristocratic esoteric Irish literature'.[20] Whatever the original purpose for such circumlocutory names, the actual place names were restored in the 1905 versions of all the Hanrahan stories although the place references were much fewer in number. In the 1905 version Hanrahan simply meets Margaret Rooney 'on the road to Colooney'. Yeats had by then become much less concerned with grounding Hanrahan's adventures in the geography around Sligo.

Similarly, in the fourth story about O'Sullivan's and Hanrahan's curse upon old age, the many specific place names of the 1894 and 1897 versions are replaced with one simple reference to Colooney in 1905. However, many of the key references in O'Sullivan's and later in Hanrahan's curse on old age in 1897 and in 1905 are based on local place names and are obviously derived from one of the most popular kinds of oral traditions in the West of Ireland—legends of the oldest animals and trees. In the 1894 version O'Sullivan begins his curse as follows:

The poet, Red O'Sullivan, under a bush of May

Calls down a curse on his own head, because it withers grey;
Then on the speckled eagle cock of Bally Gawley Hill,
Because it is the oldest thing that knows of care and ill,
And on the leaning, wrinkling ash, that many an age hath
    stood
Hollow and knarled and broken to North of Markree Wood,
And on the great grey pike that dwells in Castle Dargan Lake,
Having in his long body a many a pain and ache . . .

Ballygawley (also known as Ballydawley), Markree, and Castle
Dargan are all places near Coolooney. Yeats recalls in his *Auto-
biography* that he frequently visited relatives at Castle Dargan.
His written folklore sources do not include legends about the
oldest animals and it is likely he got his knowledge of them from
oral traditions or from conversations with Douglas Hyde. Hyde
included two such legends in *Legends of Saints and Sinners*, a
collection of oral traditions from the West of Ireland which he
translated and published in 1915, and remarked that he had
been interested in such legends of ancient animals for many
years. The first legend, 'The Adventures of Léithin', is trans-
lated from a Middle Irish manuscript which, according to Hyde,
is a variant of the ancient poem, as yet untranslated in 1915,
called the 'Colloquy between Fintan and the Hawk of Achill as
to who is the oldest'. Both Fintan and the Hawk of Achill were
6515 years old because they had each undergone many meta-
morphoses.[21] The Hawk of Achill was so old that the horn of the
anvil he had occasionally rubbed had come to be as thin and as
worn as a needle. When Fintan had been in the shape of the
salmon at Assaroe, the crow or hawk of Achill had plucked out
his eyes. The crow also has an interesting connection with Echtge,
the goddess who curses Hanrahan in the first story in the 1905
edition. After the Battle of Moytura the old crow had carried
off Echtge's father Nuada's hand, which had been a plaything
for the crow's children for seven years. The oldest of animals
motif thus has a close link with Irish mythology. Indeed, Hyde
remarks that the legend of the oldest animals is 'pre-Christian
folk-lore, and probably very much older than any documents'.
    Hyde follows his translation of the manuscript version with
a 'folk-lore version' entitled 'The Comparison as to Age between
the Four Elders; Namely, the Crow of Achill, the Great Eagle

of Leac Na Bhfaol, the Blind Trout of Assaroe and the Hag of Beare'. Léithin in Hyde's manuscript version had been an eagle who was victimised by the Hawk of Achill. An eagle is actually one of the oldest animals in the version Hyde translates from oral tradition. Hyde remarks that 'the Crow of Achill is a bird that every Irish speaker in the West has heard of, but Raftery curiously made him a "raven".' Elsewhere in oral tradition the bird was a hawk. There clearly were oral precedents either for the liberty which Yeats took in making the bird an eagle or for the ancient eagle itself. The usual blind salmon of Assaroe had become a trout in Hyde's version from oral tradition and thus suggests that Yeats's pike is merely another local variation.

Yeats knew of the ancient salmon of knowledge because that is the subject of O'Sullivan's query to Cleona in 'The Devil's Book' (1892): 'O'Sullivan asked her if Fintain the Salmon God still lived, and whether, if he did, he had not grown even wiser than he was in the time of Fionn McComhil [sic].' Yeats had also referred to the eagle of Balleygawley in *The Land of Hearts' Desire*, which was written in 1894, the same year he wrote 'The Curse of O'Sullivan the Red upon Old Age'. Michael Clancy, in Yeats's story 'Michael Clancy, the Great Dhoul, and Death' became a miraculous salmon in the river at Ballisodare rather than a will-of-the wisp as in most versions of 'the smith outwits the devil' plot. The popularity of the motif of the oldest animals in Yeats's work is probably due to such legends being among the most ancient materials available to Yeats in contemporary oral tradition and to the way the lives of such ancient animals provided a symbolic link between ancient and contemporary Ireland.

Such ancient fish and birds were obviously popular subjects in oral tradition in the West of Ireland. Sean O'Sullivan, whose *Folktales of Ireland* includes a version of the legend of the oldest animals collected in 1946 from a seventy-year old storyteller who had heard it more than fifty years earlier from his sixty-year old father, remarks that forty-three versions had been recorded as of 1966.[22] The ancient ash tree which Yeats has O'Sullivan and Hanrahan include in the curse on old age also represented a popular oral tradition concerning ancient trees and bushes which had witnessed and recorded all Irish history. Yeats changed the ash to a yew tree for the 1905 version. A yew tree was quite common in such a context; the Irish word 'éo' can mean a 'salmon' or a 'yew tree 'and the salmon or yew were both among the oldest things in Ireland according to oral tradition.[23] Lady Gregory's translation of such an oral history by a tree, 'The Story of Ireland to the Defeat at Aughrim as the Little Bush Told the Poet Raftery in Irish', is probably the best known published example.[24] The curse on old age which is the subject of the fourth Hanrahan story is thus as much a part of oral tradition as were the folksongs on which the preceding two stories were based. The situation which was the catalyst for the composition of the curse—the marriage of the young Colleen to an old man—was also a common custom in rural Ireland during the eighteenth and nineteenth centuries.[25]

Yeats had also described the poet's students playing traditional games in the first two versions of the story. His deletion of such games in 1905 reflects a subtle change of emphasis in which Hanrahan becomes less of a peasant hedge-schoolmaster and more of a bardic poet. The reference to his teaching English out of the chapbook, *Lives of Celebrated Rogues and Rapparees,* is also dropped in 1905. Moreover, Hanrahan in the 1905 version composes his curse, not outdoors as he had in the first two versions, but as bardic poets composed—on their bed in the darkness: '. . . he went and lay down on the bed for a while as he was used to do when he wanted to make a poem or a praise or a curse. And it was not long he was in making it this time, for the power of the curse-making bards was upon him.' This new detail heightens his association with the ancient Irish poetic tradition but it is integral to the plot and is not superfluous commentary or description relating him to ancient Ireland such as Yeats had removed at the beginning of 'The Twisting of the Rope' when 'simplifying' the stories for the 1905 edition.

'The Vision of O'Sullivan the Red' was not written until 1896 and represents, along with the opening and closing stories of the series, Yeats's most obvious attempt to make O'Sullivan a visionary. O'Sullivan sits on an old fairy rath where his reminiscences about his old love, Maive Lavell, and his thoughts of 'certain ancient poems that told of sinful lovers' who had gone to 'faeryland' after death generate a vision. He sees fairies, the 'divine Shee', then the spirits of famous ancient lovers 'Blanid and Deirdre and Grania' and finally the spirits of more recent and less noble lovers such as Diarmuid and Dervorgilla, whose fatal love supposedly brought the Normans to Ireland. However, O'Sullivan is incapable of comprehending who the lovers were until Dervorgilla herself explains who everyone was. The degeneration of love and nobility suggested by the contrast between the ancient lovers and twelfth-century lovers—Diarmuid is cursed always to see Dervorgilla as a rotting corpse because he had loved her physical body and not her eternal beauty—is paralleled by the implication that O'Sullivan possessed less than perfect visionary powers. He sees but does not understand what he sees; he is so terrified at what he sees that he shrieks and thus destroys the vision even though Dervorgilla wished to tell him more. In a similar manner, O'Sullivan had been incapable of loving Cleena whether she was in fairy or human form and his relationship with Maive, who is buried nearby, was also a failure. Hanrahan's visionary and amatory powers obviously represent a deterioration when they are compared to those of ancient Ireland where the gods had continually interacted with mortals and lovers had been heroic.

The only significant revisions Yeats made in this story of the vision in 1897 were the usual anglicisation of the place names and the addition of a detail about Hanrahan resting 'by that yew-tree which men believed to have been planted there by a hermit, who was thrice the age of common men, and which did not die until it was thrice the age of the hermit'. That new detail is derived from the same popular tradition about the oldest animals and trees which Yeats had integrated in the curse and dialogue of the preceding story. In *Legends of Saints and Sinners* Hyde quotes the following saying and says this one and many others are extremely popular in oral tradition :

Three wattles equal a hound's life;
Three hounds a steed;
Three steeds a man;
Three men an eagle;
Three eagles a salmon;
Three salmon a yew tree;
Three yew trees a ridge;
Three ridges from the beginning to the end of the world.[26]

The changes which Yeats made in the 1905 version of the story were more substantive. The lovers in the old poems Hanrahan thinks of at the beginning of the story now go to 'some shadowy land' rather than to 'faeryland' after death; the Sidhe in his vision are now specifically identified with 'the ancient defeated gods'. Mythological allusions have thus replaced fairy lore. Hanrahan likewise becomes more removed from ordinary peasants and poets: he is on the mountain because 'he had no mind to meet with common men' and the song he sings now has its origin in a vision—it 'had come to him one time in his dreams'.

The real Owen Roe O'Sullivan was thirty-six when he died penniless of the fever because of a relapse brought on by 'an act of self-indulgence', according to an Irish source translated by Daniel Corkery, in a hut for fever patients at Knocknagree, County Cork.[27] The death of O'Sullivan in Yeats's 1896 story and of Hanrahan in the *Secret Rose* story, in which only some of the names were changed, is significantly different. According to Yeats, O'Sullivan (and Hanrahan in 1897) passed the place where in the preceding story 'he had seen the unhappy lovers, that are in fairyland' on his way to his cabin on the mountain next to which 'the old yew . . . looked more malignant from dwelling at so great a height, an outcast from among its kind, and seemed to uplift its dark branches like withered hands, threatening the stars and the purple deep they fluttered in with the coming of decay and shadowy old age.' Once there O'Sullivan has an experience which ironically underscores how wisdom is as much beyond his powers as love had been. He seeks food from a being who could have given him knowledge:

A little black spot was moving from the hills and woods, between the mountain of Balligawley and the lake of Castle Dargan, and, while he watched, it grew larger and larger, until he knew it for a wide-winged bird, and then for a spotted eagle with something glittering in its claws. It came swiftly towards him, flying straight onward as if upon a long journey and pondering some hidden purpose; and when it was nearly overhead he saw that the glittering thing was a large fish, which still writhed from side to side. Suddenly the fish made a last struggle and leaped out of its claws, and

fell, with gasping mouth, into the branches of the yew tree.
O'Sullivan had not eaten since the previous morning, and
then but little, and, though he had been scarcely aware of his
hunger hitherto, his hunger came upon him now so fiercely
that he had gladly buried his teeth into the living fish. He
hurled a heavy stone at the eagle, which had begun to circle
with great clamour about the tree, and, having filled his
caubeen with like stones, drove it screaming over the moun-
tain eastward. He began then to climb the tree with a pas-
sionate haste, and had come to where the fish hung in the
fork between the two branches, glittering like a star among
the green smoke of some Fomorian fire, when a branch broke
under his hand and he fell heavily upon a rock, and from
this rebounded again, striking first his back and then his head,
and becoming unconscious at the last blow. The fire had
already consumed his goods, and now those creatures of earth
and air and water, that once endured his curse, had taken
him in a subtle ambuscade.

Hanrahan's physical assault on the yew tree, fish and eagle,
like his earlier curse on their antiquity, symbolises his inade-
quacies as a visionary. He curses and then subsequently drives
off the eagle and only seeks the fish for food rather than for
its legendary knowledge and wisdom. In the opening story
O'Sullivan had refused to compromise his quest for the ideal
and accept the fairy woman Cleona in human form; yet in his
curse and in his physical confrontation with the yew tree, eagle
and fish he combats and reduces these traditionally immortal
things to a purely mortal level. Like the Irish adventurers of
the eighteenth century, O'Sullivan's character represents seem-
ingly irreconcilable tendencies—longing for the ideal and lust
for the material, visionary potential and great obtuseness. The
blame must also be born by his times, in which the yew tree,
eagle and fish have perhaps lost their legendary powers. In any
event, his ironic quest of the fish causes his fall and ultimately his
death.

After he is knocked unconscious by his fall, O'Sullivan was
cared for by Whinny O'Byrne whose situation paralleled his
own in several respects. She was a grotesque old beggar who had
wandered through the countryside crying 'I am beautiful! I

am young!' O'Sullivan 'remembered that she was once so wise that the women of her village sought her counsel in all things; and had so beautiful a voice that men and women came from a distance of many miles to hear her sing at wake or wedding'. O'Sullivan too had once shared his knowledge as a hedge-schoolmaster and his gift of song as a poet. Whinny too had been enchanted by Cleena—'the people of the Shee stole her wits a summer night fifty years before, while she sat crooning to herself on the edge of the sea, and dreaming of Cleena. . . .' But Whinny's madness had enabled her to forget mortal things in a way the tormented O'Sullivan had never been able to. The withered and ugly Whinny O'Bryne is the medium of O'Sullivan's dying vision of Cleena who seemingly has finally come to claim him as her own for eternity. After his death Whinny wanders off and his body is not discovered until several days later by turf-cutters who give him a funeral befitting so great a poet.

The 1905 version ends in the same manner as the 1896 and 1897 versions, but everything else in the story was revised. Whinny O'Bryne becomes Winny Byrne, and the origin of her madness is changed so that it parallels Hanrahan's enchantment one Samhain night by Echtge—'the Others, the great Sidhe, had stolen her wits one Samhain night many years ago, when she had fallen asleep on the edge of a rath and had seen in her dreams the servants of Echtge of the hills.' Winny, like Hanrahan, is a more passive victim of Echtge than the original Whinny and O'Sullivan had been of Cleona. All traces of the legendary yew tree, eagle and fish have disappeared in this final version of the Hanrahan's death. Hanrahan slips and falls in a bog drain after being inexplicably drawn to follow Winny. Hanrahan dies, not in his own cabin, as O'Sullivan in 1896 and Hanrahan in *The Secret Rose* had, but in Winny's where he sees the four old women of the opening Hanrahan story playing cards. A 'big pot', 'flat stone', 'long rusty knife' and 'long blackthorn stick' in Winny's cabin, which were not in O'Sullivan or Hanrahan's cabin in the earlier stories, recall to Hanrahan the four Danaan symbols—'The Cauldron, the Stone, the Sword, the Spear'—he had seen during his initial encounter with Echtge which had opened the 1905 sequence of stories. These mythological objects have replaced the legendary yew tree, eagle and fish as the major symbols in the story of Hanrahan's death. But whereas O'Sullivan and Hanrahan in the earlier versions had no sense of the legendary significance of the yew, eagle and fish, this Hanrahan's sight of the four ordinary objects in Whinny's kitchen is transformed into a visionary experience of mythological significance.

O'Sullivan, in the 1892 story of his encounter with Cleena, had asked whether 'Fintain the Salmon God', the legendary salmon of knowledge still lived; Hanrahan in the 1897 version of that same Devil's Book story asked Cleona 'whether Angus the master of love still lived'. But Hanrahan in the 1905 opening story, 'Red Hanrahan', had been unable to ask any question, although each of the four treasures represent something: the old woman holding the cauldron says 'Pleasure', the old woman holding the stone says 'Power', the old woman holding the spear says 'Courage', and the old woman holding the sword says 'Knowledge'. O'Sullivan's quest for 'knowledge' had been replaced with Hanrahan's quest for 'love' in *The Secret Rose*; in 1905 the question has been significantly expanded. Although Hanrahan had been unable to ask any question about the four Danann treasures in the opening story in 1905, he is able to in the following passage from the closing story and consequently he seems finally to have earned legendary knowledge and the love of Echtge with whom he is about to be united: 'And when he saw those four things [pot, stone, knife and stick], some memory came into Hanrahan's mind, and strength came back to him, and he rose sitting up in the bed, and he said very loud and clear, The Cauldron, the Stone, the Sword, the Spear. What are they? Who do they belong to? And I have asked the question this time.' The opening story had made it clear that the treasures belonged to the gods of ancient Ireland and that they represented Pleasure, Power, Courage and Knowledge. Thus Hanrahan's question implies a quest for much more than either knowledge or love, and encompasses all the gods rather than just Fintain, the salmon-god of knowledge, or Angus the god of love. The full significance of Hanrahan's dying question is apparent in Richard Ellmann's explanation of what the four symbols meant to Yeats during the late 1890s when he wanted to found a mystical cult of Irish heroes based on them. Yeats explained their significance in an early draft of his *Autobiography*: 'At any moment of leisure, we obtained in vision long lists of symbolic forms that correspond to the cardinal points, and the old

H

gods and heroes took their places gradually in a symbolic fabric
that had for its centre the four talismans of the Tuatha De
Danaan [sic], the Sword, the Stone, the Spear, and the
Cauldron. . . .'; Ellmann goes on to summarise and explain
Yeats's notes concerning the significance of the four talismans:

> The talismans of sword, stone, spear, and cauldron are related
> to the elements of earth, air, water, and fire; each of these
> represents an aspect of the mind (a Zoa) that must be con-
> trolled. The spear is associated with passion, the sword with
> intellect, the cauldron with moving images (presumably
> imagined), and the stone with fixed ones (presumably seen).
> The man who has mastered each of these can hope to attain
> to the fifth element or final harmony ('Jerusalem'), where he
> is at one with universal forces, and where passion and intel-
> lect, desired image and actual fact, are united into one
> whole.[28]

Hanrahan's visionary powers in this final story in 1905 are
clearly superior to those possessed by himself in the earlier 1905
stories or in *The Secret Rose*, or by O'Sullivan in the earlier
periodical stories. Richard Finneran has argued that Yeats gave
the Hanrahan stories 'a mythic level of meaning' when he
changed the opening and closing stories in the 1905 edition
and that Hanrahan's adventures in the 1905 stories consequently
represented a progression through 'sin, suffering, repentance,
and redemption' which is reminiscent of the Romantic hero.[29]
In a similar manner, Carla Ackerman has shown that Han-
rahan, as portrayed in the 1905 stories, completes a kind of Grail
pilgrimage.[30] The mythic significance which both Finneran and
Ackerman see in Yeats's final version of the Hanrahan stories
is further underscored by the revisions discussed in this chapter.
The earliest versions of the Hanrahan stories—the periodical
stories about O'Sullivan—had been much more closely grounded
in the folklore and life of the peasantry. In the course of Yeats's
revisions, the fairies become gods, information about the fairies
disappears and information about the gods is added. Less and
less information is given about the customs of the peasantry.
Hanrahan becomes much less a peasant and much more a
visionary than O'Sullivan had been in the periodical stories. As
he wrote and rewrote these stories, Yeats transformed the pas-

sionate peasant poet of folk legend into a visionary who is much more in touch with ancient Ireland than with eighteenth-century Ireland. The history of the poem which Yeats eventually entitled 'Maid Quiet' provides a summary of that transformation. The poem was untitled in 'The Twisting of the Rope' in the 1892 periodical version and in the 1897 version in *The Secret Rose.* When Yeats published the poem, now entitled 'O'Sullivan the Red upon his Wanderings', in *The New Review* in August 1897, O'Sullivan has become a worshipper of the ancient gods according to the note with which Yeats preceded the poem : ' "Galeon's place of pride" is the mountain called "The Fews," and once called "Slieve Fua." It is fabled to be his (O'Sullivan's) tomb, and was doubtless the place of his worship, for Gulleon was Cullain, a god of the underworld. The "pale deer" were certain deer, hunted once by Cuchullain in his battle fury, and, as I understand them, symbols of night and shadow.'[31] In *Stories of Red Hanrahan* (1905) folklore has been transformed into mythology, the fairies have been transformed into the gods and the peasant poet has been transformed into a visionary.

Richard Finneran has argued that in the songs Yeats included in the successive versions of the Hanrahan stories, 'The movement is clearly from an Irish and folk idiom to a symbolic and esoteric idiom.'[32] What is true of the language of the songs is equally true of the substance of the stories themselves. Although Yeats wrote to John O'Leary in 1897 that the stories in *The Secret Rose* were 'an honest attempt towards that aristocratic esoteric Irish literature, which has been my chief ambition', the earliest versions of the Hanrahan stories had been grounded in folklore and quite down-to-earth. Yeats admitted in his Dedication at the beginning of the 1897 edition of *The Secret Rose* that 'I wrote these stories at different times and in different manners, and without any definite plan', but he claimed that 'they have but one subject, the war of spiritual with natural order' and 'so far, however, as this book is visionary it is Irish'.[33] In the earlier versions of the stories in *The Secret Rose* the natural order had been much stronger and more vivid than the spiritual order. Indeed, Yeats's revisions to the stories in *The Secret Rose* represent a decline in his conception of the peasantry.

Not only do details about the peasantry disappear in the

successive versions of the Hanrahan stories, the peasants them-
selves become less and less admirable as Hanrahan becomes less
a peasant and more a poet, and eventually less a poet and more
a visionary. The violent and earthy personality of the real
O'Sullivan also became increasingly unattractive to Yeats. After
1897 Yeats never reprinted the one story in *The Secret Rose*,
'The Rose of Shadow', which contained a character who resem-
bled the real O'Sullivan more closely in many ways than his
fictional O'Sullivan did. 'The Rose of Shadow', which had
originally been published in 1894 under the title 'Those Who
Live in the Storm', was the story of Oona Herne's abduction
to the other world by a demonic lover, Michael Creed, on the
first anniversary of his death. Until Oona's brother Peter had
killed Creed with a boat-hook, Creed, a ship's captain, 'had long
been the terror of the little western ports because of his violence
and brutality, and the hatred of all peaceful households, because
of his many conquests among women, whom he subdued
through that love of strength which is deep in the heart of even
the subtlest among them'.[34] Creed possessed the physical strength
and violent brutality which Yeats glossed over in his fictional
portrait of O'Sullivan by ignoring his life as a farm labourer
and his drinking. As Oona came under the dead Creed's spell,
she fittingly sang 'a fitful exultant air' which had supposedly
been composed by O'Sullivan in the 1894 version and by Han-
rahan in *The Secret Rose*. Her father struck her and said, 'Be
silent! that is an evil air, and no daughter of mine shall ever
sing it. Hanrahan the Red sang it after he had listened to the
singing of those who are about the faery Cleena of the Wave,
and it has lured, and will lure, many a girl from her hearth and
from her peace.' Her mother's response furthered Creed's asso-
ciation with Yeats's O'Sullivan or Hanrahan: 'The host of
Cleena sang of a love too great for our perishing hearts, and
from that night Hanrahan the Red is always seeking with wild
tunes and bewildered words to answer to their voices, and a
madness is upon his days and a darkness before his feet. His
songs are no longer dear to any but to the coasting sailors and
to the people of the mountain, and to those that are ill-nurtured
and foolish.' Yeats presented this story, like his stories about
O'Sullivan, as a local legend. He concluded it with details of
time and place such as characterise a legend: 'The next day

the neighbours found the dead in the ruined house, and buried them in the barony of Amharlish, and set over them a tombstone to say they were killed by the great storm of October 1765.' This sentence, as so many of the local details in the O'Sullivan stories were, was removed when the story was included in *The Secret Rose* because by then Yeats had become much less interested in recounting folk legends than in developing the occult and mythological significance of Hanrahan. Yeats's growing disenchantment with a character who represented only physical passion is apparent in the fact that he did not include 'The Rose of Shadow' in *The Secret Rose* after 1897.

Oona's materialistic parents in 'The Rose of Shadow' represent Yeats's declining opinion of the peasantry. The peasants had declined in stature with each new version of each Hanrahan story. The peasants in the stories in *The Secret Rose* which were not about Hanrahan were generally even more reprehensible. O'Sullivan and Hanrahan had become progressively more removed from the ordinary peasantry. The heroes in the other stories in *The Secret Rose* were often even more at odds with the peasantry than O'Sullivan and Hanrahan, who were peasants themselves, had been. The following analysis of other stories published in *The Secret Rose* (1897) will consider them in the order in which Yeats arranged them in *The Secret Rose* in *Collected Works* (1908).

Yeats based 'The Crucifixion of the Outcast' on a medieval Irish romance entitled 'The Vision of Mac Conglinne' which Kuno Meyer had translated and published in 1892. When Yeats reviewed 'The Vision of Mac Conglinne' he found in it an extravagance similar to that he had admired in the lives of the nineteenth-century peasantry but in a new form : 'It brings before one with very startling vividness that strange mixture of extravagant asceticism and extravagant indulgence, mystical aspiration and gross materialism which we call the Middle Ages.' Yeats's summary of this romance in his review indicates how much he changed his source : 'The whole story, too, is but a description of the gradual rout of the monks and the slow triumph of the gleeman, until it leaves him sitting at the right hand of the king.'[35] Yeats made three major changes in the original. Meyer's gleeman was to be crucified by the monks because he cursed them after he experienced how the ancient Irish custom of hospitality had become ludicrously degenerate among them. Yeats's gleeman was to be crucified because of his curse and because of his supposed allegiance to the ancient gods, Manannan, Aengus, Bridget, the Dagda and Dana, and to the fairies, Finvaragh and Cliona. Yeats's gleeman was actually crucified by the monks while the gleeman in his source was saved from crucifixion because of his vision concerning the source of the king's enchantment, a vision which led to his triumph when he exorcised and captured the demon from out of the king's body. After Yeats's gleeman was crucified, peasants stoned him and, despite his pleas, abandoned him to the birds and wolves. Yeats's hero is thus presented as much more closely associated with the ancient gods and as much more at odds with the peasantry who were not even present in Meyer's version. Yeats's peasants had no more appreciation for the literature or the mythology of ancient Ireland than the monks did. Both the peasants and monks embodied passionate violence and ferocity but they were completely devoid of vision or art.

In a similar manner, the young peasant assigned to watch over the dying medieval knight in 'Out of the Rose' loves 'stories' but has no conception of heroic or visionary action. The knight, mortally wounded while recovering the goods of materialistic, cowardly peasants from wood-thieves, was left by them under the care of the young peasant who asked the knight to tell him 'why you fought like the champions and giants in the stories and for so little a thing'.[36] The knight's dying explanation of his quest of the Rose was lost on the young peasant who said of it, 'He has told me a good tale for there was fighting in it, but I did not understand much of it, and it is hard to remember so long a story.' The young peasant appreciated neither the heroic passion and energy the knight had displayed in the fight with the wood-thieves nor the occult significance of his visionary quest. Yeats had clearly created the old knight as a man of both action and vision, as the following description of him from the 1893 version of the story made clear: 'He seemed to be that strange being who appears but seldom in the world, and, when he does, binds the hearts of men with his look of misery—doer and dreamer in one.'[37]

Although like Hanrahan the bard in the 'Crucifixion of the Outcast' and the old knight in 'Out of the Rose' each combined action and vision, the other characters in *The Secret Rose* stories suggest it had become more and more impossible for anyone to embody both passion and wisdom. The visionary powers of the king in 'The Wisdom of the King', which were bestowed upon him by the Sidhe when he was a child, distanced him from earthly passions and energies. In the 1897 version of the story, the 'common things of life . . . were hidden from him by thoughts and dreams that filled his mind like the marching and counter-marching of armies . . . his heart wandered lost amid throngs of overcoming thoughts and dreams, shuddering at its own consuming solitude.' The king's visionary powers doom the passion he offers to the beautiful girl because she is horrified by 'the mystery of the hawk feathers' which symbolises his un-earthly wisdom and she prefers to love an ordinary man. The plot of the king's subjects to have everyone wear feathers in place of hair in order to make him think he is like all men also fails. Because his wisdom is incompatible with the things of the world and with love, the king leaves. According to the 1897 version of the story, 'Some believed that he found his eternal abode among the demons, and some that he dwelt henceforth with the dark and dreadful goddesses, who sit all night about the pools in the forest watching the constellations rising and setting in those desolate mirrors.' 'The Wisdom of the King' thus suggests that heroic passion and vision, after having been crucified and misunderstood by ignorant peasants, can only find its home amidst the demons or goddesses. Phillip Marcus has pointed out in *Yeats and the Beginning of the Irish Renaissance* that this story combines the opening of Lady Wilde's nineteenth-century folktale, 'The Horned Women', with versions of the ancient legend of King Fergus MacLeide (Fergus Wry-Mouth) by Samuel Ferguson and Katharine Tynan.[38] Yeats's sources indicate that he fused contemporary folklore and ancient myth-ology in creating the story—a process which mirrors the fusion of contemporary legend and ancient legend evident throughout his writing and rewriting of the stories in *The Secret Rose*.

The remaining stories in *The Secret Rose*, most of which take place during later times, present heroic passion and ancient wisdom as increasingly incompatible. The 'very old man' who is the hero in 'The Heart of Spring' is a visionary who sees both 'the ancient gods' and 'the little people'. This combination of peasant folklore with ancient mythology, which characterises all the stories in *The Secret Rose*, is especially apparent in this story. The 1897 version contained a passage in which the old man described how he had performed the offices of what the peasantry would have called a 'fairy doctor' for an aristocratic clientele : 'I have saved all the gold and siver pieces that were given to me by earls and knights and squires for keeping them from the evil eye and from the love-weaving enchantments of witches, and by earls' and knights' and squires' ladies for keeping the people of the Sidhe, from making the udders of their cattle fall dry, and taking the butter from their churns.' As folklore becomes more and more aristocratic it becomes more mythological. Visionary wisdom has simultaneously become less and less associated with the peasantry. The old man advises his young servant not to pursue 'the search for the Great Secret' but to enjoy ordinary human passions instead. Nevertheless the old man does not abandon his own quest to 'become like the Immortal Powers themselves . . . like the Ancient Gods of the land'. Folklore and magic had been the keys to the old man's quest of the ancient gods which succeeds at the end of the story. A fairy man in a red cap told the old man how to prepare for his union with the Immortal Powers. After the old man died the young peasant concluded that 'It were better for him to have told his beads and said his prayers like another, and not to have spent his days in seeking amongst the Immortal Powers what he could have found in his own deeds and days had he willed' and saw no significance in a thrush having begun to sing among the boughs—the symbol of the old man's metamorphosis.

In 'The Curse of the Fires and of the Shadows' the pagan powers of the ancient gods and of the fairies were more powerful than either the Puritan troopers or the Christianity that the young peasant in 'The Heart of Spring' had concluded was preferable to pagan beliefs. After Sir Frederick Hamilton and his troops overcame the Abbey of the White Friars at Sligo, a group of the soldiers were themselves overcome by the combined forces of the hag known as the Washer at the Ford in Irish mythology and a fairy, 'an old man with a red cap and withered face', who enchanted the soldiers over a cliff and to their death. Yeats's story incorporated mythology and fairy lore into a local

Sligo legend which had had no supernatural overtones in Wood-Martin's *History of Sligo*:

> Cope's mountain, with its fearful precipices (bordering the valley of Glencar) is the scene of the alleged 'Protestant leap'. The legend connected with it is as follows:—A detachment of Colonel Hamilton's troops (garrisoned in Manorhamilton during the war of 1641) was making a raid into Sligo, and obtained a guide, who stipulated, in return for a certain sum of money, to enable the party to fall on the Irish unawares, at the close of the evening. 'Accordingly he led them up the mountain, directing them to a halt a little short of the precipice, of the existence of which they had not the most remote idea, while he himself moved forward to ascertain if all was favourable among the Irish, in which case he was to give them a signal, by dropping his cloak, to rush on to the work of havoc. The cloak was dropped, on perceiving which, rushing forward with eager haste, they reached the verge of the precipice, where, unable to check themselves, the rear pressing on the front rank, every man of the detachment was hurled down that fearful abyss. . . . Their deceitful guide had dropped the cloak just on the edge of the abyss towards which they accordingly rushed, and he, stepping aside, either made his way down the mountain again, or remained to gloat over the destruction of his victims.'[39]

The powers of the ancient gods and fairies had clearly declined by the eighteenth century according to the next story 'The Old Men of the Twilight'. The hero, 'old Michael Bruen', was a smuggler who lived at Rosses and was probably based on the many legends concerning smugglers which, according to William Murphy, Yeats heard when visiting his Middleton cousins who had a house at Rosses which was haunted by its builder, a smuggler named Black.[40] Michael Bruen, however, had become a fervent Christian in his old age. When he went out to shoot a heron at the beginning of the story he prayed: 'Patron Patrick, let me shoot a heron . . . if you keep me from missing I will say a rosary to you every night until the pie is eaten.' Bruen's was clearly a Christianity which involved little spiritual vision. Nor did he show any appreciation of ancient wisdom when the herons turned out to be ancient bards who

H*

had been cursed and enchanted by the druids and King Leag-
haire for having been too absorbed in their abstract poetics to be
interested in the Christianity which the king had accepted. The
latter-day Bruen's Christianity was a degenerate form of the
visions with which St Patrick had converted King Leaghaire
and the Druids. In the 1897 version of the story Bruen was
presented as 'trying in vain to understand something of this
tale'; in the version Yeats included in *Early Poems and Stories*
(1925) Bruen was 'too stupid to understand what he heard'.[41]
In all versions Bruen was more interested in getting the warm
cloak the bard wore than in any wisdom he offered. Bruen's
Christianity was neither passionate nor visionary; it was sheer
materialism.

The Christianity of earlier centuries, according to the next
story 'Where There is Nothing, There is God', had at least been
visionary. When the 'stupid and unteachable' Olioll suddenly
and miraculously grew clever under the influence of a beggar
whom the monastery had taken in, the brothers at first feared
that 'the child was trafficking with bards, or druids, or witches'.
But the beggar turned out to be 'the greatest of saints and of the
workers of miracle' named 'Aengus the Lover of God'. His
holiness and his name were an obvious inversion of the ancient
passion of Aengus the God of Love. This new Christian Aengus,
whose visionary powers were the antithesis of the ancient god's
passion, was perhaps supposed to be the legendary Oengus the
Culdee, the ninth-century hermit and scribe whose *Féilire*, a
calendar of saints and festivals with a verse for every day of the
year, represents the most extensive surviving collection of Old
Irish poetry.[42] If Yeats did base the Aengus in his story on
Oengus the Culdee, he pointedly left out any reference to
Aengus' association with Irish literature.

Yeats concluded the edition of *The Secret Rose* in his *Collected
Works* (1908) with the story 'Of Costello the Proud, of Oona
the Daughter of Dermott and of the Bitter Tongue', an account
of a tragic love affair which had occurred near Sligo in the
seventeenth century. The new arrangement of the stories thus
concluded with a character who embodied heroic passion more
than visionary powers, yet Yeats endowed the adventures of the
legendary Costello with a new visionary dimension such as he
had done when he transformed the legendary Owen Roe

O'Sullivan into Red Hanrahan. Yeats described Costello in the 1896 version of the story as follows: 'He was of those ascetics of passion who keep their hearts pure for love or for hatred, as other men for God, for Mary and for the saints, and who, when the hour of their visitation arrives, come to the Divine Essence by the bitter tumult, the Garden of Gethsemane, and the desolate rood, ordained for immortal passions in mortal hearts.'[43]

Yeats based his story of Costello on a popular legend with which Douglas Hyde had prefaced his translation of the even more popular folksong 'Fair Una' in *Love Songs of Connacht.* Hyde had declared, 'I do not think that there is any love song more widely spread throughout the country and more common in the mouth of the people than the poem which Tuamus Loidher (strong Thomas) Costello . . . composed over the unfortunate and handsome girl Una Mac Dermott, to whom he had given love.'[44] In Hyde's account of the legend, 'There was no man in Ireland in his time of greater strength and activity.' Although Una loved Costello, her father arranged for her to marry a wealthy farmer rather than the poor and wild Costello. At the betrothal ceremony Una defiantly declared her love for Costello; later she became so sick because of her love for Costello that her father finally relented and allowed her to send for him. Costello's visit restored Una's health but when he realised that they had been left alone in the house, his sense of honour made him leave. He rode slowly away expecting her father to send for him. His servant's insinuations that Mac Dermott was toying with him goaded Costello into vowing he would never return unless he was sent for before he crossed the river. He stood in the river for more than half an hour until goaded again by his servant, he rushed to the opposite bank. Almost immediately a messenger arrived to summon him back but, like an ancient hero under a geasa, Costello refused to break his vow. He killed his servant with one blow and refused to return to Una, who consequently died of grief. Hyde's legend culminated in the exquisite lament Costello supposedly composed over Una's grave.

Yeats's Costello shared the legendary Costello's strength, courage, pride and, most of all, his passionate nature. But Yeats's Costello was not a poet—instead of composing a song at

Oona's grave, Costello grieved there until Oona appeared to him amidst a crowd of 'the women of the Sidhe' who rush past and she angrily told him never to return. Costello, 'understanding nothing but that he made his beloved angry and that she wished him to go', waded into the lake and swam until, exhausted, he drowned. His passion had not generated poetry but instead had consumed him and led him to a vision, although the vision had not granted him wisdom. Oona and the Sidhe had rushed off 'in the shape of a great silvery rose' and Costello's body was found 'lying upon the white lake sand with his arms flung out as though he lay upon a rood'. According to Hyde, the legendary Costello was told to depart from Una's grave by Una's spirit after he had composed his lament and he lived to have many more adventures until he was killed by an assassin hired by his legendary enemies, the Dillons. Yeats's failure to include Costello's legendary lament for Oona in his story is all the more noteworthy because when he had based several of the Hanrahan stories on legends behind the composition of famous folksongs, he had always included the songs themselves—'The Twisting of the Rope 'and 'Kathleen-ny-Houlihan'.

Yeats split the personality of the legendary Costello in Hyde's account into two separate characters. He took the poetic powers he did not include in Costello's character and gave them to the servant, who in Yeats's story became a piper referred to as Duallach, son of Daly, and was thus a member of an ancient line of poets, the family of Ó Dálaigh. Although Duallach's tongue generates only curses and bitterness within the story or else retells older stories, his bitter tongue caused the tragedy which in turn generated the song and the legend. This is clear in the passage commenting on Duallach's death which Yeats included in the story until 1925 : '. . . and the waters swept over the tongue which God had made bitter that there might be a story in men's ears in after time'. Until 1925, Duallach's story-telling powers also played an important role in the story. Several lengthy paragraphs in the early versions of the story described how Duallach sang traditional songs and retold 'those traditional tales which were as much a piper's business'. Costello 'while the boundless and phantasmal world of the legends was a-building, would abandon himself to the dreams of his sorrow'.

Costello's response to the legends Duallach told in the following passage resembled Yeats's personal interpretation of the Cuchulain legend and recalled his declaration in his 1893 essay 'The Message of the Folk-lorist' that folklore offered 'types and symbols of those feelings and passions which find no adequate expression in common life'.

> Duallach would often pause to tell how the Lavells or Dunns or Quinns or O'Dalys, or other tribe near his heart, had come from some Lu, god of the leaping lightning, or incomparable King of the Blue Belt or Warrior of the Ozier Wattle, or to tell with many railings how all the strangers and most of the Queen's Irish were the seed of some misshapen and horned Fomoroh or servile and creeping Firbolg; but Costello only cared for the love sorrows, and no matter whither the stories wandered, whether to the Isle of the Red Lock where the blessed are, or to the malign country of the Hag of the East, Oona alone endured their shadowy hardships; for it was she, and no King's daughter of old, who was hidden in the steel tower under the water with the folds of the Worm of Nine Eyes round and about her prison; and it was she who won, by seven years of service, the right to deliver from hell all she could carry, and carried away multitudes clinging with worn fingers to the hem of her dress; and it was she who endured dumbness for a year because of the little thorn of enchantment the fairies had thrust into her tongue . . . for there was no beauty in the world but hers, no tragedy in the world but hers. . . .[45]

Yeats removed the opening reference to Irish peasants being descended from ancient gods, an obviously contrived attempt to link the peasantry with ancient Ireland, when he included the story in *The Secret Rose* (1897). He deleted the entire lengthy section describing Duallach's story-telling when he prepared the *Secret Rose* stories for *Early Poems and Stories*. By 1925 he was no longer so absorbed with linking the characters and events in the *Secret Rose* stories to ancient Ireland, as his revisions in the Hanrahan stories and other *Secret Rose* stories have already indicated. Yeats let the narrative itself convey the legendary significance of the characters and this tragedy in 1925 when only one sentence suggesting that significance remained:

'. . . the peasants came about the door and peered in, as though they understood that they would gather their children's children about them long hence, and tell how they had seen Costello dance with Mac Dermot's daughter Una. . . .'[46] In the 1896 version through the 1908 version of the story that passage had been followed by this statement: '. . . and become, by the telling, themselves a portion of ancient romance'.

The legend about Costello thus represented Yeats's deepening appreciation for the power and significance of 'the story' itself, a theme which was apparent in so many of the poems and plays he wrote while writing and revising the *Secret Rose* stories. During the 1890s Yeats became convinced that passion and vision could best be achieved not within a man's life but through the story or legend which celebrated that life. The legend that lived on after the man and commemorated his heroic passion was what immortalised them. Such a legend could be created over the generations through oral tradition and then recreated by writers like Yeats who, in so many of the stories in *The Secret Rose*, recreated legendary heroes and stories. Hanrahan, of course, is the best example of Yeats's achievement in this regard in *The Secret Rose*. Hanrahan became so much Yeats's own creation because of the visionary experiences he endowed him with that he could declare in 'The Tower'—'And I myself created Hanrahan'—and request wisdom from Hanrahan in that poem which the legendary O'Sullivan had never possessed:

> Go therefore; but leave Hanrahan,
> For I need all his mighty memories.
> Old lecher with a love on every wind,
> Bring out of that deep considering mind
> All that you have discovered in the grave . . .[47]

The lecher had become a seer because of the legend Yeats recreated in the Hanrahan stories in *The Secret Rose*. Passion had been united with vision and immortalised in legend. Richard Finneran has quoted Yeats's remark in his *Autobiography*—'I had some hope that my invention [Hanrahan] . . . might pass into legend as though he were a historical character'—to support the conclusion that with Hanrahan, Yeats 'attempted to make his contribution to the corpus of folklore'.[48] Hanrahan was a character in plays by both Douglas Hyde and Lady

Gregory. Hanrahan rather than Owen Roe O'Sullivan was the
hero in Hyde's version of 'The Twisting of the Rope' legend,
'Casadh an t-Sugain', the first play in Gaelic produced by the
Irish Literary Theatre. Hanrahan was also the subject of Lady
Gregory's play 'Hanrahan's Oath'.

Yeats's fashioning of the Hanrahan legend out of the actual
folk legend of O'Sullivan had been a significant step towards
his later method of transforming his friends and contemporaries
into legend. Yeats's admiration for the legend he created in
Hanrahan reflects the important influence which the narrative
process of legend was to have on the creation of his later works,
a matter which will be discussed in the next chapter. Yeats's
success in combining heroic passion and ancient wisdom in the
Hanrahan stories provided him with an artistic method and a
fervent lifelong belief in the power of Art to immortalise heroic
passion and ancient wisdom in human form and thus to achieve
the goal of his occult and messianic pursuits through Art. Michael
Robartes, a character in 'Rosa Alchemica' in the 1897 edition
of *The Secret Rose*, represented the occult and messianic alter-
native to Hanrahan. 'Rosa Alchemica', which Yeats separated
from both the Hanrahan stories and *The Secret Rose* stories in
his *Collected Works* in 1908, contained a passage, not deleted
until 1925, which carried the mythological and occult overtones
of the other *Secret Rose* stories still further. Michael Robartes,
who has established a mystical order based on Irish mythology
and the occult in the West of Ireland, expressed his alienation
from the Christianised peasantry and his hopes for the future
in the following words:

I and mine are long past human hurt or help, being in-
corporate with immortal spirits, and when we die it shall
be the consummation of the supreme work. A time will come
for these people [the peasants] also, and they will sacrifice
a mullet to Artemis, or some other fish to some new divinity,
unless indeed their own divinities, the Dagda, with his over-
flowing cauldron, Lug, with his spear dipped in poppy-juice
lest it rush forth hot for battle, Aengus, with the three birds
on his shoulder, Bodb and his red swineherd, and all the
heroic children of Dana, set up once more their temples of
grey stone. Their reign has never ceased, but only waned in

power a little for the Sidhe still pass in every wind, and dance
and play at hurley, and fight their sudden battles in every
hollow and on every hill; but they cannot build their temples
again till there have been martyrdoms and victories, and
perhaps even that long-foretold battle in the Valley of the
Black Pig.[49]

The success of Michael Robartes's attempts to achieve heroic
passion and ancient wisdom hinged on the return of the ancient
gods and apocalyptic cataclysms. The creation of *The Secret
Rose* stories out of traditional Irish literature and folklore had
suggested an alternative means of achieving that heroic passion
and ancient wisdom through Art.

The new sources of traditional literature and folklore which
became available to Yeats during the 1890s also influenced his
growing absorption with ancient Irish mythology and legend.
In the course of his revisions to the stories in *The Secret Rose*
Yeats had either replaced the fairies with the ancient gods or
else had associated the fairies with the gods. The peasantry be-
came more and more removed from heroic passion and ancient
wisdom. The peasantry in 'Costello the Proud', with the ex-
ception of the MacDermot and the MacNamara clans, were
nobler than in any other story in *The Secret Rose* because they
sympathised with Costello and were presented as 'wild Irish'
who continued ancient traditions. Even as late as the 1925
version they supposedly 'left the right arms of their children un-
christened that they might give the better blows, and were even
said to have named the wolves godfathers to their children.'[50]
Like Hanrahan, Costello and the other heroes in *The Secret
Rose*, the nobility of the peasantry was in direct proportion to
the extent of their relationship with ancient Ireland. Yet Yeats
had to go back to the seventeenth century to find such a peas-
antry and such a hero as Costello. Such a peasantry had dis-
appeared by the eighteenth century according to his Hanrahan
stories. But the heroic passions of ancient Irish heroes and peasant
visionary experiences of mythological dimensions had become
much more readily available to Yeats.

During the 1880s when Yeats had had reservations about the
expression of personality in literature, the old myths and legends
had been either inaccessible in Irish manuscripts or available in

unsatisfactory translations and popularisations. Earlier nine-
teenth-century collections of Irish folklore had contained mostly
folk beliefs, fairy legends, or folktales. Yeats's growing interest
in the quintessential Irish personality fortunately coincided with
the publication of several important new collections of folklore
which encouraged his new absorption with heroic passion.
Yeats's reservations about personality in literature had already
begun to disappear because of his fascination with the character
of the Irish peasant in 1890 when Douglas Hyde published
Beside the Fire: A Collection of Irish Gaelic Folk Stories. Hyde's
collection, which Yeats repeatedly praised as the best collection
of Irish folklore ever published, contained several narratives
about legendary figures such as Bran and Crinnawn, son of
the god Balor. Hyde also included several 'hero tales' such as
'The King of Ireland's Son' and 'Guleesh Na Guss Dhu', in
which legendary Irish heroes had adventures with mythological
overtones. Most of the tales in Jeremiah Curtin's two collections,
Myths and Folk-Lore of Ireland (1890) and *Hero-Tales of
Ireland* (1894) were about ancient Irish heroes. The story
'Cuculin' in Curtin's first collection was Yeats's source for his
poem 'The Death of Cuchullin' (1892). The tales in William
Larminie's *West Irish Folk-Tales* (1894) were concerned with
ancient Ireland or took place in a timeless realm more readily
identifiable with ancient than with modern Ireland. Hyde,
Curtin, and Larminie all translated their materials from the Irish
and consequently their style was not marred by the artificial sub-
limity and stale literary conventions of earlier popularisations.

These collections, especially the heroic passions and adven-
tures and the suggestion of ancient wisdom which they con-
tained, transformed Yeats's earlier attitudes about ancient Irish
myth and hero tales. The number of allusions to myths and hero
tales in Yeats's works increased throughout the 1890s. When
Yeats reviewed Larminie's *West Irish Folk-Tales* he declared
that even Hyde's *Beside the Fire*, which had contained mostly
folktales, had been 'no such heaped-up bushel of primeval
romance and wisdom as "West Irish Folk Tales" '.[51] In this
essay Yeats applied the same critical vocabulary to the legendary
heroes that he had used a few years earlier about fairy lore
and the peasants : he declared that Larminie's materials had 'the
extravagance and tumultuous movement as of waves in a

storm'. During the late 1890s when Yeats and George Russell
were working to form a mystical Irish order modelled upon
the occult wisdom of ancient Ireland, they attempted to con-
jure the heroes of an ancient mystical Ireland rather than the
fairies they had conjured in the 1880s. The ancient heroes now
personified the passion, the energy and the imaginative extra-
vagance he had been seeking in the Irish peasant and his
folklore. As Yeats declared in 1892, 'And if history and the
living present fail us, do there not lie hid among those spear
heads and golden collars over the way in the New Museum,
suggestions of that age before history when the art legends
and wild mythology of earliest Ireland rose out of the void?
There alone is enough of the stuff that dreams are made on to
keep us busy a thousand years.'[52] The ancient Irish heroes had
traditionally been viewed as half-human, half-supernatural
creatures, and thus combined the supernatural qualities Yeats
had admired in the Irish fairies with the human emotions and
energy he had sought in the Irish peasants and in the Irish
adventurers. The ancient heroes also provided Yeats with an
image of heroic action with which he tried to identify during
his attempts to pursue a life of action during the 1890s and dur-
ing his courtship of Maud Gonne.

Moreover, as Yeats had become more and more annoyed
with the factual and linguistic accuracy demanded by Irish
folklorists and with the realism inherent in Irish fiction, the
fantastic extravagance inherent in Irish myth became more and
more appealing. As he remarked in his 'Introduction' to *Repre-
sentative Irish Tales*, 'No modern Irish writer has ever had any
thing of the high culture that makes it possible for an author
to do as he will with life, to place the head of a beast upon a
man, or the head of a man upon a beast, to give to the most
grotesque creation the reality of a spiritual existence.'[53] Yeats's
note explaining the Fomoroh in *Poems* (1895) shows how his
developing conception of Irish myth encouraged rather than
limited his admiration for imaginative extravagance: 'The
Fomoroh were misshapen and had now the heads of goats and
bulls, and now but one leg, and one arm that came out of the
middle of their breasts.'[54] Yeats could say of ancient Irish myths,
'It is not necessary that [writers] should understand them with
scholar's accuracy, but they should know them with the heart,

so as not to be repelled by what is strange and *outré* in poems or plays taken therefrom. The most imaginative of all our periods was the heroic age.'[55]

Materials from ancient Irish myth also provided the seriousness and depth which Yeats had once sought in Irish fairy lore. Yeats had attempted to endow the pooka in *Fairy and Folk Tales of the Irish Peasantry* (1888) with awesome and monstrous dimensions which his materials had not justified. Yeats had presented the theory that the fairies were descended from the gods of ancient Ireland in his Introduction to *Fairy and Folk Tales*, but he explicitly rejected mythological interpretations of Irish fairy lore in the same introduction. Yet Irish myth eventually resolved his dilemma about the pooka. In the same 1895 note about the Fomoroh quoted above, he explained the Fomoroh were 'the gods of night and death and cold . . . [and] the ancestors of the evil faeries'; in 1899 he referred to 'the horse-shaped Pucas, who are now mischievous spirits, but were once Fomorian divinities'.[56]

Even though the ancient heroes replaced the peasantry as Yeats's major subject matter during the 1890s, he still valued them as a repository of ancient legends. In 1898 Yeats participated in a published debate with John Eglinton, George Russell, and William Larminie about the place of Irish myth in modern Irish literature. Yeats vehemently defended Irish myth against Eglinton's charge that the ancient legends 'obstinately refuse to be taken out of their old environment and be transplanted into the world of modern sympathies' and declared that the ancient legends were to be found both 'in popular tradition and in old Gaelic literature'. But Yeats's definition of poetry during the same debate—'a revelation of a hidden life . . . the only means of conversing with eternity left to man on earth'—indicates why ancient Irish myth, with its associations of occult wisdom, seemed preferable to the peasantry and their fairies.[57] However, the oral traditions to which Lady Gregory introduced Yeats during the late 1890s convinced him that the beliefs of the contemporary peasantry were indeed in touch with ancient Irish mythology. Yeats acknowledged his debt to Lady Gregory in this regard when he dedicated *Plays for an Irish Theatre* to her in 1903. He said he had collected folklore since he was a child but explained:

Then I went to London to make my living, and though I spent a part of every year in Ireland and tried to keep the old life in my memory by reading every country tale I could find in books or old newspapers, I began to forget the true countenance of country life. The old tales were still alive for me indeed, but with a new, strange, half unreal life, as if in a wizard's glass, until at last, when I finished 'The Secret Rose', and was half-way through 'The Wind Among the Reeds', a wise woman in her trance told me that my inspiration was from the moon, and that I should always live close to water, for my work was getting too full of those little jewelled thoughts that come from the sun and have no nation. I had no need to go to my books of astrology to know that the common people are under the moon, or to Porphyry to remember the image-making power of the waters . . . I no longer had the knowledge and emotion to write. Then you brought me with you to see your friends in the cottages, and to talk to old wise men on Slieve Echtge, and we gathered together, or you gathered for me, a great number of stories and traditional beliefs. You taught me to understand again, and much more perfectly than before, the true countenance of country life.[58]

Yeats's references to forgetting country life, to *The Secret Rose* and to his work lacking a nation, recall the revisions he made in the stories before he published them in *The Secret Rose* in 1897: the anglicisation of place names and the removal of other place names and details of peasant life. Irish folklore again inspired Yeats and brought his work back down-to-earth as it had in the late 1880s, but this time it had explicit occult and mythological overtones.

Between 1897 and 1902 Yeats published six articles based on the folklore he and Lady Gregory had collected: 'The Tribes of Danu' (1897), 'The Prisoners of the Gods' (1898), 'The Broken Gates of Death' (1898), 'Ireland Bewitched' (1899), 'Irish Witch Doctors' (1900), and 'Away' (1902).[59] He included materials from several of these articles in the revised edition of *The Celtic Twilight*. Each essay opened and closed with his commentary, but the central portions were a much more direct reportage of oral tradition than any essay in *The Celtic Twilight*.

The first article, 'The Tribes of Danu', explained that the
fairies were the tribes of the ancient Goddess Danu and that
the pagan religion of ancient Ireland had survived over the
centuries and still coexisted with Christianity. Yeats declared
the fairies to be 'the gods', yet he was equally concerned with
the legends of the ancient 'heroes and beautiful women of old
times' commemorated by local legends all over Ireland. The land-
scape of Ireland, where legend held that the ancient heroes had
enacted the 'old love tales, old battle tales', thus was a living link
with the ancient heroes just as the fairies were a living link with
the ancient gods. People taken by the fairies were thus called
'prisoners of the Gods' in the second article in which Yeats
declared 'the peasants believe in their ancient gods, and that to
them, as to their forbears, everything is inhabited and mysterious'.
Yeats concluded the third article, 'The Broken Gates of Death',
with the declaration : 'The stories of the country people, about
men and women taken by "the others," throw a clear light
on many things in the old Celtic poems and romances, and
when more stories have been collected and compared, we shall
probably alter certain of our theories about the Celtic mythology.'
The fairy legends retold tales such as had once been told about
ancient heroes : 'And when the country men and country women
tell of people taken by "the others," who come into the world
again, they tell the same tales the old Celtic poets and romance
writers told' when they told of Finn, Cormac Mac Art, and
Oisin and their encounters with 'the gods'. Yeats declared in
'Ireland Bewitched' that the folklorist who gains the peasantry's
confidence 'soon finds that they live in a very ancient world' :
'One finds the old witches and wise men still busy, and even the
crafts of the smith and of the miller touched with a shadow
of old faiths, that gives them a brotherhood with magic. The
principal crafts were once everywhere, it seems, associated with
magic, and had their rites and their gods.' In the fifth article,
'Irish Witch Doctors', Yeats associated Irish fairy doctors with
the ancient gods and 'the old Irish epic tales'. In the sixth
article, 'Away', Yeats demonstrated how legends of peasants
'taken' by the fairies parallel and make more intelligible the
ancient legends about heroes such as Cuchulain being 'taken'
by the gods because 'the country people inherit their belief'
from 'the ancient peoples'.

When Yeats interpreted the ancient legendary materials available in folklore collections published during the 1890s in the light of new theories about ancient myth, Lady Wilde's claims about the mystical meanings inherent in the legends and tales of the peasantry began to be justified. Contemporary theories about the religious nature of ancient Irish myth implied that the occult wisdom Yeats had been seeking was to be found in the ancient legends. Yeats became enthusiastic about the theories of John Rhys and Henri D'Arbois Jubainville that the beliefs of the Irish peasantry were examples of the primitive religion of mankind. In 1890 he had praised Rhys and Jubainville for having made him see in the beliefs of the peasantry 'old beautiful mythologies wherein ancient man said symbolically all he knew about God and man's soul, once famous religions fallen into ruin and turned into old wives' tales, but still luminous from the rosy dawn of human reverie'.[60] When Yeats reviewed Daniel Deeney's *Peasant Lore from Gaelic Ireland* in 1900 he declared that an Irish-speaking folklore collector like Deeney stood 'at the gates of primitive and barbaric life'.[61] His own folklore collecting expeditions in County Galway with Lady Gregory had been a crucial influence on his deepening sense of the mystical and ancient mythological overtones of contemporary folklore.

Yeats's essay 'The Celtic Element in Literature' (1897) is his definitive and best known statement of the interconnection between contemporary folklore and ancient mythology.[62] This essay also marks the culmination of his search for ancient wisdom and heroic passion in traditional Irish literature—he had originally sought wisdom and passion in the folklore and the life of the Irish peasantry, and later in their folk heroes, the rogues and rapparees of *Irish Adventurers* and the legendary poets and heroes of *The Secret Rose*. Yeats declared in the essay that folk literature was indeed in touch with ancient wisdom and passion : 'All folk literature, and all literature that keeps the folk tradition, delights in unbounded and immortal things. . . . All folk literature has indeed a passion whose like is not in modern literature and music and art, except where it has come by some straight or crooked way out of ancient times.' Yeats appropriately succeeded this last statement with an example of lyrical passion from Hyde's *Love Songs of Connacht* :

'Love was held to be a fatal sickness in ancient Ireland, and there is a love-poem in the *Love Songs of Connacht* that is like a death-cry: "My love, O she is my love, the woman who is most for destroying me . . ." ' Despite Yeats's assertion—'the ancient farmers and herdsmen were full of love and hatred, and made their friends gods, and their enemies the enemies of gods, and those who keep their tradition as not less mythological' —the gap between ancient god and modern peasant seems extensive. Yeats bridged this gap with legendary heroes who were at once divine and human. According to Yeats, the 'passions' of the 'great gods' echoed in the 'wild and beautiful lamentations' of tragedy in the old hero tales. In Oisin's lamentations—still the most popular poetry in Irish-speaking places according to Yeats—the wild Irish melancholy and passion become heroic. As Yeats tells it, the cauldron of a mythological Irish god became the Holy Grail of the legendary Arthur and 'later still Shakespeare found his Mab, and probably his Puck, and one knows how much else of his faery kingdom, in Celtic legend'. Myth evolved into heroic legend and heroic legend in turn evolved into fairy legends. Maeve was transformed from a goddess to a semi-historical heroine to the fairy queen Mab. To Yeats's credit, Alan Bruford in *Gaelic Folk-Tales and Medieval Romances* argues that a similar transformation from ancient god to legendary hero did actually take place in traditional Irish literature.

Yeats found the vision of 'the life beyond the world' he once sought in fairy lore and the 'unbounded emotion' he once sought among the peasantry and their folk heroes in ancient Irish myth and legend. He concluded 'The Celtic Element in Literature', not with reference to the ancient gods, but to the legendary heroes and heroines of ancient Ireland—Deirdre, Cuchulain, Grania and Diarmuid—and declared, 'Literature dwindles to a mere chronicle of circumstances, or passionless phantasies, and passionless mediations, unless it is constantly flooded with the passions and beliefs of ancient times.' He added a postscript to the essay in 1902 which said that he could have written the essay with more precision and better illustrations 'if I had waited until Lady Gregory had finished her book of legends, *Cuchulain of Muirthemne*, a book to set beside the *Morte d'Arthur* and the *Mabinogion*'. Yet it was fitting that Yeats wrote his definitive essay on the relationship between folklore and mythology before Lady Gregory actually published either *Cuchulain of Muirthemne* (1902) or *Gods and Fighting Men* (1904). Yeats's profuse praise of both works and his repeated referrals of his readers to these works for information about the legendary and mythological backgrounds of his own works have too often obscured the extensive and complex development his own attitudes about folklore and mythology underwent during the decade before he met Lady Gregory in 1896. His interest in ancient Irish mythology had begun with his interest in Irish folklore and had evolved through several successive subjects— fairies, peasants, rogues and rapparees, legendary poets and heroes of recent centuries, and finally ancient heroes—and through several successive genres—poetry, folk belief legends, Anglo-Irish fiction, legends of folk heroes, and finally ancient myth and legend. The title of Yeats's first twentieth-century collection of poetry, *In the Seven Woods: Being Poems Chiefly of the Irish Heroic Age* (1903), indicates how complete the transformation of Yeats's traditional Irish subject matter had become.

7

'Traditional Innovations'
in Literary Theory and Style

Irish folklore influenced the language, the subject matter, the literary theory and the style of Yeats's writings and enabled him to be at once conservative and innovative. Irish folklore provided Yeats with a 'new' subject matter and a 'new' poetic diction and syntax because the content and the Anglo-Irish idiom of Irish oral traditions were unknown to most of his readers. The influence of the Anglo-Irish dialect on Yeats's work has frequently been explored. His poems, plays and prose fiction have repeatedly been traced to sources in traditional Irish literature. The theoretical and stylistic repercussions of Irish folklore in Yeats's writings have only begun to be explored.

The innumerable sources in Irish folklore and mythology for plots, characters, details and allusions in Yeats's writings are well known. However, the pattern of development in his use of subjects from Irish folklore and mythology, which has been suggested by this book's study of his interests as an anthologist and fiction writer, is also apparent in the poetry and plays he wrote during the 1880s and 1890s. The fairies had been the subject of many of the poems which Yeats wrote in the late 1880s, but gradually the peasantry replaced the fairies as the major Irish subject of Yeats's poetry. Peasants rather than the fairies are Yeats's focus in poems as 'The Meditation of the Old Fisherman' (1886); 'The Priest of Coloony' (1888), later retitled 'The Ballad of Father O'Hart'; 'The Ballad of Moll Magee' (1889); 'The Lamentation of the Old Pensioner' (1890); 'The Ballad of Father Gilligan' (1890); 'The Man who Dreamed of Fairyland' (1891). All of these poems were included in later editions of his works, but he included only a few of the poems about the fairies in later editions of his poetry.

Yeats had declared in 1892 that 'He who studies the legends, the history, and life of his own countryside may find there all the themes of art and song.'[1] By the end of the decade the legends most associated with ancient Ireland had become his major interest, and the gods and heroes of ancient Ireland replaced both the fairies and the peasantry as Yeats's major Irish subject matter. In the list of 'Authorities on Irish Folk-lore' which Yeats appended to *Fairy and Folk Tales of the Irish Peasantry*, only the *Transactions of the Ossianic Society* had been specifically concerned with ancient Ireland. By 1892 a similar list appended to *Irish Fairy Tales* included Douglas Hyde's, Jeremiah Curtin's, and Standish J. O'Grady's works about ancient Ireland. In the list of 'best Irish books' which Yeats compiled in 1895, nine of the twelve works in the section entitled 'Folklore and Legend' were specifically concerned with ancient Ireland.[2] As Yeats's knowledge of the ancient gods and heroes increased, so too did his use of them in his writings. The notes on Irish myth which Yeats appended to his poems became longer with each succeeding collection in the 1890s. The recently published manuscript versions of *The Shadowy Waters* indicate that Yeats included new materials from ancient Irish myth, available to him in recently published works, in successive versions of the play during the 1890s.[3]

The revisions which Yeats made in his plays during the 1890s also indicate that the stature of the peasants declined as the heroes of ancient Ireland became more significant. In *The Countess Kathleen*, the ordinary, somewhat foolish peasants are more numerous and individualised in the version of 1892 than in the version of 1895, in which Yeats removed some of the peasant characters and added references to figures from ancient Irish myth. In the 1892 version, Kevin, the Irish bard familiar with legends of the ancient heroes, is a minor character whose visions are vague. By 1895 Kevin has become a much more prominent character renamed Aleel whose visions are filled with allusions to ancient Ireland. When Yeats recalled his 're-writing' of the play, he described it as 'elaborating the death scene, filling it with the old Irish mythology as that was getting an always greater mastery over my imagination'.[4] Yeats's image of the Irish peasantry also noticeably deteriorated in his play, *The Land of Heart's Desire* (1894). With the exception of the heroine, the peasants do not see the fairies and are portrayed as more concerned with getting and spending than with poets and ballads. Significantly, 'Faeryland' in the play is presented as the home of the heroes and gods of ancient Ireland as well as of the creatures of Irish fairy lore.

When collecting folklore with Lady Gregory in the late 1890s renewed Yeats's interest in fairies and peasants, these new fairies and peasants were clearly in touch with the gods and heroes of Ireland. Yeats had realised in the course of the 1890s that the ancient wisdom he had sought in fairy lore and the heroic passions he had sought in the peasants and their legendary heroes such as 'Fighting Fitzgerald' and Owen Roe O'Sullivan were both available in ancient Irish myth and legend. 'The Cradles of Gold', a story based on fairy lore and peasant life which Yeats published in 1896, mirrors the failure of his early attempts to endow the fairies with ancient wisdom and the peasantry with heroic passions. The story was set near Sligo and its hero, Michael Hearne, epitomised 'passion' such as could be found among the peasantry: 'He lived alone, because the many scars left by the fights at patterns and on fair days, and his reputation for grimness and violence, had kept him from getting a wife.'[5] When his timid brother Peter's wife Whinny was 'taken' by the fairies in order to nurse the child of Finvaragh, the king of the fairies, Peter enlisted Michael's help. The next time Whinny returned to nurse her own baby, Michael grabbed her and yelled defiantly at the fairies: 'Children of the Goddess, children of Dana, faeries of the Hill, take her from me if you dare.' The fairies were described as 'a multitude of tall, slender forms dressed in a saffron raiment, and having torques of silver and gold' but neither their wisdom nor their passion rang any truer than their supposedly ancient dress. Finvaragh said, 'I am Finvaragh, the King, and understand many things that even the archangels do not understand, and out of my knowledge I bid you let her go.' That statement and his wish to 'meditate upon the wisdom that Mongan raved out after he had drunk from the seven vats of wine' were no more than empty rhetoric. Michael referred to the fairies' 'passionate natures' but the story presented no examples. It is not surprising that Michael was able to rescue Whinny from such fairies and that Yeats did not include such a story in *The Secret Rose*. The early stories which Yeats did include in *The Secret Rose* were rewritten in order to identify the fairies more closely with ancient gods and goddesses and the peasant heroes with ancient heroes.

The mythological dimensions of the oral traditions which Yeats collected in Galway with Lady Gregory delighted him. Lady Gregory showed him that the ancient heroes were still alive in the imaginations of the Kiltartan peasantry. Although much of the material she used in *Gods and Fighting Men* was drawn from manuscript sources, she declared that stories of the Fenian heroes could be got 'from any old person in the place'.[6] Yeats's delight with the heroic tales Lady Gregory narrated in *Gods and Fighting Men* and *Cuchulain of Muirthemne* is obvious in the Prefaces he wrote for each book. He declared that, contrary to earlier translations and popularisations of ancient Irish myth and legend, Lady Gregory's works told them 'perfectly for the first time'.[7] When he praised Lady Gregory's collections for their extravagance and symbolism, their heroic passion and wildness and their mythological and visionary dimensions it is apparent he has finally found the combination of ancient wisdom and heroic passion he had been seeking.[8] Since the time of his early enthusiasm for Samuel Ferguson's work, Yeats had declared the ancient legends were full of heroic passion. He eventually came to believe that such 'passionate art' approached the condition of vision and wisdom, not only because of the mythological dimensions of the ancient legends, but because the passionate intensity of such legends were 'alluring us almost to the intensity of trance'.[9]

The development of Yeats's interest in Irish folklore and mythology was not a matter of subject matter only. His involvement with Irish folklore also affected his theories about literature significantly. Although definitions of folklore can differ widely, any definition of folklore involves its two essential characteristics: it is oral and traditional. Yeats's enthusiasm for the subjects of Irish folklore waned in the twentieth century, but he held a lifelong conviction that great literature was fundamentally oral and traditional.

The power of the spoken word is a hallmark of Yeats's poetry and his literary theory. Denis Donoghue has pointed out that Yeats usually presents experience in his writings as speech, lore, rumour, anecdote, as tale rather than fiction.[10] Yeats's interest in oral literature encouraged such an emphasis on the oral nature of experience in his writings. He declared in 1902, 'Let us get back in everything to the spoken word, even though we have to speak our lyrics to the psaltery or to the harp, for, as AE says, we have begun to forget that literature is but recorded speech, and even when we write with care we have begun "to write with elaboration what could never be spoken".'[11] He began his essay on 'Speaking to the Psaltery' in 1907 with the declaration, 'I naturally dislike print and paper.'[12] A year earlier he had argued that 'There is no poem so great that a fine speaker cannot make it greater or that a bad ear cannot make it nothing.'[13] When he explained the Abbey Theatre in a speech delivered in 1908 he said : 'In rehearsing our Plays we have tried to give the words great importance; to make speech, whether it be the beautiful and rhythmical delivery of verse, or the accurate speaking of a rhythmical dialect, our supreme end . . .'[14]

For Yeats the spoken word conveyed personality and passion, while all too frequently the written word represented abstract thought. In his essay 'Literature and the Living Voice', he declared that such an oral quality distinguished Irish literature from English literature : 'Irish poetry and Irish stories were made to be spoken or sung, while English literature . . . has all but completely shaped itself in the printing-press.'[15] He believed that the vitality of Irish and Greek literature could be traced to the oral traditions which shaped both literatures, whereas Roman and English literature lacked such vitality because they 'were founded upon the written word'.[16] Yeats never lost his convictions about the essentially oral nature of literature. He voiced such theories as late as 1937 in his essay 'An Introduction for my Plays' :

> I wanted all my poetry to be spoken on a stage or sung, and, because I did not understand my own instincts, gave half a dozen wrong or secondary reasons; but a month ago I understood my reasons. I have spent all my life in clearing out of poetry every phrase written for the eye, and bringing all back to syntax that is for ear alone. . . . 'Write for the ear', I thought, so that you may be instantly understood as when an actor or folk singer stands before an audience.[17]

Yeats reiterated the 'traditional' origins and nature of his work in another definitive essay he wrote at the end of his life,

'A General Introduction for my Work' (1937). In the section of that essay entitled 'Subject-Matter', he recalled his youthful enthusiasm for the poetry of Thomas Davis and the Young Irelanders and remarked that he knew even then 'that they were not good poetry' but 'they had one quality I admired and admire : they were not separated individual men; they spoke or tried to speak out of a people to a people; behind them stretched the generations.' Yeats declared he had never lost an appreciation for the traditional nature of literature and culture : 'Some modern poets contend that jazz and music-hall songs are the folk art of our time, that we should mould our art upon them; we Irish poets, modern men also, reject every folk art that does not go back to Olympus. Give me time a little youth and I will prove that even "Johnny, I hardly knew ye" goes back.' In the section entitled 'Style and Attitude' in the same essay, Yeats discussed how tradition had been integral to his style : 'I must choose a traditional stanza, even what I alter must seem traditional. . . . Talk to me of originality and I will turn on you with rage.'[18]

The third characteristic feature of folklore—that oral tradition involves a dynamic tension between stability and variation—also had important repercussions in Yeats's theory of literature. Because folklore is an oral process of continual creation and re-creation, any tale or song is a continually evolving process rather than a static piece of literature frozen for all time in print. Yeats declared in 1890 that Irish legends were 'ever changing, ever the same'.[19] His description of how Irish legends were created reflected his keen sense of their potential for both stability and variation : 'All that is greatest in that literature is based upon legend—upon those tales which are made by no one man, but by the nation itself through a slow process of modification and adaptation to express its loves and its hates, its likes and dis-likes.'[20] Yeats, of course, never considered any of his own works 'finished'. He rewrote his poems, plays and stories throughout his life and consequently they were both 'finished' and 'un-finished' simultaneously. The process of creation which he saw at work in oral tradition universalised the artistic practices and philosophy of his father, John Butler Yeats, who was notorious for never completing his portraits, preferring to continue to work on them.

A secondary characteristic of folklore, its reliance on formulas for its literary structure and style, is also apparent in Yeats's writings. On its simplest level, this can be seen in his use of stock phrases from oral tradition. Many such phrases have been pointed out in analyses of his poetic diction. His prose also echoed formulas from oral tradition, as in his essay 'What is "Popular Poetry"?' when he declared: 'I pick my examples at random, for I am writing where I have no books to turn the pages of, but one need not go east of the sun or west of the moon in so simple a matter. On the other hand, when Walt Whitman writes in seeming defiance of tradition, he needs tradition for protection, for the butcher and the baker and the candlestick-maker grow merry over him when they meet his work by chance.'[21] Much more significant than such allusions to oral tradition, is Yeats's having grounded his poetry in the forms and stylistic features of oral tradition throughout his life. His declaration at the end of his life that even what he altered must seem 'traditional' reflects a lifelong attempt to express himself through traditional forms. The influence of ballads and folksongs on Yeats has been noted by many commentators on his poetry. G. S. Fraser has analysed the significance of the 'ballad style' in Yeats's posthumous volume, *Last Poems and Plays*. Michael Yeats has written an essay examining how his father's 'surprisingly wide knowledge of Gaelic folksongs' influenced his works, especially the implications of his father having often followed the traditional practice of composing his poetry to remembered airs. Several recent studies have continued to analyse the implications of that practice on Yeats's poetry. Colin Meir's discussion of how Yeats composed 'The Song of the Old Mother' to a tune in the 'gapped scale' of folk song is part of his book-length analysis of *The Ballads and Songs of W. B. Yeats*. Seán Lucy has demonstrated how Yeats achieved a counterpoint of rhythms in 'The Cold Heaven' by mounting the stress line of the Gaelic amhrán, or 'song poetry', on a regular iambic line. David R. Clark has pointed out several instances of how Yeats's poetry echoes the lyrics and metres of Irish folk song.[22]

The narrative traditions of Irish folklore, especially legend, also illuminate many of Yeats's distinctive literary forms and techniques. The preceding chapters have demonstrated that

Yeats's interest in Irish folklore during the 1880s and 1890s was essentially an interest in legends rather than in folktales or in mythology. As an anthologist and collector of folklore in *Fairy and Folk Tales, Irish Fairy Tales* and *The Celtic Twilight*, Yeats preferred fairy legends and other contemporary supernatural legends. *Representative Irish Tales* and *Irish Adventurers* continued this 'legendary' focus but his interest had switched to passionate heroic personalities in those anthologies. Yeats presented *Dhoya* and all the stories in *The Secret Rose* as legends. Many of Yeats's early ballads and poems recounted legends. Thus, during the pre-1900 phase of his career when his writings have so often been labelled 'escapist', Yeats ignored the more purely imaginative and escapist folktale and selected the most realistic narrative genre of Irish folklore, the legend, as his most characteristic narrative form.

Yeats's subject matter has often been labelled 'mythology' and so it is, to a point, but Yeats himself perceptively recognised and emphasised its more 'legendary' nature. Yeats used the term 'legend' much more frequently than 'myth' or 'mythology' in referring to his materials. His earliest surviving prose article, 'The Poetry of Sir Samuel Ferguson' (1886), referred to Ferguson's ancient heroic materials as 'legends' and declared 'of all the many things the past bequeathes to the future, the greatest are great legends.'[23] Although fairy legends and other contemporary supernatural legends fascinated him at first, by 1898 he considered legends as essentially grounded in heroic personality, as a matter of both passion and vision—'legends are the magical beryls in which we see life, not as it is, but as the heroic part of us, the part which desires always dreams and emotions greater than any in the world . . .'[24] Yeats generally discussed legend and mythology as distinct genres, as in the following passage: 'Emotions which seem vague or extravagant when expressed under the influence of modern literature, cease to be vague and extravagant when associated with ancient legend and mythology, for legend and mythology were born out of man's longing for the mysterious and the infinite.'[25] Generally when Yeats used the term 'mythology' he used it precisely as a folklorist would today, in reference to the gods and superhuman heroes who lived in a world supposed to have preceded the present order. The six articles Yeats wrote between 1897 and 1902 to explain the 'mythological' origins and significance of Irish folklore all use 'mythology' to refer to gods and semi-divine heroes. Yeats was well aware that the heroes of ancient legend were at once mythological and human. Christianity had de-mythologised the ancient gods into human heroes and consequently Yeats was able to reverse the process and declare that the 'immense energy' and the 'something extravagant and superhuman' about legendary heroes and tales was 'something almost mythological'.[26] Such a concept of legend illuminates a suggestion which Denis Donoghue made in his essay 'Yeats: The Question of Symbolism': 'I propose to say that there is a middle term between the Symbolist Yeats, at one extreme, and, at the other, the Yeats who made his art from the roughage of daily experience, chance, choice, and history. The middle term I propose is legend, which Yeats sometimes called myth, and we may think of it as situated between the unseen world of Symbolism and the indisputable world of act and time.'[27]

Modern scholarship about the folktale and about early Irish literature has confirmed the validity of Yeats's recognition of the pseudo-historical or legendary nature of early Irish literature. The antiquity and the ancient setting of Yeats's materials did not necessarily make them myths for, as Stith Thompson pointed out in his classic study of traditional narrative, *The Folktale*, legends recount events which happened in ancient times or in the more recent historical past.[28] Gerard Murphy, in *Saga and Myth in Ancient Ireland*, concluded that mythological elements made up only a relatively small part of the Mythological, the Ulster and the Fenian cycles of early Irish literature. Myles Dillon has also emphasised the pseudo-historical quality of these cycles. Gerard Murphy argued that the tales of the Tuatha de Danaan, Cuchulain and Finn had survived because of their narrative interest rather than because of their significance to ancient Irish religious belief.[29] Yeats, who accepted Rhys and Jubainville's theory that Cuchulain and other heroes had once been gods, was well aware that Irish legends contained remnants of Irish mythology, indeed he frequently praised their mystical significance. But he realised that the two subjects he took from Irish folklore—the ancient Irish heroes and the beliefs of the contemporary peasants—were not only the most uniquely Irish of the materials available to him from Irish folklore, but

I

also the most legendary, since they were much more closely grounded in the real world than myths or folktales. Both subjects contained as much the marvellous and supernatural as many myths and folktales did, but because of their vivid sense of specific place, their supposedly historical personalities and their tragic incidents, they were legends rather than myths or folktales.

Legends, such as Lady Gregory and Yeats collected together in the late 1890s, often represent a kind of oral history unknown and disconcerting to people who have been accustomed to think of history as a written, chronological account of the past, as an objective, systematic and, above all, accurate presentation of facts. Folk-history legends, even when recorded and written down by a folklorist, present an *oral* memory of the past which contains as much, if not more, fiction as fact. A brief description and analysis of the materials in Lady Gregory's *Kiltartan History Book* will provide a basis on which to consider the significance of Yeats's preference for legends.

Although Lady Gregory arranged the individual accounts from various informants in *The Kiltartan History Book* in chronological sequence, the individual anecdotes themselves confuse more often than imply accurate chronology. The Viking invasions are simultaneous with the life of Finn, although Finn supposedly lived in the third century and the Vikings did not arrive until centuries later. St Brigit, who could only have lived centuries after the crucifixion, is nevertheless said to have been the companion of Christ and his mother and to have been present at the crucifixion. Events are chronological in Raftery's major poem about Irish history, 'The Story of Ireland to the Defeat at Aughrim as the Little Bush Told the Poet Raftery in Irish', of which Lady Gregory gives a prose translation in *The Kiltartan History Book*. But Raftery telescoped centuries of Irish history into the oral memory of a little bush in Co. Galway which had witnessed all events in Ireland since the Biblical flood. The little bush relates Irish history as a sequence of personalities rather than events, as do most of the accounts in *The Kiltartan History Book*. This emphasis on personality is apparent in the following vivid description of Queen Elizabeth I :

Queen Elizabeth was awful. She was a very lustful woman.
Beyond everything she was. When she came to the turn she
dyed her hair red, and what ever man she had to do with,
she sent him to the block in the morning, that he would be
able to tell nothing. She had an awful temper. She would
throw a knife from the table at the waiting ladies. Very
superstitious she was. Sure after her death they found a card,
the ace of hearts, nailed to her chair under the seat. She
thought she would never die while she had it there. . . . It
was a town called Calais broke her heart and brought her to
her death the same as the Boer War did with Queen Victoria,
and she lay chained on the floor three days and three nights.
The Archbishop was trying to urge her to eat, but she said,
'You would not ask me to do it if you knew the way I am,'
for nobody could see the chains. After her death they waked
her in Whitehall, and there were six ladies sitting beside her
body every night. Three coffins were about it, the one nearest
the body of lead, and then a wooden one, and a leaden one
on the outside. And every night there came from them a great
bellow. And the last night there came a bellow that broke
the three coffins open, and tore the velvet, and there came
out a stench that killed the most of the ladies and a million
of the people of London with the plague. Queen Victoria
was more honourable than that. It would be hard to beat
Queen Elizabeth.[30]

Such personal immediacy is typical of folk history in which
historical personages and events are reduced to the most funda-
mental human dimensions and relationships and in which local
landmarks, such as Raftery's bush, are a visible reminder of
events which occurred long ago. Thus we are told by Lady
Gregory's informants: 'Samson was of the Irish race, all the
world was Irish in those times.' Or that Aristotle was a Druid
out of Greece who wandered in Ireland; one of Douglas Hyde's
informants referred to Aristotle familarly as 'Harry'. Lady
Gregory points out how the immediacy of folk history frequently
reduced even the glorious heroes of ancient Ireland to quite
human, ordinary, even ridiculous dimensions: Finn has 'the
blood of the gods' but, according to one informant, is 'the son
of an O'Shaughnessy who lived at Kiltartan Cross'; the ancient

goddess Aine is confused with Queen Anne of England; 'Goibniu, the divine smith of the old times' became a saint and finally the builder of the round towers and Norman castles; Brigit, once a goddess, became a saint and now healed the poor at blessed wells in the form of 'a very civil fish, very pleasant, wagging its tail'. Conversely, the legends about more contemporary figures like Daniel O'Connell and Parnell were elaborated according to the patterns and motifs of traditional legends.

Yeats's preference for legendary materials was not new. Legends about ancient Ireland and the fairy lore of the contemporary peasantry had been the major focus of collections and literary popularisations of Irish folklore throughout the nineteenth century. But earlier writers such as Thomas Davis and Standish J. O'Grady and folklorists such as Thomas Croker had imposed English literary forms and styles on the subject matter of Irish legends. Yeats's editorial criteria and emendations in *Fairy and Folk Tales of the Irish Peasantry* demonstrate how he tried to remove such elaborate literary conventions from Irish folklore. Douglas Hyde's careful recording of the language and form of Irish folk literature demonstrated to Yeats, Synge and Lady Gregory the literary potential of some of the stylistic and formal elements of oral tradition. Not surprisingly then, Yeats found many of his own distinctive literary forms and techniques in, or paralleled in, Irish legend. Because a legend is not defined on the basis of subject matter alone, and because formal and stylistic elements are crucial in defining a legend, Yeats's preference for legendary materials had structural and stylistic repercussions in his work.

The most well-known of Yeats's innovations in literary form having to do with Irish legends is his use of them as vehicles for personal expression. Phillip Marcus has argued that this was not an Irish innovation, that Yeats was only the first to apply to Irish literature a technique which originated in English literature with Shelley and Tennyson.[31] Yet there was a precedent for such a technique in Irish folklore which Yeats recognised. While anonymity is generally a definitive characteristic of folklore, Yeats and Lady Gregory, as their fascination with Raftery demonstrates, were aware of the role of the personality of the original creative artist and of the narrator in the creation and transmission of folklore decades before contemporary folklorists were. According to Yeats, whether the narrator of an oral tradition was presenting words 'the poet had put into his mouth' or 'that he had made himself', he 'will not allow you for any long time to forget himself. Our own Raftery will stop the tale to cry, "That is what I, Raftery, wrote down in the book of the people" . . . He knows how to keep himself interesting that his words may have weight—so many lines of narrative, and then a phrase about himself and his own emotions.'[32] The vivid personalities of many of the tradition-bearers in Yeats's early works—Hanrahan, Paddy Flynn, Mary Battle—and of his later peasant *personae* such as Crazy Jane attest to his keen sense of the importance of personality in the transmission and expression of oral literature. Yeats's combination of personal voice, whether his own or a *persona*'s, with traditional material, though reinforced by the example of Shelley and Tennyson, had a definite precedent in Irish oral tradition, so there is some justification for claiming this technique as something of an Irish innovation in literary form.

An ever-altering oral dimension distinguishes all folklore, whether oral history or oral literature, from written history and written literature. Legend is generally considered the most 'oral' of all traditional oral narrative genres. Folklorists have discovered legends are so 'oral' that it is difficult to capture them in writing for they are much more fragmentary and less complex in structure, and consequently much more subject to oral variation than myths and folktales. The depiction of events in legends demonstrates how the materials and the style of legends are more subject to oral variation than those of myths and folk tales. Legend transcends history and time by depicting past events as simultaneous rather than chronological. According to Patrick O'Farrell, this was especially true until the end of the nineteenth century in Irish oral tradition where there was not a strongly developed sense of the movement of time and the tendency was to compress all the past into 'one living yesterday'.[33] Yeats experienced this firsthand when he collected Fenian legends with Lady Gregory from peasants in Galway who he said, 'know so little about ancient customs that they will tell you about Finn MacCool flinging a man over a haystack on his way to the assizes in Cork'.[34] A simultaneous rather than chronological sense of time is a characteristic feature of Yeats's work.

In *Coole Park and Ballylee* Daniel Harris describes how Yeats
realised moments of time simultaneously in many of his later
poems, as in 'The Black Tower' where he used the present tense
in the refrain and thus narrated a 'present medieval event'.[35]
Harris argues that Yeats broke with earlier traditional forms
of narrative, but considers the ballad form as the only possible
traditional precedent for Yeats's technique. However, place
legends and folk history in Irish oral tradition are characterised
by a simultaneous sense of time as Lady Gregory's *Kiltartan
History Book* has demonstrated.

Yeats's 'innovation' can be traced to techniques he discovered
very early in his career in Irish legendary materials. He des-
cribed such a simultaneous sense of time in his Notes to 'The
Wanderings of Oisin': 'The events it describes, like the events
in most of the poems in this volume, are supposed to have taken
place in the indefinite period, made up of many periods, des-
cribed by the folk-tales, than in any particular century; it there-
fore, like the later Fenian stories themselves, mixes much that
is medieval with much that is ancient.'[36] Likewise, he said that
in 'The Countess Kathleen', which he had based on a legend
he had included in *Fairy and Folk Tales of the Irish Peasantry*,
he 'tried to suggest throughout the play that period, made out
of many periods, in which the events in the folk-tales have
happened'.[37] Yeats dispenses with the sequential order of written
history in his 'Reveries over Childhood and Youth'. He opens
that first section of his *Autobiography* with the declaration that
'My first memories are fragmentary and isolated and contem-
poraneous . . . It seems as if time had not yet been created, for
all thoughts connected with emotion and place are without
sequence.'[38] Yeats continues this technique of remembering
the events of his life simultaneously rather than sequentially
with remarks such as 'All these events seem at the same distance'
and 'events of this period have as little sequence as those of
childhood'.

Irish legends typically contain as much, if not more, fiction
as fact and thus transcend history by exhibiting what Matthew
Arnold called the Celt's characteristic reaction against 'the des-
potism of fact'. Yeats had valued legends from the beginning
because of their displacement of factual accuracy and their sym-
bolic depiction of reality. As much as he admired Douglas Hyde

as a folklorist, Yeats refused to accept Hyde's argument that Irish legends were to be valued for the historical information they contained rather than their imaginative extravagance. When Yeats reviewed Hyde's *The Story of Early Gaelic Literature* in 1895 he criticised Hyde for considering Irish legends as 'history coloured by legend' rather than 'legend coloured by history' because in doing so Hyde had forgotten 'the noble fantasy and passionate drama which is their crowning glory'.[39] When Yeats reviewed Standish J. O'Grady's *The Flight of the Eagle* in 1897 he declared his preference for legendary history rather than factual history. Yeats could not accept O'Grady's account of Irish noblemen co-operating with their Elizabethan conquerors—whether O'Grady had evidence to support his account or not: 'Mr O'Grady may be right, for I am no historian, and human nature is a nearly incalculable thing, but I will find it difficult to follow him until the Gaelic tongue has given up its dead and I know what was sung and repeated at the hearths of the people, and how the tradition of hunters and shepherds magnified or diminished policies and battles.'[40] For Yeats the final proof would be that of oral history. Such a conviction about the importance of oral history was still apparent in 1939 when Yeats wrote his essay 'Ireland after the Revolution': 'let every schoolmaster point out where in his neighbourhood this or that thing happened, or is said to have happened.'[41]

The symbolic depiction of reality and the displacement of factual accuracy by imaginative extravagance which Yeats so admired in legend is paralleled in his literary ideals. According to Yeats, a country does not begin to produce great literature until it ceases to consider history 'merely as a chronicle of facts' and begins to consider history 'imaginatively'.[42] His disdain for scholarly accuracy and the slipperiness of his poetic and autobiographical memory are well known. Joseph Ronsley's immediate declaration at the beginning of his book-length study of Yeats's *Autobiography* that 'I have made no attempt to annotate the book or to correct it for the sake of factual accuracy' speaks for itself.[43] William Murphy was less subtle in his recent biography of Yeats's father: 'No fact or figure or name or title or ascription of any kind given by W. B. Yeats should be accepted without independent verification.'[44] A legend's characteristic technique of presenting reality through an imaginative process of memory while claiming to be historical fact proved irresistible to Yeats. Such a process of memory characterises his *Autobiography* and so many of his poems, such as 'Under Saturn' and 'The Tower' where his own memory expands to include the memory of the Irish countryside.

What a legend selects to remember and how it recreates reality also influenced Yeats. Legends celebrate the most dramatic, sensational and passionate aspects of human experience. History thus becomes more a matter of personality than of event: Devorgilla's passions caused the Norman invasion of Ireland just as Helen's caused the Trojan War; Parnell's love for Kitty O'Shea ended his career and Irish hopes for Home Rule. The majority of folk-history legends are personal legends about vivid historical personalities whose actions are associated with specific places. Yeats was well aware of how much place mattered in Irish legends: 'Our legends are always associated with places, and not merely every mountain and valley, but every strange stone and little coppice has its legend, preserved in written or unwritten tradition. Our Irish romantic movement has arisen out of this tradition, and should always, even when it makes new legends about traditional people and things, be haunted by places.'[45] Yeats's own poetry, of course, was frequently 'haunted by places'.

Yeats modelled many of his writings on the memory of personality and of place. As he remarks in his *Autobiography*, 'I only seem to recall things dramatic in themselves and that are somehow associated with unforgettable places.'[46] This emphasis on the legendary memory of personality and place is echoed in his 1913 recollection of his youthful researches in Irish folklore: 'I sought some symbolic language reaching far into the past and associated with familiar names and conspicuous hills that I might not be alone among the obscure impressions of the senses.'[47] In his *Autobiography* Yeats recalls York Powell's definition of history as 'a memory of men who were amusing or exciting to think about'.[48] That a famous Oxford Professor of History's view of history so closely paralleled the presentation of history Yeats had found in Irish legend must have delighted him. Thus, when he identified the definitive moments in history with the personalities of great men in *A Vision*, he echoes the techniques of Irish legends as well as his father, Carlyle, and Nietzsche.

Yeats's sense of legendary memory, of the process of celebrating noteworthy personalities and places, had an early and extensive influence on his work. Frank Murphy, in a recent study of Yeats's early poetry, remarks that in *Crossways* (1889) 'gesture, like a physical description, is rare; the figures appear and move in an abstract pattern, like the impersonal, stylized figures in an ancient fairy tale.'[49] Murphy's 'fairy tale' analogy refers to the Cinderella-like märchen, folktales whose impersonal, stylised characters and abstract plots indeed remind one of the original versions of Yeats's earliest poems. In his Notes to *Crossways* Yeats declares that 'many of the poems in *Crossways*, certainly those upon Indian subjects or upon shepherds and fauns, must have been written before I was twenty, for from the moment when I began *The Wanderings of Oisin*, which I did at that age, I believe, my subject-matter became Irish.'[50] Yeats's style as well became more and more similar to the style of the legendary materials which became his major subject matter: more dramatic, more immediate in time and place. The poems in *The Rose* (1893) reflect these qualities. As Frank Murphy points out, the dramatic structure of 'Fergus and the Druid', with its dialogue and present tense, makes the past as immediate as the present. Yeats also began to fill his poems with supposedly historical characters and Irish place names in the late 1880s. He thus achieved the aura of historical reality, and the greater immediacy of time and of place which folklorists argue distinguishes legends from myths and folktales.[51]

What many commentators have referred to as Yeats's 'mythologising' of contemporary persons, events and places is, of course, a major example of the kind of historical memory Yeats had discovered in Irish legends. Lady Gregory's autobiography demonstrates how quickly anyone who collects oral legends among the peasantry realises that the legendary process is not dead in the modern world. In an early chapter, 'Folklore in Politics: Mr Gladstone in Ireland', she discusses how oral traditions in rural and in urban Ireland made Gladstone as much a figure of folk-history as Finn or Daniel O'Connell by celebrating his personality in numerous apocryphal anecdotes and ignoring the more mundane facts and events of his political career. Her chapter on 'The Folk-Lore of the War' describes how rapidly the traditional motifs and apocryphal incidents of oral tradition replaced facts. She quotes a letter from Yeats in which he said that censors in Dublin received the most detailed reports from all over Ireland and that all were lies. Her quotation of his response to her chapter 'the Rising' reflects his conception of history as legend and his appreciation of the importance of legendary accounts of contemporary events:

> You have given us the most important part of history, its lies . . . I don't believe that events have been shaped so much by the facts as by the lies that people believed about them.
> When I had my political year I noticed that every prominent man was hated by somebody because of some anecdote told of him in a whisper by somebody else . . . Some of the fine things [concerning the events of the Rising] had been said and done but many were legends. Dublin cynicism had passed away and was inventing beautiful, instead of derisive, Fables.[52]

Yeats tried to perpetuate the memory of his friends by celebrating their personalities in legends and anecdotes. He filled his letters, poems, essays and autobiography with anecdotes—a type of legend which illustrates some of the most distinctive characteristics of legends: the reduction of a personality or an event to its simplest, most essential form; a conversational rather than a highly structured format. Yeats recalls in his *Autobiography* that the only memory his branch and other branches of his family had about an ancestor was an anecdote about boiled pork and remarks that, 'Were we country people, we could have summarised his life in a legend.'[53] Yeats frequently used the anecdotal form with its drama and condensation when trying to transform his contemporaries into the stuff of legend.

Yeats's works also reflect another aspect of legend: the re-organisation and re-creation of history in terms of traditional patterns and motifs. Yeats applied this technique to all human history in *A Vision* and to an individual's life in his literary treatment of Parnell. Both he and other Irish writers transformed Parnell into a legendary hero by echoing how the popular imagination had reshaped and reinterpreted historical fact in remembering Parnell. F. S. L. Lyons devotes the last chapter of his recent biography of Parnell to carefully separating Parnell the man from Parnell the legendary hero—a necessary task because Parnell's enigmatic personality and the dramatic, sensational aspects of his life and death soon became the very stuff of folk legend.[54] Padraic Colum, in his Foreword to Lady Gregory's *Kiltartan History Book* noted that in legends 'actual happenings are made to fit into traditional patterns.'[55] Such was the case with Parnell. Legends about him abound in motifs which had been common in Irish and other national legends for centuries: portents at the death or burial of the hero; the supposedly dead hero who has really only disappeared and will return one day to help Ireland in her time of need; the noble hero betrayed by the mob; the ignominious death of the hero; the role of women and adultery in the hero's downfall; the aristocratic, proud hero, aloof from and disdainful of the common people. Of course, many of these motifs had also characterised the personality of the legendary Cuchulain. Yeats, who did not begin writing about Parnell until twenty years after his death, incorporated all the above legendary motifs, which Lyons's biography has demonstrated were often at odds with historical fact, into his poems about Parnell. Yeats expanded his legend-making process to identify Parnell with motifs from pagan mythology, as when he uses the motif of the pagan god Dionysus' murder in 'Parnell's Funeral' to portray the Irish as devouring the sacrificed hero's heart. Yeats's transformation of history into legend also underscores how very 'traditional' his view and treatment of history were. Thomas Whitaker has argued that Yeats's unique view of history was a combination of pattern and panoramic vision, plus the drama of individual human experience.[56] Such is the basic structure of folk legend: traditional pattern plus dramatic personality. Yeats's use of traditional legendary motifs, as in his poems about Parnell, enabled the speaker in the poems to unite individual drama (his own and Parnell's) with larger historical patterns.

For Yeats, then, the meaning of history resided in the motifs and patterns of oral legend rather than in the facts of written history. He believed that legends acquired a symbolic truth over the centuries. As Allen Grossman suggested in his book *Poetic Knowledge in the Early Yeats*, legends reflect Yeats's doctrine of the 'moods'—'Whatever the passions of men have gathered about, becomes a symbol in the Great Memory.'[57] In 'A General Introduction for my Work' (1937) Yeats praised the literary and philosophical significance of the legendary treatment of a lady-in-waiting to Mary, Queen of the Scots, in the ballad 'Mary Hamilton': 'The maid of honour whose tragedy they sing must be lifted out of history with timeless pattern, she is one of the four Maries, the rhythm is old and familiar, imagination must dance, must be carried beyond feeling into the aboriginal ice.' According to Yeats, such 'timeless pattern' made the tragedy of human history as 'cold and passionate as the dawn'.[58] Historical facts are indeed hopelessly lost in 'Mary Hamilton' because of the 'timeless pattern' imposed on history by oral memory.[59] But for Yeats the symbolic energy of the ballad is what mattered.

Yeats believed that, just as meaning in legends derived from symbolic motifs and patterns, much of the literary effect of legend came from a lack of intellectual understanding and coherence. He praised Irish oral tradition because it 'trembles on the verge of incoherence with a passion all but unknown among modern poets'.[60] He praised an enigmatic conversation between Cuchulain and Emer in Lady Gregory's *Cuchulain of Muirthemne* for its 'obscurity', its reliance on 'symbol' and 'enigma', explaining that meaning had been lost after centuries of oral and written transmission.[61] He actually sought such an enigmatic effect in some of his writing by reducing the intellectual coherence of his legendary materials. For example, when he included Carleton's 'Wildgoose Lodge' in *Representative Irish Tales* he deliberately omitted two final paragraphs of factual background information about the legend. Yeats's poem 'The Black Tower' presents a legendary event to an audience lacking the traditional background details necessary to understand it. A background knowledge of Irish legends is often as necessary to understand one of Yeats's poems as it is to understand a legend in oral tradition. Yeats's prose writings and notes frequently amplify the meaning of enigmas in his poetry and thus function much as an audience's background knowledge of Irish legends did in oral tradition.

Thus the relative, symbolic nature of truth and the obscure nature of reality in Yeats's writings have parallels, if not their origin, in Irish legends, in which the ever-altering oral dimension makes truth relative and symbolic by allowing imagination to transcend time and historical fact, and obscures original meaning. A line from 'The Song of the Happy Shepherd'—'Words alone are certain good'—has frequently been cited as an example of Yeats's aestheticism and escapism. But it also reflects the oral and imaginative dimensions of reality which Yeats discovered in Irish legend. Irish legend was the form of traditional narrative which was, in a sense, the least aesthetic because of its lack of a fixed artistic structure, and the least escapist because it was so carefully grounded in the places and the history of the actual world. Legend provided Yeats with a literary form in which truth was embodied rather than actually known. Reality in legends is a matter of emotional and imaginative experience rather than intellectual and factual certainty. In legends one experiences rather than knows truth. Such is the nature of much of Yeats's poetry, of his *Autobiography* where he disguises his research into the old letters and diaries as memory, and his articles and essays where he repeatedly declares he is writing from memory because his books and papers are not with him. All such techniques are derived from the oral memory process of legends. When Yeats summed up his entire career in 'A General Introduction for my Work' he declared that 'even what I alter must seem traditional'. An examination of the generic characteristics of legends demonstrates that many of the most distinctive characteristics of Yeats's writings, his seeming innovations which have placed him in the forefront of modern literature, are indeed 'traditional'.

ABBREVIATIONS

Works by W. B. Yeats:

Auto	*The Autobiography of W. B. Yeats*
BIV	*A Book of Irish Verse*
E & I	*Essay and Introductions*
Exp	*Explorations*
FFT	*Fairy and Folk Tales of the Irish Peasantry*
IFT	*Irish Fairy Tales*
Letters	*The Letters of W. B. Yeats*
LKT	*Letters to Katharine Tynan*
LNI	*Letters to the New Island*
RIT	*Representative Irish Tales*
SC	*Stories from Carleton*
SR	*The Secret Rose*
UP	*Uncollected Prose by W. B. Yeats*
Var Plays	*The Variorum Edition of the Plays of W. B. Yeats*
Var Poems	*The Variorum Edition of the Poems of W. B. Yeats*

Periodicals:

DLM	*Dublin and London Magazine*
DUM	*Dublin University Review*
IUR	*Irish University Review*
JAF	*Journal of American Folklore*
JIL	*Journal of Irish Literature*

See the Bibliography for complete bibliographic citation of works referred to in Notes.

Notes

Preface
(pp. 1–4)
1. Yeats, *IFT*, 297.
2. Jeffares, 'Chairman's Address', *IUR*, 294.
3. Yeats, 'A General Introduction for My Work' (1937), *E & I*, 523.
4. Yeats, 'The Message of the Folk-Lorist' (1893), *UP* I, 284.
5. Bramsbäck, 'W. B. Yeats and Folklore Material', *Hereditas*, 56–68.
6. Jochum, *W. B. Yeats: A Classified Bibliography*; Finneran, 'W. B. Yeats', 304.
7. Kelleher, 'Yeats's Use of Irish Materials', 115-25.
8. Henn, *Lonely Tower*, xiii.

Chapter 1
YEATS AND NINETEENTH-CENTURY IRISH LITERARY
TRADITION : FROM POETRY TO FOLKLORE
(pp. 5–31)
1. Yeats, 'The Message of the Folk-Lorist', 228.
2. Yeats, 'The Rhymers' Club' (1892), *LNI*, 148.
3. Yeats, 'A Ballad Singer' (1891), *LNI*, 137–8.
4. Yeats, 'Browning' (1890), *LNI*, 103–104.
5. Yeats, 'Nationality and Literature' (1893), *UP* I, 268.
6. Yeats, 'The Trembling of the Veil' (1922), *Auto*, 77.
7. Yeats, 'Discoveries' (1906), *E & I*, 294.
8. Yeats, 'Irish Folk Tales' (1891), *UP* I, 187.
9. Froude, *English in Ireland*, 15–16.
10. Froude, 22–3.
11. Froude, 23.
12. Quoted by Lady Gregory in *Gods and Fighting Men*, 355.
13. Dowling, *Hedge Schools of Ireland*, 82.
14. Nutt, *Legend of the Holy Grail*, xiii.

15. Yeats, *Letters*, 307.
16. Yeats, 'Mr William Wills' (1889), *LNI*, 75.
17. Yeats, 'A General Introduction for My Work', 510.
18. O'Leary, *Inaugural Address*, 4–5.
19. Quoted in Duffy, *Young Ireland*, 80.
20. Davis, *Poems of Thomas Davis*, 69.
21. Yeats, 'Irish Nationalist Literature, I' (1895), *UP* I, 361; 'Introduction', *BIV*, xiii.
22. Lucy, *IUR*, 151–77.
23. Yeats, 'What is "Popular Poetry"?' (1901), *E & I*, 3.
24. Yeats, 'Poetry and Tradition' (1907), *E & I*, 256.
25. Yeats, 'Irish National Literature, I' 362.
26. *Poems and Ballads of Young Ireland*, 72.
27. Bourke, *John O'Leary*, 183.
28. 'Historicus', *Best Hundred Irish Books*, 48.
29. Yeats, 'Popular Ballad Poetry of Ireland' (1889), *UP* I, 147.
30. O'Driscoll, *Ascendancy of the Heart*, 57–8.
31. Taylor, *Irish Poetry of the Nineteenth Century*, 59.
32. Yeats, 'Introduction', *BIV*, xviii.
33. Meir, *Ballads and Songs*, 49–53; O'Driscoll, *Ascendancy*, 70.
34. Clarke, 'Gaelic Ireland Rediscovered', 32.
35. Yeats, 'A General Introduction for My Work', 511.
36. Ferguson, *Congal*, viii; Yeats, 'The Poetry of Sir Samuel Ferguson—I' (1886), *UP* I, 81–7.
37. O'Grady, *History of Ireland* II, 28, 44.
38. Yeats, 'General Introduction', 512–13.
39. Marcus, *Standish O'Grady*, 18.
40. Yeats, *LKT*, 64, 76.
41. Yeats, 'The Poetry of R. D. Joyce' (1886), *UP* I, 112.
42. Yeats, 'Tales from the Twilight' (1890), *UP* I, 170.
43. Yeats, 'Poetry of R. D. Joyce', 113.
44. Corkery, *The Hidden Ireland*, 272–3.
45. Yeats, *Var Poems*, 799.
46. Yeats, 'The Legendary and Mythological Foundation of the Plays and Poems', *Var Plays*, 1283.
47. Sidnell, *Druid Craft*, 4, 5, 16.
48. Yeats, *John Sherman and Dhoya*, 125.
49. Eddins, *Yeats: The Nineteenth Century Matrix*, 64.
50. Ellmann, *Yeats: The Man and the Masks*, 139–40.
51. Zimmermann, 'Yeats, the Popular Ballad and the Ballad Singers', 588.
52. Yeats, 'Popular Poetry', 3–12.
53. Yeats, 'The Poet of Ballyshannon' (1888), *LNI*, 172.

54. Taylor, *Irish Poetry*, 5, 8.
55. Yeats, 'A Poet We Have Neglected' (1891), *UP* I, 212.
56. Yeats, 'Message of the Folk-Lorist', 285.
57. Frayne, *UP* I, 146.
58. Yeats, *Letters*, 213
59. Zimmermann, *Songs of Irish Rebellion*, 78; Allingham, 'Irish Ballad Singers', 16.
60. Clarke, 'Gaelic Ireland Rediscovered', 37.
61. Yeats, 'Popular Poetry', 4.

Chapter 2
YEATS AND IRISH FOLKLORE: THE NINETEENTH-CENTURY TRADITION
(pp. 32–73)

1. Ellmann, *Yeats*, 23.
2. Murphy, *The Yeats Family*, 18.
3. Quoted in Murphy, *Yeats Family*, 19.
4. Yeats, *Auto*, 33.
5. Ellmann, *Yeats*, 56–86.
6. Yeats, 'Irish Fairies, Ghosts, Witches, etc.' (1889), *UP* I, 130.
7. Yeats, *Letters to John O'Leary*, 9.
8. Yeats, 'Invoking the Irish Fairies' (1892), *UP* I, 245–7.
9. Yeats, *Letters to John O'Leary*, 13–14.
10. Yeats, 'Magic' (1901), *E & I*, 46.
11. Yeats, *A Vision*, xi.
12. Yeats, 'A General Introduction for My Work', 517.
13. Dorson, *British Folklorists*, 440. Much of the following discussion is indebted to Dorson's excellent study.
14. Johnson, *Journey to the Western Islands*, 86.
15. Johnson, *Journey*, 81.
16. Brand, *Observations on Popular Antiquities* I, xiv.
17. Briggs, *The Fairies*, 182.
18. Dickens, 'Frauds on the Fairies', 97.
19. Thackeray, *Irish Sketch-Book* I, 281.
20. Dillon, 'The Archaism of Irish Tradition', 1.
21. Dorson, *Folklorists*, 162–3.
22. Dorson, *Folklorists*, 174.
23. Fitzgerald, 'Early Celtic History and Mythology', 192–259.
24. Stokes, 'Remarks on Mr Fitzgerald's "Early Celtic History and Mythology" ', 370.
25. Croker, *Fairy Legends* I, 357–9.
26. Keightley, *Fairy Mythology* I, xi.
27. O'Kearney, 'Folklore', 35–7.

28. W. Wilde, *Irish Popular Superstitions*, 44, 50.
29. Lady Wilde, 'Fairy Mythology of Ireland', 73.
30. Scott, *Waverley*, 491–2.
31. Parsons, *Witchcraft and Demonology*, 285.
32. Scott, *Waverley*, 492.
33. Dorson, *Folklorists*, 92.
34. Thompson, *The Folktale*, 8, 9; Bascom, 'The Forms of Folklore: Prose Narratives', *JAF*, 3–20.
35. Croker, *Researches*, 3.
36. Croker, *Researches*, 329, 340, 334, 99, 334.
37. Ó Casaide, 'Crofton Croker's Irish Fairy Legends', 289–90.
38. Croker, *Fairy Legends* I, 362–3.
39. Dorson, 'Collecting in County Kerry', *Folklore and Fakelore*, 189–90.
40. Croker, *The Keen of the South of Ireland*, xxiii.
41. Hyde, *Beside the Fire*, x-xi.
42. 'Legends and Tales of the Queen's County Peasantry. No III—The Sheoge', *DUM*, 581–2.
43. 'Legends and Tales of the Queen's County Peasantry. No.I—The Banshee', *DUM*, 367.
44. 'The Sheoge', 580.
45. 'The Banshee', 366.
46. 'Superstitions of the Irish Peasantry—No I', *DLM*, 31.
47. 'Superstitions', 31.
48. Carleton, 'Preface to First Series' (1830), xxv; *Tales and Sketches*, viii-ix.
49. Quoted in Delaney, 'Patrick Kennedy', 58.
50. Webb, *A Compendium of Irish Biography*, 272.
51. Kennedy, *Legendary Fictions*, viii.
52. Kennedy, *Fireside Stories*, viii, x.
53. Kennedy, *Fireside Stories*, viii, 2.
54. Brown, *Ireland in Fiction*, 153–4.
55. Yeats, *FFT*, 7.
56. Quoted in Delaney, 'Patrick Kennedy', 83.
57. 'Lageniensis', *Legend Lays of Ireland*, 102–103, ix.
58. Delargy, 'Royal Hibernian Tales', 200–201.
59. Yeats, *Letters*, 206–207.
60. Yeats, 'Tales from the Twilight', 170.
61. Flanagan, *Irish Novelists*, 325.
62. Hyde, *Beside the Fire*, xiv.
63. Lady Wilde, *Ancient Legends*, 33.
64. Lady Wilde, *Ancient Legends*, xi; *Ancient Cures*, 1–2.
65. McClintock, 'Folk Lore of the County Donegal' (1876), 607.

66. Hyde, *Literary History of Ireland*, xv.
67. Daly, *Douglas Hyde*, 173; discussion of Hyde's life is based on Daly and on Conner.
68. Hyde, *Beside the Fire*, x-xvii.
69. Yeats, *FFT*, 6.
70. Yeats, *Letters*, 88.
71. Hyde, *Beside the Fire*, 158–9, 153.
72. Yeats, 'Irish Folk Tales', 188.
73. Yeats, 'Tales from the Twilight', 170.
74. Myles, *Academy*, 266.
75. Yeats, 'Poetry and Science in Folklore' (1890), *UP* I, 174.
76. Yeats, 'The Story of Early Gaelic Literature' (1895), *UP* I, 359.
77. Yeats, *BIV*, xxiii.
78. Yeats, 'Introduction to "The Cat and the Moon" (1934), *Exp*, 401.
79. Yeats, *Auto*, 147.
80. Yeats, *Letters*, 249.

Chapter 3
THE FOLKLORE ANTHOLOGIES: *FAIRY AND FOLK TALES OF THE IRISH PEASANTRY* AND *IRISH FAIRY TALES*
(pp. 74–105)
1. Yeats, *Letters*, 45, 57.
2. McHugh, ed., *LKT*, 43.
3. Yeats, *Letters*, 57, 74–5, 78–9.
4. Yeats, *Letters*, 42; *LKT*, 43.
5. Wood-Martin, *History of Sligo*, 55, 385, 64, 359.
6. Yeats, 'Introduction', *FFT*, 3–9.
7. O'Kearney, 'The Story of Conn-eda', 4.
8. Yeats, *Letters*, 79.
9. Yeats, *LKT*, 67.
10. Yeats, 'Irish Wonders' (1889), *UP* I, 139.
11. Thuente, 'A List of Sources', *Fairy and Folk Tales of Ireland*, xvii-xxvi.
12. Hoffman, *Barbarous Knowledge*, 96.
13. Mc Anally, *Irish Wonders*, 93.
14. Yeats, 'A Ballad Singer', 138.
15. Yeats, 'Poetry of Samuel Ferguson—I', 81.
16. Keightley, *Tales and Popular Fictions*, 177.
17. Kennedy, *Legendary Fictions*, 132.
18. Yeats, 'Poetry of Samuel Ferguson—I', 85.
19. Yeats, 'The Scholar Poet' (1890), *LNI*, 205.

20. Yeats, 'Irish Folk Tales', 189.
21. Yeats, 'Irish Folk Tales', 188; 'Poetry and Science in Folk-Lore', 174.
22. Yeats, *Auto*, 146.
23. Wilde, *Ancient Legends*, 10.
24. Yeats, 'Tales from the Twilight', 171.
25. Yeats, 'Irish Wonders' (1889), *LNI*, 192; 'Irish Wonders', *UP* I, 138–41.
26. Yeats, 'Irish Folk Tales', 187.
27. Croker, *Fairy Legends* I, 44–6.
28. Croker, *Fairy Legends* I, 53–4.
29. Croker, *Fairy Legends* I, 70–71.
30. 'Legends and Tales of the Queen's County Peasantry. No. II', *DUM*, 491.
31. 'Queen's County Peasantry. No II', 492–3.
32. Yeats, *FFT*, 7.
33. Yeats, 'Irish Folk Tales', 187; Kennedy, *Legendary Fictions*, 180.
34. Yeats, *FFT*, 6–7.
35. Croker, *Fairy Legends* I, 168.
36. Yeats, 'Popular Ballad Poetry of Ireland', 162.
37. Yeats, 'Tales from the Twilight', 173.
38. Yeats, 'Irish Folk Tales', 187.
39. Yeats, *IFT*, 299.
40. Yeats, *LKT*, 61.
41. Raine, 'Foreword', *Fairy and Folk Tales of Ireland*, x.

Chapter 4
FROM FAIRY TO FOLK : *REPRESENTATIVE IRISH TALES* AND *THE CELTIC TWILIGHT*
(pp. 106–156)

1. Yeats, *Letters*, 127.
2. Yeats, *Letters*, 143.
3. Yeats, 'Introduction', *RIT*, 25–32.
4. Yeats, 'William Carleton' (1889), *UP* I, 145.
5. Carleton, 'Preface to First Series', xxv.
6. Wilde, *Ancient Legends*, 144–5.
7. Flanagan, *Irish Novelists*, 37–8.
8. Yeats, 'Irish Wonders', *UP*, 139; 'The Three O'Byrnes' (1889), *LNI*, 89.
9. Yeats, 'Chevalier Burke and Shule Aroon' (1889), *LNI*, 91.
10. Yeats, *Auto*, 138.
11. Yeats, 'Introduction', *SC*, reprinted in *RIT* (1979), 363.

12. Yeats, 'Irish National Literature, I', 363.
13. Yeats, 'Poetry of Samuel Ferguson', 87.
14. Carleton, *SC* (1889), 23.
15. Yeats, *Letters*, 143.
16. Yeats, 'Carleton as an Irish Historian' (1890), *UP* I, 168.
17. Kiely, *Poor Scholar*, 195.
18. Hall, *Stories of the Irish Peasantry*, 5.
19. Brown, *Ireland in Fiction*, 184.
20. 'Historicus', *Best Hundred Irish Books*, 10, 28.
21. Carleton, 'Author's Introduction' (1842), *Tales and Stories* I, xxxi.
22. Yeats, 'Irish National Literature, IV' (1895), *UP* I, 385.
23. Yeats, 'Old Gaelic Love Songs' (1893), *UP* I, 295.
24. Yeats, 'Samhain : 1908', *Exp*, 235.
25. Yeats, 'Irish National Literature, I', 364.
26. Yeats, 'Samhain : 1908', 235.
27. Unterecker, 'Countryman, Peasant and Servant', 178–9.
28. Yeats, 'A General Introduction for My Work', 513.
29. Yeats, *Var Plays*, 232.
30. Raine, 'Foreword', v–xvi.
31. Yeats, *The Celtic Twilight*, 31.
32. Yeats, *LKT*, 74.
33. Dorson, 'Foreword', *Folktales of Ireland*, xvii.
34. Ó hÓgáin, 'The Visionary Voice', *IUR*, 44–61.
35. Dorson, 'Foreword', xix–xx.
36. Dorson, 'Esthetic Form in British and American Folk Narrative', 307.
37. Yeats, 'Samhain : 1906', *Exp*, 215.
38. Danaher, 'Folk Tradition and Literature', *JIL* 1/2 (1972), 67.
39. Yeats, *IFT*, 301.
40. Yeats, *Auto*, 46.
41. Dorson, 'Defining the American Folk Legend', *Hereditas*, 115–16.
42. Wade, *Bibliography*, 30.
43. Evans-Wentz, *Fairy Faith*, 44, 72.
44. Mac Manus, *Middle Kingdom*, 15.
45. Deeney, *Peasant Lore from Gaelic Ireland*, ix.
46. Flanagan, 'Yeats, Joyce, and Ireland', 50.
47. E. Estyn Evans, 'Peasant Beliefs', 54.
48. Mac Lochlainn, 'Gael and Peasant', 24.
49. Yeats, 'The Four Winds of Desire', originally published as 'Irish Folk Tales' (1891), *UP* I, 188.
50. Yeats, 'A Ballad Singer', 139.

51. Arensberg, *The Irish Countryman*, 189.
52. Griffin, *RIT*, 265.
53. O'Sullivan, 'Introduction', *Legends from Ireland*, 11.
54. 'Humoriensis', *Memoir*, 3.
55. Yeats, *Letters*, 143.
56. Yeats, 'William Carleton', 396.
57. Yeats, 'At Stratford-on-Avon' (1901), *E & I*, 109–10.
58. Yeats, 'The Galway Plains' (1903), *E & I*, 211–12.
59. Yeats, *The Celtic Twilight*, 32.
60. Kelleher, 'Yeats's Use of Irish Materials', 115–25.
61. Wood-Martin, *History of Sligo*, 354.
62. O'Sullivan, *Handbook*, 447–8, 493.
63. O'Sullivan, *Types of the Irish Folklore*, 65–7.
64. O'Sullivan, *Storytelling in Irish Tradition*, 16.
65. 'Céatach', *Folktales of Ireland*, 38–56.
66. 'The Coming of Oscar', *Folktales of Ireland*, 60–74.
67. Gregory, *Kiltartan Books*, 210.
68. Yeats, 'Irish Folk Tales', 190.
69. Yeats, 'Bishop Berkeley' (1931), *E & I*, 411.
70. Harmon, 'Cobwebs before the Wind', 130.
71. McCaffrey, 'Daniel Corkery', 41.
72. Danaher, 'Folk Tradition and Literature', 71–2.
73. Starkie, 'Introduction', *Celtic Twilight*, xviii.

Chapter 5
RAKES AND RAPPAREES: *IRISH ADVENTURERS*
(pp. 157–194)
1. Yeats, 'Poetry of Samuel Ferguson', 82.
2. Yeats, 'The Poetry of Sir Samuel Ferguson—II' (1886), *UP* I, 103.
3. Yeats, 'The Children of Lir' (1889), *LNI*, 190.
4. Yeats, 'Message of the Folk-Lorist', 287–8.
5. Yeats, 'Modern Poetry' (1936), *E & I*, 495; 'Discoveries', 284.
6. Quoted in Ellmann, *Yeats*, 15.
7. Ellmann, *Yeats*, 27, 70–71.
8. Yeats, 'Poetry of Samuel Ferguson—I and II', 87, 82, 93–5.
9. Yeats, 'Poetry of R. D. Joyce', 109, 113, 106, 114.
10. Yeats, 'Clarence Mangan' (1887), 118–9.
11. Yeats, 'Popular Poetry', 4.
12. Ellmann, *Yeats*, 28–9.
13. Quoted in Ellmann, *Yeats*, 28.
14. Yeats, *Letters*, 154–6.
15. Yeats, *Letters*, 171, 173.

16. Yeats, 'A Reckless Century' (1891), *UP* I, 198–202.
17. Yeats, *Letters*, 214.
18. Garnett, reader's report on *Irish Adventurers*, Berg Collection, NYPL.
19. Yeats, *Letters*, 223, 227.
20. Danaher, 'Oral Tradition and the Printed Word', *IUR*, 34, 39, 32–3, 36.
21. Dowling, *Hedge Schools*, 79–80.
22. 'Irish Literature', *DLM*, 277.
23. Wilde, *Irish Popular Superstitions*, 86.
24. Walsh, *Ireland Sixty Years Ago*, 86.
25. Croker, *Researches*, 55.
26. Zimmermann, *Songs*, 24.
27. Marshall, *Irish Tories, Rapparees and Robbers*, 59.
28. *Dublin Penny Journal* I/47 (18 May 1833), 372.
29. Duffy, *Ballad Poetry*, 203–5.
30. Yeats, *Letters*, 227–8.
31. *Narrative of Col. Blood*, 15.
32. Yeats, *Auto*, 12.
33. Walsh, *Ireland*, 96–107.
34. Walsh, *Ireland*, 9–10.
35. *DUM* XVI (October 1840), 370.
36. *Life and Times of G. R. Fitzgerald* (1787), 13.
37. Somerville-Large, *Irish Eccentrics*, 157-71. Account of Fitzgerald is from this source unless otherwise indicated.
38. *Life and Times*, 44.
39. *Life and Times*, 67.
40. Yeats, *Auto*, 34–5.
41. Yeats, 'Reckless Century', 200–201.
42. Walsh, *Ireland*, 29–30.
43. Wilde, *Irish Popular Superstitions*, 63, 76.
44. Mac Killop, 'Finn Mac Cool', 90, 98.
45. O'Grady, *History of Ireland* I, 28.
46. Carleton, 'The Irish Rake', 358.
47. Carleton, *Redmond Count O'Hanlon*, 40, 70, 95–6.
48. Marshall, *Irish Tories*, 25.
49. Cosgrave, *History*, 33.
50. Marshall, *Irish Tories*, 28.
51. McLysaght, *Irish Families*, 171.
52 Walsh, *Ireland*, 87.
53. Account which follows is from Freney's autobiography unless otherwise indicated.
54. Walsh, *Ireland*, 84–7.

55. Prim, 52–61.
56. Cosgrave, *History*, 98, 39.
57. Walsh, *Ireland*, 88–93.
58. 'Michael Dwyer', *Dictionary of National Biography VI*, 1921–22, 277.
59. Zimmermann, *Songs*, 141.
60. Quoted in Colum, *Treasury*, 259–63.
61. Yeats, *Var Poems*, 115.
62. Yeats, 'A Reckless Century', 198–202.
63. Walsh, *Ireland*, 17.
64. Frayne, *UP* I, 199.
65. Yeats, 'Chevalier Burke and Shule Aroon', 90–91.
66. Walsh, *Ireland*, 10.
67. Yeats, 'Michael Clancy, the Great Dhoul, and Death' (1898), *UP* I, 310–17.

Chapter 6
POETS AND HEROES : *THE SECRET ROSE*
(pp. 195–238)
  1. Wade, *Bibliography*, 40–41.
  2. Yeats, quoted in Finneran, 'Old Lecher with a Love on Every Wind', 349.
  3. Bradford, *Yeats at Work*, 325.
  4. Yeats, 'Message of the Folk-Lorist', 287; 'Old Gaelic Love Songs', 293, 295.
  5. Finneran, 'Old Lecher', 350–51.
  6. Walsh, *Reliques of Irish Jacobite Poetry*, 6, 14.
  7. Gregory, *Poets and Dreamers*, 69.
  8. Corkery, *Hidden Ireland*, 184.
  9. Walsh, *Reliques*, 5, 7.
10. Corkery, *Hidden Ireland*, 184.
11. Sidnell, 'Versions of the Stories of Red Hanrahan', 119–74; quotations from *Stories of Red Hanrahan* (1905) are from Yeats, *Collected Works* V, (1908).
12. Walsh, *Reliques*, 8.
13. Quoted in Wade, *Bibliography*, 74.
14. Yeats, *Mythologies*, 1.
15. Rhys, *Lectures*, 124.
16. McGarry, *Place Names*, 45.
17. Finneran, 'Old Lecher', 352.
18. Gregory, *Poets and Dreamers*, 197.
19. Walsh, *Reliques*, 8.
20. Yeats, *Letters*, 286.

21. Hyde, *Legends*, 40–62.
22. O'Sullivan, *Folktales of Ireland*, 260.
23. Hull, 'The Hawk of Achill', 382.
24. Gregory, *Kiltartan Books*, 92–4.
25. Arensberg, *Irish Countryman*, 105–35.
26. Hyde, *Legends*, 57.
27. Corkery, *Hidden Ireland*, 202–203.
28. Ellmann, *Identity of Yeats*, 29.
29. Finneran, 'Old Lecher', 351, 354.
30. Ackerman, 'Yeats's Revisions of the Hanrahan Stories', 505–24.
31. Yeats, *Var Poems*, 171.
32. Finneran, 'Old Lecher', 356.
33. Yeats, 'Dedication' *SR* (1897), VII.
34. Yeats, 'Those Who Live by the Storm' and 'The Rose of Shadow', *UP* I, 328–32.
35. Yeats, 'The Vision of Mac Conglinne' (1893), *UP* I, 261–3.
36. Yeats, *SR* (1908), 27. All quotations from this edition unless otherwise indicated.
37. Yeats, 'Out of the Rose' (1893), 41.
38. Marcus, *Yeats*, 54–5.
39. Wood-Martin, *History of Sligo*, 384–5.
40. Murphy, *Prodigal Father*, 91.
41. Yeats, *Mythologies*, 195.
42. Cleeve, *Dictionary of Irish Writers* III, 104.
43. Yeats, 'Costello the Proud, Oona Mac Dermott and the Bitter Tongue' (1896), 9.
44. Hyde, 'Costello', in Colum, *Treasury*, 236.
45. Yeats, 'Message of the Folk-Lorist', 287; 'Costello the Proud' (1896), 8–9.
46. Yeats, *Mythologies*, 202.
47. Yeats, *Var Poems*, 413.
48. Finneran, 'Old Lecher', 353.
49. Yeats, 'Rosa Alchemica', *SR* (1908), 123–4.
50. Yeats, *Mythologies*, 203.
51. Yeats, 'The Evangel of Folk-Lore' (1894), *UP* I, 328.
52. Yeats, 'The Irish National Literary Society' (1892), *LNI*, 159.
53. Yeats, *RIT*, 32.
54. Yeats, *Var Poems*, 795.
55. Yeats, 'Ireland's Heroic Age' (1890), *LNI*, 107.
56. Yeats, *Var Poems*, 795, 808.
57. Yeats, in Eglinton, *Literary Ideals in Ireland*, 17, 19, 36.
58. Yeats, *Var Plays*, 232.
59. Yeats, 'The Tribes of Danu' (1897), *UP* II, 54–70; 'The

Prisoners of the Gods' (1898), *UP* II, 74–87; 'The Broken Gates of Death' (1898), *UP* II, 94–108; 'Ireland Bewitched' (1899), *UP* II, 167–83; 'Irish Witch Doctors' (1900), *UP* II, 219–36; 'Away' (1902), *UP* II, 267–82.

60. Yeats, 'Browning', 101.
61. Yeats, 'Irish Fairy Beliefs' (1900), *UP* II, 218.
62. Yeats, 'The Celtic Element in Literature' (1897), *E & I*, 173–88.

Chapter 7
'TRADITIONAL INNOVATIONS' IN LITERARY THEORY AND STYLE
(pp. 239–259)

1. Yeats, 'The Irish Intellectual Capital: Where Is it?' (1892), *UP I*, 224.
2. Yeats, 'Irish National Literature, IV', 386.
3. Sidnell, *Druid Craft*, 16–42, 122.
4. Yeats, *Memoirs*, 77.
5. Yeats, 'The Cradles of Gold' (1896), *UP* I, 413–18.
6. Gregory, *Cuchulain*, 5.
7. Yeats, 'Preface' to Lady Gregory's *Cuchulain*, 11.
8. Yeats, 'Preface' to *Cuchulain*, 11–17; 'Preface' to *Gods and Fighting Men*, 11–20.
9. Yeats, 'The Tragic Theatre' (1910), *E & I*, 245.
10. Donoghue, *Yeats*, 19.
11. Yeats, 'Samhain: 1902', *Exp*, 95.
12. Yeats, 'Speaking to the Psaltery' (1907), *E & I*, 13.
13. Yeats, 'Literature and the Living Voice' (1906), *Exp*, 212.
14. Yeats, 'Speech' (1908), *UP* II, 367.
15. Yeats, 'Literature and the Living Voice', 206.
16. Yeats, *Var Plays*, 573.
17. Yeats, 'An Introduction for My Plays' (1937), *E & I*, 529.
18. Yeats, 'A General Introduction for My Work', 510, 516, 522.
19. Yeats, 'Bardic Ireland' (1889), *UP* I, 166.
20. Yeats, 'Nationality and Literature', 273.
21. Yeats, 'Popular Poetry', 7–8.
22. Fraser, 'Yeats and the Ballad Style, 177–94; Clark, 'Yeats', 25–41.
23. Yeats, 'Poetry of Samuel Ferguson—II', 92.
24. Yeats, 'Mr Rhys' Welsh Ballads' (1898), *UP* II, 92.
25. Yeats, 'Miss Fiona MacLeod as a Poet' (1896), 423.
26. Yeats, 'At Stratford-on-Avon', 109.
27. Donoghue, 'Yeats: The Question of Symbolism', 109.

28. Thompson, *Folktale*, 8.
29. Murphy, *Saga and Myth*, 22–3, 51; Dillon, *Early Irish Literature*, 52.
30. Gregory, *Kiltartan Books*, 83–4.
31. Marcus, *Yeats*, 240–41.
32. Yeats, 'Literature and the Living Voice', 215.
33. O'Farrell, 'Millenialism', 58.
34. Yeats, 'Irish Witch Doctors', 231.
35. Harris, *Yeats*, 10, 248.
36. Yeats, *Var Poems*, 793.
37. Yeats, 'Plans and Methods' (1899), *UP* II, 161.
38. Yeats, *Auto*, 3.
39. Yeats, 'Story of Early Gaelic Literature', 359.
40. Yeats, 'Mr Standish O'Grady's Flight of the Eagle', 49.
41. Yeats, 'Ireland after the Revolution' (1839), *Exp*, 439.
42. Yeats, 'Samhain : 1908', 236.
43. Ronsley, *Yeats's Autobiography*, 1.
44. Murphy, *Prodigal Father*, 582.
45. Yeats, 'The Poems and Stories of Miss Nora Hopper' (1898), *UP* II, 127.
46. Yeats, *Auto*, 20.
47. Yeats, 'Art and Ideas' (1913), *E & I*, 349.
48. Yeats, *Auto*, 78.
49. Murphy, *Yeats's Early Poetry*, 48–9.
50. Yeats, *Var Poems*, 841.
51. Dundes, 'On the Psychology of Legend', 24.
52. Gregory, *Seventy Years*, 56–70, 518, 549.
53. Yeats, *Auto*, 12.
54. Lyons, 'Myth and Reality', *Parnell*, 608–25.
55. Colum, 'Foreword', *Kiltartan Books*, 5.
56. Whitaker, *Swan and Shadow*, 135.
57. Grossman, *Poetic Knowledge*, 71; Yeats, 'Magic', 50.
58. Yeats, 'A General Introduction for My Work', 523.
59. Friedman, *Folk Ballads*, 183.
60. Yeats, 'The Literary Movement in Ireland' (1899), *UP* II, 188.
61. Yeats, *Cuchulain*, 264–6.

Bibliography

This Bibliography, which includes all works either quoted or cited in the text, provides complete bibliographic citations for works referred to in abbreviated form in the Notes. Page references in the Notes refer to the most recent edition of a book cited in the Bibliography.

Anon., *Ancient Irish Tales, A Collection of the Stories Told by the Peasantry in the Winter Evenings*, Dublin 1829.
'Irish Literature', *DLM* (August 1825), 275–8.
'Legends and Tales of the Queen's County Peasantry. 'No I—The Banshee', *DUM* (September 1839), 366–74; 'No II—The Bewitched Butter', *DUM* (October 1839), 487–94; 'No III—The Sheoge', *DUM* (November 1839), 580–86.
Life and Times of G. R. Fitzgerald, Dublin 1787; reprinted *DUM* (July-October 1840).
Narrative of Col. Thomas Blood, London 1680.
Remarks on the life and death of the fam'd Mr. Blood; giving an account of his plot in Ireland, London 1680.
'Superstitions of the Irish Peasantry—No I', *DLM* I (1825), 31–4.
Aarne, Antti and Stith Thompson, *The Types of the Folktale: Classification and Bibliography*, Helsinki 1961.
Ackerman, Cara, 'Yeats's Revisions of the Hanrahan Stories, 1897 and 1904, *Texas Studies in Literature and Language*, XVII (Summer 1975), 505–24.
Allingham, William, 'Irish Ballad Singers and Irish Street Ballads', *Household Words* 94 (10 January 1852), reprinted in *Coel*, III (1967), 2–20.
Arensberg, Conrad, *The Irish Countryman*, 1937, Garden City, N. Y. 1968.
Arnold, Matthew, *On the Study of Celtic Literature*, London 1867.
Barrington, Sir Jonah, *Personal Sketches of His Own Times*, London 1869.

Bascom, William, 'The Forms of Folklore : Prose Narratives', *JAF*
LXXVIII (1965), 3–20.
Bourke, Marcus, *John O'Leary: A Study in Irish Separatism*,
Athens, Georgia 1967.
Bradford, Curtis, *Yeats at Work*, Carbondale, 1965.
Bramsbäck, Birgit, 'W. B. Yeats and Folklore Material', *Hereditas*,
56–68.
Brand, John, *Observations on the Popular Antiquities of Great
Britain: Chiefly Illustrating the Origin of our Vulgar and Pro-
vincial Customs, Ceremonies and Superstitions*, 3 vols, London
1877.
Briggs, Katharine, *An Encyclopedia of Fairies*, New York 1976.
Briggs, Katharine, *The Fairies in Tradition and Literature*, Lon-
don 1967.
Brooke, Charlotte, *Reliques of Irish Poetry: Consisting of Heroic
Poems, Odes, Elegies, and Songs, translated into English Verse*,
Dublin 1789.
Brown, Stephen, *Ireland in Fiction: A Guide to Irish Novels, Tales,
Romances and Folklore*, Dublin 1915.
Bruford, Alan, *Gaelic Folk-Tales and Medieval Romances*, Dublin
1969.
Bryant, Sophie, *Celtic Ireland*, London 1889.
Cambrensis, Giraldus, *The Historical World of Giraldus Cam-
brensis containing the Topography of Ireland, and the History
of the Conquest of Ireland*, trans. Thomas Forester, London
1863.
Carleton, William, 'The Irish Rake', *Irish Life and Character*,
London n.d.
  'Preface to First Series' (1830) of *Traits and Stories* in *Tales
and Stories of the Irish Peasantry*, 4 vols., ed. D. J. O'Donoghue,
London 1896.
  Redmond Count O'Hanlon, The Irish Rapparee (1862) in
Tales and Stories of the Irish Peasantry, New York 1875.
  Stories from Carleton, ed. W. B. Yeats, London 1889.
  *Tales and Sketches, Illustrating the Character, Usages, Trad-
itions, Sports and Pastimes of the Irish Peasantry*, Dublin 1845.
Clarke, Austin, 'Gaelic Ireland Rediscovered : The Early Period'
in *Irish Poets in English*, ed. Seán Lucy, Cork 1972.
Clarke, David R., 'Yeats : "Out of a People to a People" ', *Malahat
Review XXII* (1972), 25–41.
Cleeve, Brian, *Dictionary of Irish Writers*, 3 vols, Cork 1969.
Colum, Padraic, *A Treasury of Irish Folklore*, New York 1967.
Comyn, Michael, 'The Land of Youth', *Transactions of the*

Ossianic Society IV, ed. Bryan O'Looney, Dublin 1859, 228–79.

Conner, Lester, 'The Importance of Douglas Hyde to the Irish Literary Renaissance', *Modern Irish Literature*, eds. R. J. Porter and J. D. Brophy, New York 1972, 95–114.

Corkery, Daniel, *The Hidden Ireland*, Dublin 1967.

Cosgrave, J., *A Genuine History of the Lives and Actions of the Most Notorious Highwaymen, Tories and Rapparees*, Belfast 1776.

Croker, T. Crofton, *Fairy Legends and Traditions of the South of Ireland*, 3 vols, London 1825–28.

Croker, T. Crofton, *The Keen of the South of Ireland*, London 1844.

Croker, T. Crofton, *The Legends of the Lakes*, 2 vols, London 1829.

Croker, T. Crofton, *Researches in the South of Ireland*, London 1824.

Curtin, Jeremiah, *Hero Tales of Ireland*, London 1894.

Curtin, Jeremiah, *Myths and Folk-Lore of Ireland*, London 1890.

Daly, Dominic, *The Young Douglas Hyde: The Dawn of the Irish Revolution and Renaissance 1874–1893*, Totowa, N. J. 1974.

Danaher, Kevin, 'Folk Tradition and Literature', *JIL* 1/2 (1972), 63–76.

Danaher, Kevin, 'Oral Tradition and the Printed Word', *IUR* IX/1 (Spring 1979), 31–41.

Davis, Thomas, *The Poems of Thomas Davis*, Dublin 1846.

Deeney, Daniel, *Peasant Lore from Gaelic Ireland*, London 1900.

Delaney, James, 'Patrick Kennedy', *The Past* 7 (1964), 9–88.

Delargy, Seamus, 'The Royal Hibernian Tales', *Béaloideas* X (1940), 148–203.

Dickens, Charles, 'Frauds on the Fairies', *Household Words* VIII (1 October 1853), 97.

Dillon, Myles, 'The Archaism of Irish Tradition', *Reprints in Irish Studies* 5 (January 1969).

Dillon, Myles, *Early Irish Literature*, Chicago 1948.

Donoghue, Denis, *William Butler Yeats*, New York 1971.

Donoghue, Denis, 'Yeats : The Question of Symbolism', *Myth and Reality in Irish Literature*, ed. Joseph Ronsley, Waterloo, Ontario 1977.

Dorson, Richard, *The British Folklorists: A History*, Chicago 1968.

Dorson, Richard, 'Defining the American Folk Legend', *Hereditas*, 112–26.

Dorson, Richard, 'Esthetic Form in British and American Folk Narrative', *Medieval Literature and Folklore Studies*, eds Jerome

Mandel and Bruce Rosenberg, New Brunswick, N. J. 1970, 305–21.

Dorson, Richard, *Folklore and Fakelore: Essays Toward a Discipline of Folk Studies*, Cambridge, Mass. 1976.

Dorson, Richard, *Folktales of Ireland*, ed. Sean O'Sullivan, Chicago 1966, v – xxxii.

Dowling, Patrick J., *The Hedge Schools of Ireland*, Dublin 1935.

Duffy, Charles Gavan, *Ballad Poetry of Ireland*, New York 1886.

Duffy, Charles Gavan, *Young Ireland: A Fragment of Irish History 1840–1850*, New York 1881.

Dundes, Alan, 'On the Psychology of Legend', *American Folk Legend: A Symposium*, ed. Wayland Hand, Berkeley 1971.

Eddins, Dwight, *Yeats: The Nineteenth Century Matrix*, University of Alabama 1971.

Eglinton, John et al, *Literary Ideals in Ireland*, London 1899.

Ellmann, Richard, *The Identity of Yeats*, 2nd ed., New York 1964.

Ellmann, Richard, *Yeats: The Man and the Masks*, New York 1948.

Evans, E. Estyn, 'Peasant Beliefs in Nineteenth-Century Ireland', *Views of the Irish Peasantry 1800–1916*, 37–56.

'Feis Tigh Chonain', ed. Nicholas O'Kearney, *Transactions of the Ossianic Society* II, Dublin 1855.

Ferguson, Samuel, *Congal*, Dublin 1872.

Finneran, Richard, ' "Old Lecher with a Love on Every Wind" : A Study of Yeats's *Stories of Red Hanrahan*', *Texas in Literature and Language* XIV (1972), 347–58.

Finneran, Richard, ed., 'W. B. Yeats', *Anglo-Irish Literature: A Review of Research*, New York 1976, 216–314.

Fitzgerald, David, 'Early Celtic History and Mythology', *Revue Celtique* VI (1883–85), 192–259.

Flanagan, Thomas, *The Irish Novelists: 1800–1850*, New York 1959.

Flanagan, Thomas, 'Yeats, Joyce, and Ireland', *Critical Inquiry* II/1 (Autumn 1975), 43–67.

Folktales of Ireland, O'Sullivan, Sean, ed. and transl., Chicago 1966.

Fraser, G. S., 'Yeats and the Ballad Style', *Shenandoah* XXI/3 (1970), 177–94.

Freney, James, *The Life and Adventures of James Freney*, Dublin, n.d.

Friedman, Albert, *The Penguin Book of Folk Ballads*, New York 1956.

Froude, James A., *The English in Ireland in the Eighteenth Century* I, London 1881.

Garnett, Edward, reader's report on *Irish Adventurers*, Berg Collection, New York Public Library.

Gregory, Lady, *Cuchulain of Muirthemne*, London 1902, Gerrards Cross 1973.

Gregory, Lady, *Gods and Fighting Men: The Story of the Tuatha de Danaan and the Fianna of Ireland*, London 1904, Gerrards Cross, 1970.

Gregory, Lady, *The Kiltartan Books: Comprising the Kiltartan Poetry, History and Wonder Books*, 1909–19, New York 1971.

Gregory, Lady, *Poets and Dreamers: Studies and Translations from the Irish*, 1903, Port Washington, N. Y. 1967.

Gregory, Lady, *Seventy Years: Being the Autobiography of Lady Gregory*, ed. Colin Smythe, New York 1974.

Gregory, Lady, *Visions and Beliefs in the West of Ireland*, 1920, Toronto 1976.

Grossman, Allen, *Poetic Knowledge in the Early Yeats: A Study of the Wind among the Reeds*, Charlottesville, Virginia 1969.

Hall, Mr and Mrs Samuel C., *Ireland: Its Scenery, Character, Etc.*, London 1846.

Hall, Mrs S. C., *Stories of the Irish Peasantry*, Edinburgh 1840.

Hardiman, James, *Irish Ministrelsy, or the Bardic Remains of Ireland with English Poetical Translations*, 2 vols, London 1831.

Harmon, Maurice, 'Cobwebs before the Wind: Aspects of the Peasantry in Irish Literature from 1800–1916', *Views of the Peasantry*, 129–59.

Harris, Daniel, *Yeats: Coole Park and Ballylee*, Baltimore 1974.

Henn, T. R., *The Lonely Tower: Studies in the Poetry of W. B. Yeats*, London 1965.

Hereditas: Essays and Studies Presented to Professor Séamus Ó Duilearga, ed. Bo Almquist, Dublin 1975.

'Historicus', *The Best Hundred Irish Books: Introductory and Closing Essays by 'Historicus' and Letters*, Dublin 1886.

Hoffman, Daniel, *Barbarous Knowledge: Myth in the Poetry of Yeats, Graves, and Muir*, New York 1967.

Hull, Eleanor, 'The Hawk of Achill, or the Legend of the Oldest of the Animals', *Folk-Lore* XLIII (1932), 376–409.

'Humoriensis, Gulielmus Dubliniensis', *Memoir of the Great Original Zozimus*, Dublin 1871.

Hyde, Douglas, *Beside the Fire: A Collection of Irish Gaelic Folk Stories*, London 1890.

Hyde, Douglas, *Leabhar Sgeulaigheachta*, Dublin 1889.

Hyde, Douglas, *Legends of Saints and Sinners*, Dublin 1915, Shannon 1973.

Hyde, Douglas, *A Literary History of Ireland from Earliest Times to the Present Day*, London 1899, revised ed. 1967.

Hyde, Douglas, *Love Songs of Connacht*, Dublin 1893.

Hyde, Douglas, 'The Necessity for De-Anglicising Ireland', *The Revival of Irish Literature*, London 1901.

Hyde, Douglas, *The Story of Early Gaelic Literature*, London 1895.

Jeffares, A. Norman, 'Chairman's Address', *Irish University Review* I (Spring 1971), 294.

Jochum, K. P. S., *W. B. Yeats: A Classified Bibliography of Criticism including Additions to Allan Wade's Bibliography of the Writings of W. B. Yeats*, Urbana, Illinois 1976.

Johnson, Samuel, *A Journey to the Western Islands of Scotland*, ed. Allan Wendt, Boston 1965.

Joyce, Patrick Weston, *Old Celtic Romances*, London 1879.

Jubainville, Henri D'Arbois de, *Le Cycle Mythologique Irlandais et la Mythologie Celtique*, Paris 1884.

Keightley, Thomas, *The Fairy Mythology*, 2 vols, London 1828.

Keightley, Thomas, *Tales and Popular Fictions; their Resemblance and Transmission from Country to Country*, London 1834.

Kelleher, John V., 'Yeats's Use of Irish Materials', *Tri-Quarterly* 4 (Fall 1965), 115–25.

Kennedy, Patrick, *The Banks of the Boro*, Dublin 1867.

Kennedy, Patrick, *The Bardic Stories of Ireland*, Dublin 1871.

Kennedy, Patrick, *Evenings in the Duffrey*, Dublin 1869.

Kennedy, Patrick, *The Fireside Stories of Ireland*, Dublin 1870.

Kennedy, Patrick, *Legendary Fictions of the Irish Celts*, London 1866.

Kennedy, Patrick, *Legends of Mount Leinster*, Dublin 1855.

Kiely, Benedict, *Poor Scholar: A Study of the Works and Days of William Carleton*, London 1947.

'Lageniensis' (John O'Hanlon), *Irish Folklore: Traditions and Superstitions of the Country*, Glasgow 1870.

'Lageniensis' (John O'Hanlon), *Legend Lays of Ireland*, Dublin 1870.

Larminie, William, *West Irish Folk-Tales*, London 1894.

Lover, Samuel, *Legends and Stories of Ireland*, Dublin 1831, 1834.

Lucy, Seán, 'Metre and Movement in Anglo-Irish Verse', *Irish University Review* VIII/2 (Autumn 1978), 151–77.

Lyons, F. S. L., *Charles Stuart Parnell*, London 1977.

McAnally, D. R., *Irish Wonders: The Ghosts, Giants, Pookas, Demons, Leprechawns, Banshees, Fairies, Witches, Widows, Old Maids, and Other Marvels of the Emerald Isle*, Boston 1888.

K

McCaffrey, Lawrence, 'Daniel Corkery and Irish Cultural Nationalism', *Eire-Ireland* VIII/1 (Spring 1973), 35–41.

McClintock, Letitia, *A Boycotted Household*, London 1880.

McClintock, Letitia, 'Fairy Legends of the County Donegal', *All The Year Round* XXVIII (21 January 1882), 461–9.

McClintock, Letitia, 'Folk-Lore of the County Donegal', *All The Year Round* XXIV (10 April 1880), 464–8.

McClintock, Letitia, 'Folk-Lore of the County Donegal', *DUM* (November 1876), 607–14.

McClintock, Letitia, 'Folk-Lore of the County Donegal : Fairy Tales', *DUM* (February 1877), 241–9.

McClintock, Letitia, 'Ulster Folklore', *All the Year Round* XXV (10 September 1881), 16–20.

McGarry, James, *Place Names in the Writings of W. B. Yeats*, Toronto 1976.

MacKillop, James, 'Finn Mac Cool : The Hero and the Anti-Hero in Irish Folk Tradition', *Views of the Irish Peasantry 1800–1916*, 86–106.

MacLochlainn, Alf, 'Gael and Peasant—A Case of Mistaken Identity?', *Views of the Irish Peasantry 1800–1916*, 17–36.

MacLysaght, Edward, *Irish Families*, Dublin 1972.

MacManus, D. A., *The Middle Kingdom: The Faerie World of Ireland*, London 1959.

M'Skimin, Samuel, *The History and Antiquities of the County and Town of Carrickfergus, from the Earliest Records to the Present Time*, Belfast 1832.

Mangan, James Clarence, *Poets and Poetry of Munster*, ed. John O'Daly, Dublin 1849.

Marcus, Phillip, 'Possible Sources of Yeats's *Dhoya*', *Notes and Queries* XIV (1965), 383–4.

Marcus, Phillip, *Standish O'Grady*, Lewisburg, Pa. 1970.

Marcus Phillip, *Yeats and the Beginning of the Irish Renaissance*, Ithaca, N. Y. 1970.

Marshall, John G., *Irish Tories, Rapparees and Robbers*, Dungannon, 1927.

Mason, William Shaw, *Statistical Account or Parochial Survey of Ireland, drawn up from the communications of the Clergy*, 3 vols, Dublin 1814–18.

Meir, Colin, *The Ballads and Songs of W. B. Yeats: The Anglo-Irish Heritage in Subject and Style*, New York 1974.

Mitchell, John, *Jail Journal*, New York 1854.

Murphy, Frank, *Yeats's Early Poetry*, Baton Rouge, La. 1975.

Murphy, Gerard, *Saga and Myth in Ancient Ireland*, Dublin 1955.

Murphy, William M., *Prodigal Father: The Life of John Butler Yeats*, Ithaca, N. Y. 1978.

Murphy, William M., *The Yeats Family and the Pollexfens of Sligo*, Dublin 1971.

Myles, Percy, Review of *Ancient Cures*, *Academy* XXVIII (20 September 1890), 266–7.

Nutt, Alfred, *Studies on the Legend of the Holy Grail*, London 1888.

Ó Casaide, Séamus, 'Crofton Croker's Irish Fairy Legends', *Béaloideas* X (1940), 289–91.

O'Curry, Eugene, *Lectures on the Manuscript Materials of Ancient Irish History*, Dublin 1861.

O'Driscoll, Robert, *An Ascendancy of the Heart: Ferguson and the Beginnings of Modern Irish Literature in English*, Toronto 1976.

O'Farrell, Patrick, 'Millenialism, Messianism and Utopianism in Irish History', *Anglo-Irish Studies* II (1976), 45–68.

O'Grady, Standish Hayes, *Silva Gaedelica*, 2 vols, London 1892.

O'Grady, Standish J., *History of Ireland*, 2 vols, London 1878–80.

Ó hÓgáin, Dáithi, 'The Visionary Voice : A Survey of Popular Attitudes to Poetry in Irish Tradition', *IUR* IX/1 (Spring 1979), 44–61.

O'Kearney, Nicholas, 'Folklore', *Transactions of the Kilkenny Archeological Society* II (1852–53), 32–9.

O'Kearney, Nicholas, transl., 'The Story of Conn-eda', *Transactions of the Ossianic Society* II, London 1855.

O'Leary, John, *Inaugural Address to the Young Ireland Society, January 19, 1885*, Dublin 1885.

O'Shea, Edward, *Yeats as Editor*, Dublin 1975.

O'Sullivan, Sean, *A Handbook of Irish Folklore*, Dublin 1942, 1963.

O'Sullivan, Sean, *Legends from Ireland*, Totowa, N. J., 1977.

O'Sullivan, Sean, *Storytelling in Irish Tradition*, Cork 1973.

O'Sullivan, Sean and Reidar Christiansen, *The Types of the Irish Folktale*, Helsinki 1963.

Parsons, Coleman O., *Witchcraft and Demonology in Scott's Fiction*, London 1964.

Poems and Ballads of Young Ireland, Dublin 1888.

Power, John, *List of Irish Periodical Publications (Chiefly) Literary from 1729 to the Present Time*, London 1866.

Prim, J. G. A., discussion of Freney, *Journal of the Kilkenny and*

South-East of Ireland Archeological Society I, New Series, Dublin 1858, 52–61.

Raine, Kathleen, 'Foreword', *Fairy and Folk Tales of Ireland,* Gerrards Cross 1977.

Rhys, John, *Lectures on the Origin and Growth of Religion as Illustrated by Celtic Heathendom*, London 1888.

Ronsley, Joseph, *Yeats's Autobiography: Life as Symbolic Pattern,* Cambridge, Mass. 1968.

Scott, Sir Walter, 'Letters on Demonology and Witchcraft', *The Miscellaneous Works of Sir Walter Scott* XXIX, Edinburgh 1871.

Scott, Sir Walter, *Minstrelsy of the Scottish Border*, 3 vols, Edinburgh 1803.

Scott, Sir Walter, *Waverley*, 1814, New York 1965.

Sidnell, Michael J., 'Versions of the Stories of Red Hanrahan', *Yeats Studies* I (May 1971), 119–74.

Sidnell, Michael J., George Mayhew and David R. Clark, *Druid Craft: The Writing of the Shadowy Waters*, University of Massachusetts 1971.

Somerville-Large, Peter, *Irish Eccentrics*, London 1975.

Starkie, Walter, 'Introduction', *The Celtic Twilight*, New York 1962.

Stokes, Whitley, 'Remarks on Mr Fitzgerald's "Early Celtic History and Mythology" ', *Revue Celtique* VI (1883–85), 358–70.

Taylor, Geoffrey, *Irish Poets of the Nineteenth Century*, London 1951.

Thackeray, William, *The Irish Sketch-Book*, 2 vols, London 1843.

Thompson, Stith, *The Folktale*, Berkeley 1977.

Thuente, Mary Helen, 'A List of Sources', *Fairy and Folk Tales of Ireland*, Gerrards Cross 1977.

Unterecker, John, 'Countryman, Peasant, and Servant in the Poetry of W. B. Yeats', *Views of the Irish Peasantry 1800–1916*, 178–91.

Views of the Irish Peasantry 1800–1916, eds Daniel Casey and Robert Rhodes, Hamden, Conn. 1977.

Wade, Allan, *A Bibliography of the Writings of W. B. Yeats*, 3rd ed., London 1968.

Walsh, Edward, *Irish Popular Songs*, Dublin 1847.

Walsh, Edward, *Reliques of Irish Jacobite Poetry*, ed. John O'Daly, Dublin 1844.

Walsh, John Edward, *Ireland Sixty Years Ago*, Dublin 1847; reprinted as *Rakes and Ruffians: The Underworld of Georgian Dublin*, Dublin 1979.

Webb, Alfred, *A Compendium of Irish Biography: Comprising*

Sketches of Distinguished Irishmen and of Eminent Persons Connected with Ireland by Office or by Their Writings, Dublin 1878.

Wentz, W. Y. Evans, *The Fairy Faith in Celtic Countries*, Oxford 1911, 1966.

Whitaker, Thomas, *Swan and Shadow: Yeats's Dialogue with History*, Chapel Hill 1964.

White, Carolyn, *A History of Irish Fairies*, Cork 1976.

Wilde, Lady, *Ancient Cures, Charms, and Usages of Ireland*, London 1890.

Wilde, Lady, *Ancient Legends, Mystic Charms and Superstitions of Ireland with Sketches of the Irish Past*, London 1887, 1899.

Wilde, Lady, 'The Fairy Mythology of Ireland', *DUM* XC (1877), 70–83, 193–204.

Wilde, Sir William, *Irish Popular Superstitions*, Dublin 1853.

Wood-Martin, W. G., *History of Sligo County and Town, from the Earliest Ages to the Close of the Reign of Queen Elizabeth*, Dublin 1882.

Yeats, Michael, 'W. B. Yeats and Irish Folk Song', *Southern Folk-Lore Quarterly* XXXI (June 1966), 153–78.

Yeats, W. B., *The Autobiography of W. B. Yeats*, 1938, New York 1967.

A Book of Irish Verse, London 1895.

The Celtic Twilight, Men and Women, Dhouls and Fairies, London 1893; *The Celtic Twilight*, 2nd ed., London 1902, New York 1962.

'Costello the Proud, Oona MacDermott and the Bitter Tongue', *The Pageant* (1896), 2–13.

Essays and Introductions, 1961, New York 1968.

Explorations, New York 1962.

Fairy and Folk Tales of Ireland, ed. W. B. Yeats, Gerrards Cross 1977. Reprint of *Fairy and Folk Tales* and *Irish Fairy Tales*. Page reference in Notes are to this edition.

Fairy and Folk Tales of the Irish Peasantry, ed. W. B. Yeats, London 1888. Reprinted in *Fairy and Folk Tales of Ireland*.

Irish Fairy Tales, ed. W. B. Yeats, London 1892. Reprinted in *Fairy and Folk Tales of Ireland*.

John Sherman and Dhoya, ed. Richard J. Finneran, Detroit 1969.

'The Legendary and Mythological Foundation of the Plays and Poems', *Var Poems*, 842–3.

The Letters of W. B. Yeats, ed. Allan Wade, London 1954.

Letters to Katharine Tynan, ed. Roger McHugh, New York 1953.

Letters to the New Island, ed. Horace Reynolds, Harvard University 1934.

Memoirs: Autobiography—First Draft; Journals, ed. Denis Donoghue, London 1972.

Mythologies, 1959, New York 1969.

'Out of the Rose', *The National Observer* (27 May 1893), 41–3.

Representative Irish Tales, 2 vols, ed. W. B. Yeats, London 1891; Gerrards Cross, 1979. This edition also reprints Yeats's 'Introduction' to *Stories from Carleton* (1889) in an Appendix.

The Secret Rose, London 1897.

The Secret Rose in *The Collected Works of W. B. Yeats* VII, Stratford-on-Avon 1908.

Some Letters from W. B. Yeats to John O'Leary and His Sister, ed. Allan Wade, New York 1953.

Stories from Carleton, London 1889.

Stories of Red Hanrahan, 1905; *Collected Works of W. B. Yeats* V, Stratford-on-Avon 1908.

Uncollected Prose by W. B. Yeats : I—*First Reviews and Articles 1886–1896*, ed. John P. Frayne, New York 1970; II—*Reviews, Articles and Other Miscellaneous Prose 1897–1939*, ed. J. P. Frayne and Colton Johnson, New York 1976.

The Variorum Edition of the Plays of W. B. Yeats, ed. Russell K. Alspach, London 1969.

The Variorum Edition of the Poems of W. B. Yeats, eds Peter Allt and Russell K. Alspach, New York 1957.

A Vision: An Explanation of Life Founded upon the Writings of Giraldus and Upon Certain Doctrines Attributed to Kusta Ben Luka, London 1925.

Zimmermann, Georges-Denis, *Songs of Irish Rebellion: Political Street Ballads and Rebel Songs 1780–1900*, Dublin 1967.

'Yeats, the Popular Ballad and the Ballad Singers', *English Studies*, L (1969), 585–97.

Index

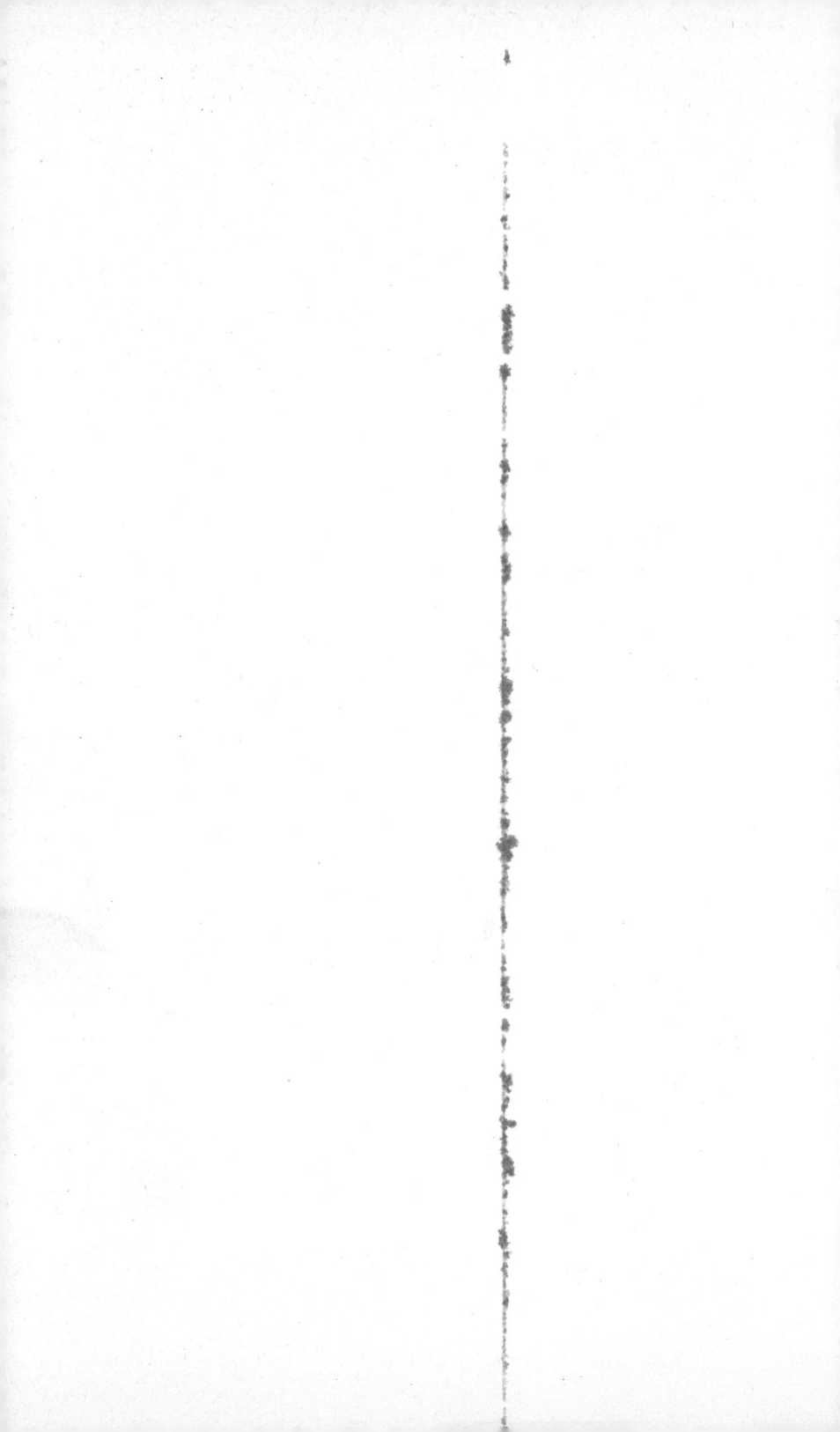